A VOLUME IN TI
Culture, Politics, and ..., Cold War

EDITED BY

Christian G. Appy and Edwin A. Martini

OTHER TITLES IN THE SERIES

Making the Desert
MODERN

Making the Desert
MODERN

Americans, Arabs, and Oil on the Saudi Frontier,
1933–1973

CHAD H. PARKER

University of Massachusetts Press • *Amherst & Boston*

Copyright © 2015 by University of Massachusetts Press
All rights reserved
Printed in the United States of America

ISBN 978-1-62534-157-0 (paper); 156-3 (hardcover)

Designed by Jack Harrison
Set in Adobe Minion Pro
Printed and bound by The Maple-Vail Book Manufacturing Group

Library of Congress Cataloging-in-Publication Data

Parker, Chad H., 1973–
Making the desert modern : Americans, Arabs, and oil on the Saudi frontier, 1933–1973 /
Chad H. Parker.
pages cm. — (Culture, politics, and the Cold War)
Includes bibliographical references and index.
ISBN 978-1-62534-157-0 (pbk. : alk. paper) — ISBN 978-1-62534-156-3 (hardcover : alk. paper)
1. Arabian American Oil Company.
2. Petroleum industry and trade—Saudi Arabia—History—20th century.
3. Economic development—Saudi Arabia—History—20th century.
4. Saudi Arabia—Foreign relations—United States. 5. United States—Foreign relations—Saudi Arabia.
6. Saudi Arabia—Economic conditions. 7. Saudi Arabia—Social conditions.
8. Saudi Arabia—History—1932–   I. Title.
HD9576.S35A763 2015
338.7′62233809538—dc23
2014050135

British Library Cataloguing-in-Publication Data
A catalogue record for this book is available from the British Library.

Contents

Acknowledgments

Obviously no project of this magnitude can be completed without the help of a number of people. I want to express my deepest gratitude to Nick Cullather, who supervised my graduate work and has continued to offer support and advice over the years. Michael McGerr, Ann Carmichael, and Claude Clegg each deserve many thanks as well. A number of other people kindly read early drafts of various chapters. Matt Stanard and Jason Lantzer agreed to be the earliest guinea pigs, reading drafts straight off the printer as I began the project. I am forever indebted to them. John Baesler, Phil Guerty, and Chris Stone also generously lent their expertise as I worked through chapters. Rich Frankel, Sara Ritchey, and John Troutman, friends and colleagues at the University of Louisiana at Lafayette, deserve a great deal of thanks as well. Each read drafts, offered advice, and kept me sane. Thanks to Juan Hinojosa, who helped in Washington. A special thanks, too, to everyone at the University of Massachusetts Press, particularly Clark Dougan.

My research was made much easier by the expert librarians at Indiana University, the University of Louisiana at Lafayette, the National Archives in Washington, D.C., the Truman Presidential Library, the Eisenhower Presidential Library, the Johnson Presidential Library, the Rockefeller Archive, the National Archives in Kew, the special collections at Georgetown University and the University of Virginia, the Bancroft Library in Berkeley, the Hoover Institution at Stanford University, and the archive and library of the World Health Organization. I could never have conducted this research without the financial support of the Indiana University Department of History, the Indiana University Graduate School, the Department of History at Indiana University Purdue University Columbus, the Department of History at Ivy Tech Community College, the Carmony family, the Weisman family, the McNutt family, the Truman Presidential Library, the Eisenhower Presidential Library, the Johnson Presidential Library, the American Heritage Center at the University of Wyoming, the American Association for the History of Medicine, the Graduate and Professional Student Association at Indiana University, the Indiana University College of Arts and Sciences, the Organization of American Historians, and the University of Louisiana at Lafayette.

I also want to say a special thanks to all those who have supported me over the years as I've worked on this project. My mother, Katie, has always been a source of strength for me. She knows what to say and when to say it and has supported me no matter how many times I called. My father, Bill, always showed a genuine interest in what to many others would certainly be mundane, and his encouragement has been critical as well. Sydney was my sidekick as I wrote this book, and while some might shy away from recognizing a dog in their acknowledgments, the lonely moments I spent in front of the computer were made much easier by having him at my side, supervising every keystroke. I wish he were still here. Emily Deal deserves my utmost thanks not only for her support but also for her intelligence, perceptiveness, patience, and love.

Parts of chapter 1 are adapted from "Aramco's Frontier Story: The Arabian American Oil Company and Creative Mapping in Postwar Saudi Arabia," in *Oil Culture,* ed. Ross Barrett and Daniel Worden (Minneapolis: University of Minnesota Press, 2014). Parts of chapters 3 and 4 are adapted from my article "Controlling Man-Made Malaria: Corporate Modernisation and the Arabian American Oil Company's Malaria Control Program in Saudi Arabia, 1947–1956," *Cold War History* 12.3 (2011): 473–94. I am grateful to the editors for their permission to reproduce this material.

Making the Desert
MODERN

Introduction

In 1963 Robert H. SCHOLL, the public relations director at Standard Oil Company of New Jersey, outlined for Congress his company's guiding principles for operating in host countries: development and use of resources, both man and material; assistance in social and economic development; and support for and sensitivity to cultural conventions. Quoting the journalist Edward R. Murrow, he said of private enterprise, "It is what we do—not what we say—that has the greatest impact overseas." He noted that Standard Oil Company affiliates were guided by that principle in developing positive relations with foreign governments and people, transferring new technologies, and raising standards of living, all the while, he added, "scrupulously avoid[ing] involvement in political activity of any kind." Road construction, educational improvements, disease prevention, and agricultural development all served, he said, to stimulate the "economic and social health" of host countries. Scholl's story is an uplifting one, but it is not entirely true. What companies said and what they did were not always the same.[1]

Oil executives like Scholl often spoke of American corporate investment in the Middle East in grand terms, stressing the modernizing influence their practices stimulated. John R. Suman, the director of Standard Oil Company of New Jersey, spoke of the Middle East in 1948 as "one of the most depressed areas on the globe," but "as a result of pouring hundreds of millions of dollars into the drilling of wells, the building of docks and refineries, the laying of pipe lines and the construction of whole communities, this area can be transformed into one of promise and its society into one of hope."[2] This sort of development work represented exactly what the U.S. government promoted in the early Cold War. President Harry Truman's

Point Four Program of technical aid, announced in 1949, stressed cooperation with private businesses to improve the global economy and standards
of living, and the Arabian American Oil Company (Aramco) and other oil
giants soon surfaced as models for realizing the outcomes Point Four imagined.[3] Stanley Andrews, the administrator of the agency that coordinated
Point Four aid, argued that oil firms were well positioned for this work.
They had been doing it for some time. "American companies," he stated,
"have brought employment and in many instances training to thousands
of people; have built hospitals, schools, housing and water facilities; have
introduced standards of efficiency and fair dealing that reach to all levels of
the population."[4] During the mid-twentieth century in Saudi Arabia, corporate development aid surfaced in various forms, but less as a Truman-
inspired, antipoverty campaign or Cold War imperative than as corporate
diplomacy and a means for securing workers.[5] Aramco's projects highlight
how corporate mythmaking intersected with private diplomacy, and they
uncover important connections between corporate relations, Saudi state
formation, and growing ideological forces at play in twentieth-century U.S.
foreign relations. Americans employed by Aramco served Saudi Arabia as
technical experts, at times consciously working toward nation building in
service of the monarchy. Often, however, their work attended to corporate
objectives, many of which had roots in a nascent development discourse
within the United States and globally.[6]

Development is as much a story as it is a policy. Aramco, jointly owned
by Standard Oil Company of New Jersey, the Texas Company, Standard Oil
Company of California, and Standard Oil Company of New York–Vacuum, held the sole concession in Saudi Arabia in the mid-twentieth century.
Signed in 1933, the agreement gave Aramco rights to Saudi oil for the next
sixty years. While expanding its operations, the company indeed engaged
in many of the activities Scholl mentioned, but so did other American businesses. The Creole Petroleum Corporation in Venezuela, United Fruit in
Central America, and Firestone Tire and Rubber in Liberia each organized
housing, education, health and sanitation, and other services for their employees. In each case, they promoted these activities as part of corporate
citizenship.[7] These were stories of progress, ones that foretold of a different kind of future, one in which standards of living improved at the hands
of American business. Conditions on the ground tell a different story.
Aramco's labor troubles, for instance, which stemmed in part from its ra-

cial segregation in housing, illustrate the difficulty the company had in balancing its story with its actions. Aramco's significance, however, lies not solely in its mythmaking but also in its engagement with the Saudi monarchy and the people of Saudi Arabia.[8] Since Middle Eastern oil came to represent power and wealth in the mid-twentieth century, understanding how this American oil giant shaped its policies in Saudi Arabia is all the more critical.

Saudi Arabia would begin its own "Decade of Development" with its first five-year plan in 1970, just as the UN's Decade of Development came to a close. What had triggered this growth initiative in Saudi Arabia was a shift in oil consumption that brought unprecedented wealth to the kingdom, allowing for lavish expenditures on everything from a medical center, roads, and a new airport to fantastic schemes to import ice from Antarctica to increase the potable water supply. Yet development was far from new to Saudi Arabia in 1970, just as it was far from new to the United Nations in 1960. American oilmen initiated the first major development push when they arrived in numbers in the early 1930s, and Aramco came to represent American corporate development in Saudi Arabia in the aftermath of the Second World War. Symbolizing what American corporate expansion had to offer, Aramco promoted its own projects for a variety of reasons, stressing more efficient resource extraction and better relations with the Saudi monarchy, all the while situating itself as a "partner in growth."[9]

The American relationship to the Middle East dates back hundreds of years, but the U.S. government's economic interest in the region emerged after the First World War and its strategic interest during the Second World War. The search for oil greatly defined the West's enthusiasm about the region in the early 1920s. Oil quickly became a commodity that states could not do without, and, to countries that had access to them, Middle East reserves came to represent future security.[10] The importance of oil in the rapidly industrializing world intensified as the nations of Europe rebuilt their war-torn economies and the Cold War came to dominate global politics. Until the 1920s American oil companies mainly drilled in the United States, but soon they turned to the Middle East for crude. Britain's Anglo-Persian Oil Company (APOC) struck oil in Iran in 1908, eventually prompting the government's purchase of a controlling share of the firm. Nearby, in what would become Iraq, APOC and Royal Dutch Shell worked out a deal to gain control of the Turkish Petroleum Company. While major American firms remained comfortable with their reserves in the Western Hemisphere, Middle East crude had a certain allure. Despite President Woodrow Wilson's pleas to British and French authorities, in 1920 the Europeans shut the Americans out, prompting fears of price wars within the State Department and among oil companies. Crude-poor Standard Oil Company of New York (Socony) and others appealed to American open-door ideology, turning to the State Department, which used the threat of trade sanctions to gain the Americans a place in a newly formed agreement in 1922. Socony and Jersey Standard would now have 25 percent control of what soon became known as the Iraq Petroleum Company (IPC).

Not a party to the IPC agreement but already operating on the island of Bahrain, the Standard Oil Company of California (Socal), later partnering with Texaco, looked west to Saudi Arabia for more crude. At the same time, American-based Gulf Oil had an eye on the Middle East and, with State Department help, secured a 50 percent stake in APOC's Kuwaiti oil interests. During the interwar period the U.S. government supported the efforts of American corporations to gain greater access to Middle East crude, recognizing its increasing value.[11] While the first American missionaries arrived in the Ottoman Empire as early as 1819, however, and American oil firms successfully turned to their government for help in opening the door to Middle East crude after the First World War, even in the late 1930s one U.S. diplomat still referred to the region as a "sideshow."[12]

The Second World War heightened the strategic centrality of Saudi Arabia's petroleum reserves.[13] The administration of Franklin D. Roosevelt, earlier content to pursue oil diplomacy through private firms, soon attempted to secure greater influence over Middle East oil. Secretary of the Interior Harold Ickes tried to impose U.S. government control on the Saudi venture in 1943 but found little backing from American companies. After a failed attempt to purchase APOC's share of Kuwaiti oil the next year, Ickes tried to establish American control of the transport of Saudi oil through the construction of a trans-Arabian pipeline. Again thwarted by American companies, he finally worked to ensure joint American–British management of oil markets. This time it was less the oil giants that fought him than American independent enterprises, which feared being driven out of business by such an agreement. Unable to take more direct control of oil operations, the U.S. government instead allowed companies to lead the way.[14]

The partnership between private firms and the government marked the start of the postwar order, as national security, economic development, and corporate interests centered on the Middle East.[15] Aramco became the most important American firm to gain access to Middle East oil at stable prices. As the private–public symbiosis strengthened, government and corporate interests merged, but oil companies took the lead in America's foreign oil policy. After Ickes's failed wartime attempts to gain a controlling stake in Saudi crude, the reliance on private firms came to serve the interests of the U.S. government, producing governments, and oil companies alike. The recognition that American oil firms represented the easiest means of achieving the country's goals drove this approach. The government recognized that corporate interests were in line with its foreign policy interests and acceded to the role of the companies.[16] Historians have expertly described and analyzed these public–private relationships but not from the corporate perspective.[17]

Aramco's expansion after the war enriched the company and the kingdom alike as well as promoted American interests in the Middle East as the national foreign policy transformed to confront the Soviet Union and rebuild Europe. In early 1946 Socal and Texaco looked to expand their markets and began discussions to partner with the IPC members Jersey Standard and Socony–Vacuum, which had large global operations but limited Middle East holdings. The Red Line Agreement of 1928, however, prevented IPC members from operating in the Middle East without other members and therefore made this particular joint venture difficult. At the same time, APOC seemed to be holding the Americans back, since it held vast reserves in Iran and Kuwait and had few holdings elsewhere. Anglo-American negotiations eventually led to an agreement in early 1947 that the IPC partnership had dissolved, clearing the way for Jersey Standard's and Socony–Vacuum's participation in Aramco.

Aramco's profits and American foreign policy soon became linked, as the Truman administration made the Middle East and Saudi oil central to the emerging Cold War. The announcement of the Truman Doctrine in March 1947, as one scholar put it, "laid the foundation" for the American military's involvement in the Middle East and confronted head-on American "maneuvers to replace the British in the region."[18] Soon after, the Marshall Plan fueled European economic recovery through the use of Middle East oil, channeling substantial amounts of American aid dollars to American oil companies in the Middle East and thereby ensuring markets and stabilizing American relations with the producer states.[19]

Oil constituted a key to American relations with Saudi Arabia from the start, but so did geography. If the First World War marked Middle East oil as an economically valuable global resource, then the Second World War announced the geostrategic prominence of the Arabian Peninsula. Saudi Arabia's location between Europe and the Far East, along critical shipping routes and beneath strategic airspace, led in 1943 to the kingdom's receiving American lend-lease aid. After the war Dhahran airfield in Saudi Arabia became a crucial military base for the projection of American power in the region and a potential launching point for an attack on the Soviet Union. As the Cold War became more pronounced, Americans sought to fashion an international system of security. Defense planners in the Pentagon hoped to construct a global base system and acquire landing and air transit rights across the globe, and the Middle East was essential to those designs.[20] The Truman administration was cognizant of the vital need of keeping the Kremlin at bay in the Middle East, and in 1947 looked to the British as a senior military partner in the region. Only a few years later, in 1950, however, U.S. defense strategists warned in National Security Council Paper 68 that the Soviets might be looking to threaten Western oil interests in the Middle East. A more intensive approach would be needed, and in May of that year the United States, Britain, and France jointly pledged to protect the territorial integrity of the region. This Tripartite Declaration, as it was known, was a start, but the Western allies hoped to organize a military pact centered on Egypt to contain the communist threat. Egypt's concern, however, remained British imperialism, not the Soviet Union, and it refused to join. President Dwight Eisenhower shifted to a so-called northern tier strategy, attempting to create a defensive line from Turkey to Pakistan, but he continued to court Egyptian participation. In 1954, after an Anglo–Egyptian agreement led to a pledged withdrawal of British troops from Egypt by summer 1956, Eisenhower may have thought he had succeeded in winning over the Egyptians, but the United Kingdom's signing of what became known as the Baghdad Pact effectively precluded any Egyptian interest in Western security designs.[21] Egypt's rejection of Eisenhower's Arab–Israeli peace proposal further irritated Americans, and when the United States retracted its offer to help fund the Aswan dam in 1956, the Egyptians nationalized the Suez Canal and brought on the subsequent Suez crisis that year. British influence

in the region crumbled, as the Americans assumed the role of regional he-
gemon. The Eisenhower administration soon looked to Saudi Arabia as an
indispensable regional bulwark against Soviet communism, a position the
United States would retain well into the 1980s.[22]

Religion also tied Saudi and American interests together early in the
Cold War, in defense of the region both from communism and from Ga-
mal Abdel Nasser's Arab nationalism. Many American Middle East experts
from the late 1940s through the 1950s believed that Islam might constitute a
totalizing force that could pit Muslims against the West, yet others thought
it could act as a defense against communism in the region. Whether the
area would retreat into tradition or advance toward modernity seemed un-
clear to them. At this time Islam began to be seen through the lens of development discourse. Eisenhower's secretary of state, John Foster Dulles,
stressed an emotional aspect that he claimed Islam had, highlighting Muslims' susceptibility to fanaticism. As an emotional and totalitarian religion,
experts argued, Islam could either steer Muslims into the Soviet embrace or
it could stand guard against the atheistic force of communism. No consensus formed until events in the Middle East compelled action by the United
States. Nasser not only began to promote a secular Arab nationalism that
called for neutrality in the Cold War but also readily accepted communist aid. The Eisenhower White House then turned to religion and would
soon come to rely on appeals to the Saudi king's claimed religious status as
the protector of Islam's two holy cities, Mecca and Medina, to strengthen
America's ties to the region.[23]

The burgeoning American relationship with Saudi Arabia became a salient backdrop to Aramco's role in the kingdom. Ultimately, the company,
not the U.S. government, served as the principal American representative in
Saudi Arabia in the mid-twentieth century. When government officials began to arrive in the country in the early 1940s to discuss wartime diplomacy
with the Saudi government, company officials provided introductions and
coordinated meetings, travel, housing, and food. The company assumed
this role well into the 1950s, fulfilling many of the duties of an embassy. Aramco constructed various modernization programs on the ground in Saudi
Arabia, merging everyday operations with broader notions of development
and erecting a corporate modernization framework built on technical aid
and service to the Saudi monarchy. To Aramco, development was less an
altruistic deed than a function of business policy, one related to resource

extraction, concession protection, labor expansion, and corporate good-will. Development became business strategy and diplomacy.

The role nonstate actors have played in what has been variously called in U.S. foreign relations, depending on the era, the civilizing mission, reconstruction, development, modernization, and nation building has proved to be a leading one. Governments have certainly not monopolized the promotion of new technologies and the cultures that come with them. Missionaries, medical societies, cooperative societies, international and transnational organizations, intergovernmental organizations, and corporations have had and continue to make their presence felt in these activities. In the second decade of the twenty-first century, as the United States draws down its commitments in Iraq and Afghanistan, nonstate actors continue to be influential. But historians are just beginning to unravel the fundamental role American corporations played in mid-twentieth-century modernization. Scholars need to expand their notion of international society to include more of these extragovernmental actors in their proper social, political, and diplomatic contexts.[24]

Early works on the history of development show the impact that state-led modernization had on both policy and a way of seeing the world. More recent treatments have refocused on country-specific studies or, even more recently, begun to globalize the study of modernization in exciting ways.[25] These histories place development at the center of U.S. foreign policy during the Decade of Development, illustrating how authoritarian models supplanted democratic-capitalist models.[26] By looking beyond the single-state approach, historians can uncover development's longer history in the twentieth century, prior to the Cold War.[27] This book builds on country-specific approaches—with Saudi Arabia as the focus—but also globalizes development's history in new ways by looking beyond states to include many diverse actors, from U.S. and Saudi Arabian government officials to agricultural specialists, doctors, corporate executives, employees of various international organizations, and research and government relations specialists working for Aramco. These people worked in Saudi Arabia for a variety of reasons, and their oft-competing roles contributed to the ad hoc nature of nation building as it came to be practiced on the Saudi frontier.

In the second half of the twentieth century, modernization served as a guide for policymakers in Washington who saw American social and economic advances as models for global change. These ideas constituted a primary way for the United States to engage the global south and served to buttress American corporate relations in Saudi Arabia. Perhaps President John F. Kennedy articulated the idea of modernization most simply in his inaugural address of 1961 when he suggested that the United States should support those living in "huts and villages" and "struggling to break the bonds of mass misery." Americans, establishing a new, yet somehow familiar, postwar, global role, he argued, should "convert our good words into good deeds . . . to assist free men and free governments in casting off the chains of poverty."[28] Along these lines, both the U.S. government and private institutions nurtured an understanding of the newly independent, nonindustrialized nations of the world as new frontiers where the transplantation of American values, technologies, and institutions could coincide with, if not facilitate, the cultural, economic, and military reach of the United States and the expansion of corporate profits. Increasing Cold War anxieties engendered even greater interest in modernization theories that established, if not rationalized, America's increasing presence in a rapidly changing global order.[29]

American corporate agents, as this story of Aramco illustrates, often improvised modernization practices on the Saudi frontier, and much of that work predated its articulation as a theory by academics in all the interested disciplines. Prior to the 1960s, theorists ranging from the fields of sociology to psychology to economics stressed various mechanisms for comprehending the attractions, challenges, and effects of development at work as postcolonial states such as Saudi Arabia moved toward a supposed modernity. Where the sociologist Daniel Lerner saw a psychological transition occurring, the scholar of comparative politics Lucian Pye emphasized ideological drives to become modern.[30] All recognized the difficulty in imposing modernization on the ground. In terms of policy, the U.S. government came to favor more authoritarian mechanisms during the Cold War to hasten this transition.[31] The governmental preference to work with authoritarian regimes, however, followed the determination by Aramco oil executives in the 1930s to do the same in Saudi Arabia. Aramco's was a pragmatic business decision, not a program directed by political directives or theory, though it seemed to establish a precedent for decades of governmental policy to follow. In fact, Aramco's history demonstrates that theory often came after the implementation of development programs.[32] Leading modernization theorists such as Gabriel Almond, Lerner, and Walt Rostow later suggested a unified, linear path to modernity in which modern, rational modes of life modeled and promoted by the West overtook allegedly traditional social and cultural arrangements. The practice of Islam, Lerner argued specifically, was no match for the power of the modern world.[33] In postwar Saudi Arabia, however, corporate economic interests and changing political and social conditions guided Aramco's programs as practitioners sought to build on some Saudi traditions and modify others. American corporate policymakers nurtured certain modes of Saudi and Islamic culture, all in the service of corporate objectives. Modernization often turned less on theory than on immediate corporate needs, and corporate agents grasped these challenges implicitly.

The oil company's engagement with the Saudi monarchy through various development schemes is a way to uncover the techniques employed by one of the most powerful and influential entities in the world as it carried out its private diplomatic relations in Saudi Arabia. It illustrates the unplanned nature of modernization as it evolved before and during the Cold War, and it highlights how nations, communities, and foreign relations are shaped and defined by local and global interactions. As the company vice president James Terry Duce once said to an audience at the Council on Foreign Relations in 1956, "The general reputation the Americans had acquired in the Middle East through the actions of many generous and patriotic citizens over the years" meant that American private enterprise could be actively involved in bringing civilization to the Middle East.[34] As we have seen, his assessment was fairly typical of those made by American private enterprise in the mid-twentieth century, but it speaks volumes about the impact Aramco claimed it had as it exploited the region for its profit. It also points to the delicate balance corporate citizens had to account for as they sought greater access to oil by cultivating favorable relations with the Saudi monarchy.

By looking more closely at the company's public relations and a wealth of recently available documentary evidence from inside the company, historians have shown how a corporate myth of social and economic uplift masked a reality of exploitation in Saudi Arabia. Public relations experts created an exceptionalist narrative—as selective and purposeful as any—to extend American hegemony in Saudi Arabia. Company programs, organized under the rhetoric of development, helped propel corporate interests.[35] This book builds on current trends along these lines to consider this corporate narrative as an essential part of the company's modernization strategy in Saudi Arabia. More than just a façade, it established the framework for

Aramco's relationship with the Saudi monarchy. Development was much more than rhetoric. The company's programs in construction, agriculture, and medical issues operated within and were informed by theoretical and practical models of nation building being debated at the time. Corporate mythmaking was not just a public relations ploy or an exceptionalist frontier narrative. It was an essential part of Aramco's identity and corporate strategy and, by extension, of U.S. policy in the Middle East. This narrative of uplift established the corporation's underlying principles and helped Aramco officials explain their mission to themselves, to the Saudi monarchy, and to the U.S. government. During this era the monarchy initiated its own nation-building agenda in Saudi Arabia and looked to Aramco's experts for assistance. Postwar American modernization theory began to materialize in Saudi Arabia as the company engaged in a series of initiatives intended to preserve its oil concession. Aramco employed Western technology and American cultural forms in an effort to transfer and promote ideas of economic and social progress to Saudi Arabia as part of a strategy to secure and maintain its financial stake in the kingdom. In the process, the company attempted to establish itself as what it called a vital partner in growth. A look at Aramco's foreign relations unveils an untold story of the links between American corporate contributions to Middle East state building, U.S. foreign relations, and the cultural and political impact of development as it was constructed on the ground.

The first chapter argues that Aramco served as the primary American political and diplomatic agent in Saudi Arabia from the 1940s into the 1950s, establishing the company as an agent of change. Aramco's concession history in Saudi Arabia is the backdrop to the study, initiating the company's presence in the kingdom's Eastern Province and its emergence as a powerful player in global oil politics. An often-tense relationship developed between the U.S. government and the company as a result of Aramco's status in the kingdom, but the Saudi monarchy understood well the role corporate technocrats played in helping it justify its part in transforming many Saudi social practices.[36] The company and the monarchy, therefore, sought to establish a modern Saudi nation-state, and development would be the lens through which both the company and the kingdom viewed power and persuasion. In this process, the company constructed a self-image as a partner in growth, one it employed as a tool of corporate diplomacy.

Technical and political aspects of modernization proved difficult to implement in some cases. The second chapter assesses some of the cultural aspects of corporate development in Saudi Arabia. Aramco's interaction with Saudi Islamic customs was just one of the many spaces where Western-styled state building confronted boundaries. The monarchy and the company faced a variety of difficulties as certain new cultural and technological forms began to overlay Saudi Islamic society. While development theory being formulated in the United States would maintain that religion served as an impediment to modernization, nation building in Saudi Arabia worked differently. Often by upholding the monarchy's position on Islamic law and its self-promotion as the rightful protector of Islam, Aramco attempted to balance Saudi religion and corporate initiatives. In particular, it supported Saudi Islamic customs when they were connected to Saudi Arabia's identity as an Islamic state, but when American domestic culture came up against Saudi practices that Aramco deemed less vital, the company sought a middle ground that would allow for greater cultural expression of Aramco's American employees, all with an eye toward maximizing resource extraction.

The third chapter explores the implementation of Western medical practices to Saudi Arabia by analyzing Aramco's medical programs. The deployment of Western medicine helps illustrate how development discourse and practice diverged when met with the reality of life in the extremely pious and religiously austere environs of Saudi Arabia. Aramco's American employees represented Saudi Arabia as being an ancient land and narrated their presence as modernizers through the use of Western medicine. An analysis of how the Saudi national body came to be defined, observed, shaped, and controlled demonstrates how Aramco measured progress and fashioned an authoritative role for the corporation in Saudi society. In the name of health, the company reconstructed domestic space to include air-conditioning and sewers. Corporate officials worked with the Ministry of Agriculture to find more effective, healthier means of fertilization. They helped organize educational opportunities to promote their views on proper hygiene, child and maternal care, and nutrition. Aramco designed its efforts as much to prepare the Saudi body for labor and to promote diplomatic goodwill as it did to develop the Saudi state. For some time Aramco was able to create a dependence on its expertise, not only with respect to the production of oil but also through the transmission of medical technology and culture.

Chapter 4 examines preventive medicine, focusing on Aramco's malaria abatement efforts from 1947 through 1956, when the Saudi government assumed jurisdiction of eradication and control programs. Aramco's primary interest in disease control revolved around maintaining a healthy workforce but demonstrating goodwill was also a diplomatic objective. The chapter reconstructs the control efforts led by Aramco scientists, showing how public health remained secondary as the company sculpted its role in service to the king. Control of malaria came about eventually in the Eastern Province but only, in the end, by dispensing with disease-development models practiced by global public health officials that saw disease as an impediment to economic growth. Officials at Aramco and, later, at the World Health Organization wrestled with these ideas, eventually turning to social and economic practices to bring about control rather than relying on technological ones alone. I also show in the chapter how corporate interests drove early attempts, often to the detriment of effective disease management. Ultimately, the chapter reveals the malleability of development ideas as practiced on the ground.

Agriculture was a central means by which the Saudi monarchy tried in the postwar years to establish its stewardship of the Arabian Peninsula and promote new economic and social organizations related to the land. In chapter 5 I analyze Aramco's transfers of technology and attempts to categorize Saudi Arabian agriculture through a series of agricultural aid programs. The title of the chapter, "Aramco's Eden," comes from Richard Drayton's discussion of imperial botany. If botanic gardens represented to early modern Europeans a return to an antediluvian paradise brought about by science, in like manner Aramco worked to create an alternative paradise in Saudi Arabia, one centered on ideas of modernity.[37] Through agriculture Aramco promoted technical advancements and modeled American practices to local Arabs. The promotion of agricultural modernization, however, took on unexpected forms. Agricultural experts ignored a history of monocropping in colonial territories and instead advocated crop diversity. Aramco's presence also helped the monarchy with one of its own nation-building projects—placement of the migratory Bedouin in agricultural settlements—and allowed the company to come closer to its own goal of creating a settled workforce, albeit while reluctantly backing Saudi-designed schemes. In the end, cultural and economic changes precipitated by the oil company profoundly altered traditions in Saudi Arabia and redefined the future of Saudi national development. The uncovering of this untold story of the links between American corporate power and state building in the Middle East reveals powerful forces, many of which continue even today to shape global affairs. The origins of this influence stemmed from how the company began to carve out its independent diplomatic role in Saudi Arabia in the mid-twentieth century.

1

Aramco's World

ARAMCO's public relations arm often boasted in the 1940s that the oil giant was a unique organization. In many ways it was. In the middle of the twentieth century the company dominated Saudi oil exploration and had a more substantial impact on life in Saudi Arabia's enormous Eastern Province than any other Western institution, including the U.S. government. This distinctiveness, expressed in corporate public relations, implied much more, however. It spoke to a self-defined corporate agenda of enlightened capitalism. Much of the energy behind this legend stems from the company's Government Relations Organization, which consisted of divisions for government affairs, local affairs, and research and translation. George Rentz, a historian and Arabist with a doctorate from UCLA, led the department from 1946 to 1963 and hired enthusiastic men, notably the anthropologist Federico Vidal, who prepared numerous regional studies for the company and the kingdom, and William Mulligan, who wrote about the company for the corporate magazine and other publications. These men conducted extensive research and produced a wealth of reports on Saudi Arabia and the corporation, carefully crafting a story of corporate enlightenment. The narrative served multiple objectives, but probably most important it laid the foundation for the company's engagement with the monarchy, whose continued backing Aramco required if it hoped to exploit the kingdom for its riches. To fashion and promote its image, the company published simplified annual reports that had mass appeal, an employee magazine, and official histories of both the company and Saudi Arabia. But the project did more than position the company rhetorically alongside the monarchy. It elevated Aramco's status as the U.S.

representative in the kingdom, entangling it in both local politics and international diplomacy.[1]

The oil company worked alongside the king of Saudi Arabia, 'Abd al-Aziz ibn Sa'ud, as he turned to science, technology, and expert advice to expand his authority.[2] The two parties were building a nation dependent on new technologies for communication, transportation, and administration, and Aramco situated itself as an indispensable partner in this social and economic advancement. To promote the "distinctly American flavor" of Saudi oil, as company publications put it, Aramco constructed its own frontier epic.[3] After initial contact in the deserts of the Eastern Province, geologists began their search for oil in 1933.[4] With the help of local Bedouin, who acted as guides, American oilmen confronted what they saw as an ancient, backward society as they probed the desert for riches. Soon after the discovery of oil in marketable quantities, American oilmen became the guides, ushering the kingdom into the twentieth century through various development schemes. Petroleum engineers, construction experts, doctors, agricultural specialists, and more began erecting transportation, communication, and industrial infrastructure and transferring not just objects but also the ideas that came with them.[5]

The above story composed by Aramco culminates in the successful transfer of new, Western values. Saudi Arabia emerged as a modern nation-state, institutionalizing new technologies and ideas and eventually taking control of oil operations. While nationalization of oil operations in other parts of the world meant conflict, Aramco's transfer to the Saudi Arabian government proceeded smoothly, owing in large part to the mutually respectful relationship forged by corporate executives for decades. The story is compelling, for sure, but the image of a corporation with a soul shepherding an ancient civilization into the modern age obscures much of the exploitation occurring on the Saudi frontier, and it ignores the powerful corporate interests at work.[6] Aramco constructed its world through an allegory meant to position the company as a partner in Saudi nation building, helping promote it as the catalyst for modernization in Saudi Arabia.[7] This project found partial success, as the company indeed acted as the primary diplomatic representative of the United States for years. With the onset of the Cold War and evolving American stake in the Middle East after the Second World War, however, Aramco's private diplomacy faced challenges on many fronts, forcing the company to contend with the influence of the U.S. government.

Aramco's official engagement with the Saudi monarchy and Saudi Arabs began with Socal during negotiations for an oil concession in the early 1930s. To acquire the Saudi concession, the Socal representative, Lloyd Hamilton, with the aid of the hydrologist Karl Twitchell, had to compete with the Iraq Petroleum Company (IPC), a consortium of Western oil firms effectively managed by the Anglo-Persian Oil Company, a British-controlled entity. Both the British and Socal believed they had a man working for them inside the kingdom, Hector St. John B. Philby. A former British colonial official and confidante to the Saudi king, Philby also worked for the American oil company. His primary loyalty, however, lay with his friend 'Abd al-Aziz, and he persuaded the British to back off, knowing that their interest—to own the Saudi concession but not develop it since they had other large oil holdings in the region—and their financial offer, which was much lower than Socal's, did little to help the king. Desperate for money to secure his newly formed kingdom, 'Abd al-Aziz accepted Socal's offer.[8] While financial concerns likely dictated his interest in granting the concession to the American company, some evidence suggests (and the Aramco story maintains) that his predilection for the Americans extended beyond payments in gold. He is said to have told the former head of Socal, Gwen Follis, that he "knew that if [he] gave it to the British or the French and we had a falling out, I'd have a gunboat here."[9] The Americans, the king contended, would never react that way. This story raises an important point with regard to corporate diplomacy. The king perhaps believed American corporations represented a kind of imperial venture different from that of the British, one dissimilar to traditional European interests in controlling and manipulating indigenous governments.[10] In the 1930s this was not a fanciful belief. American oil companies indeed operated relatively freely in the Middle East. After the Second World War, growing appetites for oil in the West, combined with the anxieties of the United States over Soviet interests in the region, altered the strategic balance between corporate and government leadership of American oil diplomacy. American oil companies, however, would maintain a crucial place in the newly emerging postwar petroleum order, despite increasing U.S. government involvement in the Middle East.

The Saudi turn to an American corporation produced a similar response more popularly in the United States. 'Abd al-Aziz's relationship with Socal was portrayed as a rejection of European imperial politics. News coverage by the late 1930s substantiated much of what Follis asserted, noting that the king strengthened his standing in the Arab world by granting Socal the rights to Arabian oil.[11] The king was said to have found balance with the oil giant. By turning to an American *company,* he gained the authoritative support of American prestige without having to worry about government attempts to interfere politically. The king could bolster his newly proclaimed position in the Middle East without fear of European meddling.[12] The idea that American ventures across the globe somehow represented a different kind of imperialism was not new in the 1930s. Americans had boasted ever since the days of continental conquest in the mid-nineteenth century that theirs was an enlightened imperialism, so by the time American oilmen made their way to Arabia a narrative of America's unique brand of imperialism had long existed. Aramco hitched its fortunes to a well-founded story of American interactions abroad, long before encountering any unrest in response to corporate policy in Arabia.[13]

The assertion that the U.S. government would not interfere in the internal affairs of the kingdom had circulated widely by the end of the Second World War. When President Roosevelt, on his way home from the Yalta Conference in February 1945, made a detour to meet with 'Abd al-Aziz, the two men reached a general understanding respecting America's imperial ambitions. The translator William Eddy, the only other person present at the meeting and later an employee of Aramco (as well as of the CIA), recalled the king stating, "The U.S.A. never colonizes nor enslaves."[14] After the war, popular accounts of this story continued to point to the king's history and discomfort with European imperialism as well as to his belief that a private company meant no direct connection with the government. The British could not offer as much. If not a primary reason, it was a point the king repeated later.[15] As the struggle in Palestine began to erupt after the Second World War, American oilmen faced a situation in which American championing of Israeli independence threatened the oil concession. The king insisted, however, that there was a distinct difference "between American companies and government, which makes policy."[16]

King 'Abd al-Aziz's apprehension regarding European imperialism had its foundation in his own history with the British. Beginning with the First World War, the British relationship with the Arabian Peninsula and the surrounding regions made an indelible impression on his thinking. Legends of British advances in Arabia had been made famous in the West through the writings of Colonel T. E. Lawrence and others.[17] While Lawrence emphasized a personal bond with the Arabs, British policies operated with a much heavier hand. During the war Britain's Arab Bureau, located in Cairo, backed the Arab Revolt against the Ottoman Empire in the northwestern regions of the Arabian peninsula. The revolt was being directed by Sharif Husayn of the Hashemite family, who ruled the Hijaz, the western region of Arabia containing the holy cities of Mecca and Medina. At the same time, British authorities from the British India Office continued their long-standing policy in the Eastern Province of negotiating treaties with various local leaders. They had signed such a treaty with 'Abd al-Aziz, then the amir of the Najd, located in central Arabia, in 1917 and began making payments to him in exchange for his allegiance. Their aim was to establish a stable sphere of influence in order to ensure secure trade routes to India. Prior to the war 'Abd al-Aziz had been engaged in local battles to regain for his family control of the Najd and its central city, Riyadh. During the war he expanded his reach, battling the al-Rashidi family in the north and later the British-backed Hashemites in the west. In the summer of 1919 'Abd al-Aziz turned south toward Jeddah, where he encountered a stern British reproach. If 'Abd al-Aziz did not retreat, the British warned, they would act. 'Abd al-Aziz complied, but in a show of force the British moved troops and aircraft to the region anyway. The future king would soon have little doubt of Britain's support for the Hashemites, as it subsequently withdrew military aid to him.

In the 1920s the British government would install Hashemite rulers in its neighboring League of Nations mandates of Trans-Jordan and Iraq. 'Abd al-Aziz then watched the British annex Aqaba and Maan in northern Arabia, domains he believed rightfully belonged to his nascent kingdom.[18] These experiences no doubt colored his thoughts on British machinations in the Middle East.[19] And if this history was not enough, he had had previous dealings with British oil concerns. 'Abd al-Aziz had granted an oil concession to a group with British ties, the Eastern and General Syndicate of London, in 1923. He anticipated royalties that would pay for the construction of infrastructure, medical services, and agricultural development.[20] Six years later, after failing to receive any revenue, 'Abd al-Aziz canceled the concession, and when the syndicate came calling again in 1933, he quickly dismissed it.[21]

Whatever favor American oilmen had in 1933, they immediately developed a presence in Saudi Arabia unlike that of the popular image of Lawrence, separating themselves from their Arab hosts in meaningful ways.

Aramco's Arabia would contain as much American culture as possible. As the corporate presence expanded after the discovery of large quantities of oil in 1938 and particularly after the Second World War, Americans who worked for the company increasingly lived exclusively American lives in Arabia. Even before transferring to Saudi Arabia they learned to see themselves as being separate. The employee handbook and instruction at the company's Long Island training center, opened in 1948, guaranteed that. After being hired by the company, many new employees began their service in New York, traveling to a former airbase in Riverhead, Long Island, where they were instructed in how to handle life in Saudi Arabia. They learned basic Arabic vocabulary and pronunciation intended for Americans working in the Foreign Service. Essential Arabic greetings and phrases required to shop at local markets were combined with necessary industrial language such as "pass the wrench" or "I'm expected. I must go." Sections of the textbooks they used outlined the conversational skills one might draw on if a truck breaks down, if one is laying pipe, or if one needs to communicate with "a new houseboy."[22] The buildings and living quarters of the center were constructed to mirror those found in the company compound in Dhahran. The main difference, however, was that these facilities contained no air-conditioning, a luxury Americans serving in Saudi Arabia enjoyed.[23] Along with their six-week immersion in Arabic, new employees received instruction in Islam and other aspects of Saudi culture, all taught by Saudi Arabs. The lessons extended beyond the classroom, too. The company encouraged the students to spend as much time as possible socializing with their Arab instructors. After six weeks, they received dental work and immunizations and began their voyage abroad.[24] In 1951 Aramco moved the school to Sidon, Lebanon, but its purpose was unchanged. The company wanted its American employees to have a basic understanding of Saudi culture and some colloquial Arabic, believing it would help them serve as better representatives of the company, even as they lived segregated lives in the oil towns.[25]

The memories of those who attended Aramco's immersion language training illustrate clearly Americans' impressions of Saudi Arabia before departing. Long after his service with the company in Saudi Arabia, Bob Waters remembered the language lessons being taught by "young Saudi boys out of the Aramco dining halls."[26] In reality, the instructors, who were both young and old, came from many places in Saudi Arabia. One of them,

Sami Hussein, traveled to New York with Aramco and began working in a company store in New York. He aspired to become an American citizen and return to Saudi Arabia in the future to help his countrymen in some way. Hussein eventually landed a job teaching at Aramco's Long Island training center, married, had children, and purchased a home in Levittown.[27] There, he lived his own version of the American dream. At times while in Saudi Arabia, Waters faced what he called inconveniences. He "dreaded having the Arabs working in the house." Nevertheless, when Arab workmen installed his "sweet water"—or filtered, drinking water—tap, he found "it wasn't too bad. . . . I was so pleased I offered them tea, so we had a cup together. That seemed to please them." If Waters's memories are any indication, Aramco's American employees likely carried with them from their training through their stay in Saudi Arabia paternalist perceptions that would be hard to overcome.[28]

Regardless of these negative impressions, the oil company promoted its relationship with the Saudi monarchy as one centered on goodwill and respect. While language and culture training in Long Island afforded the trainees some insight into the company's operations, the employee hand-book *Aramco and World Oil,* first published in 1950, gave many new employees their first real glimpse of Aramco's world and helped immerse them in the corporate narrative.[29] The "miracle of American production" relied on American employees who would help deliver civilization to Saudi Arabia. The "Arabian–American partnership" required it.[30] Employees represented much more than a slice of the company; they symbolized, the handbook stressed, "the *American* way of doing things." It was crucial that they recognize their "responsibility to the American nation," which was to acknowledge the great obligation they shouldered as America's representatives in Saudi Arabia. "All of the Americans in Arabia come into contact with Arabs," and therefore "a large proportion of the American employees are engaged in teaching the Arab new skills and in supervising their work. Others contribute indirectly to the development of the country."[31] The appropriate role for Americans in Saudi Arabia, it seemed, was tutorial, although segregated living often made the sort of engagement the company highlighted difficult.

In the 1930s, long before training facilities and manuals inculcated in employees the corporate narrative, Aramco founded the city of Dhahran as an oil camp, and it served as the company headquarters shortly after the Second World War. Like the nearby company towns of Abqaiq and Ras Tanura, Dhahran revolved around the oil industry. Towns like these had become common in oil-producing countries, something companies learned from mining syndicates over a half century earlier. By the mid-1950s over twenty thousand people lived in these three towns, only about three thousand of whom were Americans. The American Camp in Dhahran served as the home of the American staff, while Saudi and Italian workers and others lived in segregated compounds nearby. American Camp housed the residents in air-conditioned, ranch-style homes complete with white picket fences. American children stood on the curb and waited for the bus to take them to school, and after school and on weekends residents could enjoy swimming at the pool, playing tennis, and bowling. The best homes were reserved for supervisors, executives, and those with families. Unmarried American employees working in jobs that required less skill often lived in barracks but had similar amenities. Intermediate Camp, as it was known, housed Italians, Pakistanis, Palestinians, Indians, and others in barracks also. Saudi workers lived in General Camp, which was similar but did not have the same recreational facilities and other opportunities for residents. American Camp was much like a sundown town in the United States in that Saudis who worked there were not allowed to stay in camp after work.[32]

The racial division of residents combined with the failure of the company to grant better employment opportunities to Saudis led to two decades of labor disputes. Saudi Arabia experienced its first labor strike in the summer of 1945 when 137 drillers, soon followed by many others, demonstrated against the company's racial discrimination. Eventually, over 9,000 striking workers protested living conditions and pay. While the Saudi government punished the strikers and came down on the side of the company, even the king reportedly noted his displeasure at the unequal treatment. Future strikes compelled Aramco to make some changes, like installing floors in the huts where Saudis lived, but the division of life and labor remained a central feature of Aramco's world in Saudi Arabia. Even the vocational training offered to Saudis fell short of the corporate rhetoric trumpeting uplift. Those few sent abroad for university training, the company understood, often came back and agitated for more rights.[33]

Despite these problems, by the Second World War the relationship American oilmen had fostered with the Saudi monarchy positioned the company to be the primary American representative in the kingdom. The U.S. government had not aided the Americans in acquiring the concession and at the time had no diplomatic representation in the region. After the First World War the State Department did begin furnishing some diplomatic aid to American oil companies looking to break into the region, but diplomats generally accepted British hegemony on the Arabian Peninsula. The U.S. government formally recognized the new Saudi kingdom in 1931, and two years later signed an agreement that would allow for an exchange of diplomats. American oilmen, however, would not see U.S. government agents appear until growing tension in Europe began to threaten Saudi oil, a danger exaggerated by oil executives who worried about the security of the concession. President Roosevelt appointed the first envoy to Saudi Arabia in July 1939, but permanent representation would not come for four more years. American agricultural specialists served as early government representatives until a permanent ambassador arrived in 1943. The consulate in the company town of Dhahran opened in September 1944. All the while, Aramco's executives and the staff in the Government Relations Organization had been establishing close working partnerships with representatives of the Saudi government.[34]

Early interactions between the company and the consulate in Dhahran were generally positive, but American officials soon began to complain. Parker T. Hart, who opened the consulate in 1944, reported that Aramco laid a good foundation for American relations in eastern Arabia and that the company seemed pleased with the consulate's presence. Within months, however, internal correspondence signaled a shift. Hart observed that his dealings with American companies in the region "seem to be satisfactory" but added about Aramco that "in many respects, we are just another department within the company structure, struggling to get our share of the attention of garage mechanics, plumbers, carpenters, et cetera."[35]

Finding out what the company was up to, it seems, proved hard work for consular officials. Within the first year of Hart's presence he began to issue formal complaints to the Near East Division of the State Department in Washington. He outlined what he called a "lack of perspective" on the part of the company. The consulate, he wrote, relied on the oil company for "a variety of . . . services which could only be handled by their personnel." After months of repeated prodding, for example, Aramco eventually installed a flagpole but never built a document storehouse, as requested. By the summer of 1945 the consular offices still did not have central air-conditioning, and no fans were available, resulting in extremely uncomfortable temperatures that rose above 110 degrees. In addition, Hart was unable to book travel on company flights. Moreover, he noted, the company proved generally unhelpful with agricultural operations at al-Kharj after it relinquished them to U.S. officials in 1945. Aramco's management argued that government operations should not rely on the company, a position Hart accepted, but one made problematic owing to the fact that the consulate was less than a year old and not well established in eastern Arabia.[36] As the consulate saw it, Aramco "has always considered us here for its own convenience, to do passports and notarials, for its employees, as part of ARAMCO's 'service,' and to be at their (the company) beck and call at all times."[37] The more the consulate discovered about Aramco, the more the company's activities worried government officials.

Negotiations over construction of permanent consulate facilities further eroded the initial positive feelings among American officials in Dhahran. After settling on rents with the monarchy, Hart identified land in the concession area near Aramco facilities, a tract which company management hoped to use for future expansion and was reluctant to give up. After tense discussions and deflections of the company's attempts to push the consulate to nearby Dammam, the government secured the site for construction.[38] American officials continued to face difficulties even as the site was being built, all the while relying on Aramco to house employees as the consulate's operations expanded. Ambassador J. Rives Childs remarked in 1948 that Aramco was "unsympathetic [to] our housing crisis."[39]

Although there is evidence that Aramco pushed for American involvement in the kingdom, early corporate encounters with the consulate suggest that the company intended to maintain its independence, carrying out its operations and turning to State Department officials only when it was advantageous to do so. One early example of such behavior took place during the first Arab–Israeli war in 1941–48. Former ambassador Herman Elits, an economic and political officer in Saudi Arabia at the time, remembers that Aramco's American employees were the "principal and initial" representative of U.S. interests in Saudi Arabia and that it took some work to convince Saudis they should look to U.S. government representatives when it came to political matters. In the end, Elits argued, President Truman's recognition of Israel in 1948 altered this dynamic, as Aramco "was not anxious to get itself involved" in the matter. Elits is correct in saying that Aramco hoped to avoid dealing with the prickly subject of Israel, but it was a bit premature for him to suggest that the company's attitude led to a recognition "by the Saudi authorities that they had to deal with official U.S. representatives."[40] Ultimately, the company backed the Saudis during discussions at the United Nations over the future of Palestine, and it furnished material aid in the renewed military conflict in 1948.[41] The Saudis, like company officials, took their concerns where they could be heard, and it was not long before another regional diplomatic dispute prompted corporate engagement with the monarchy. From 1949 through the mid-1950s the monarchy looked to the company for assistance during border disputes with the British protectorates of Oman and Abu Dhabi. The U.S. government, Saudi officials believed, did not uphold their interests. The company proceeded carefully, communicating with State Department officials, the British Foreign Office, and Saudi government officials, as it continued to assert its independent diplomatic agenda. The company alternated between fearing British encroachment on its oil concession and making sure it provided the right backing to the Saudi monarchy.

'Abd al-Aziz surprised nearly everyone in 1949 when he declared the Buraymi oasis, located in the border regions in the kingdom's southeast, part of his domain. Even maps drafted by oil company cartographers and used in Saudi schools since 1945—subsequently pulled from classrooms in 1949—showed no Saudi claim on the region.[42] The company's response illustrated corporate strategy clearly, as the public relations team, through studies compiled by Vidal and Rentz, mapped out Aramco's independence and charted Saudi Arabia's future through a selective historical narrative. Vidal conducted the research for his study *The Al-Hasa Oasis* in the early 1950s in an attempt to understand the people who inhabited that area. As company operations moved south of Dhahran into the kingdom's interior through the construction of railroads and exploitation of new oil fields, it became clear that construction material, labor, agricultural supplies, oil contract work, and other supplies and services would need to come directly from that region. By studying al-Hasa, Vidal hoped to measure the effects the company was having on the residents of the oasis and on Bedouin in the area and, more important, to gauge whether local residents would be willing and able to work for Aramco.[43] The study built on an earlier work about the region by Rentz and Mulligan, one which outlined the Saudi influence on the eastern frontier. Rentz's subsequent study of Oman addressed this subject again, this time focusing more specifically on boundaries. Here, he detailed the status of territory he said was still undefined or, he said, under the control of neighboring governments. While much of the region actually had been defined and controlled by others for some time, this study, not incidentally, helped strengthen the Saudi monarchy's claims on territory outside the kingdom.[44]

Using reports from travelers and other evidence, Rentz placed the disputed Buraymi oasis well within Saudi authority, arguing that the British protectorates of Oman and Abu Dhabi had little historic claim to the region. The disagreement ignited a conflict between the Saudis and the British, who hoped to preserve their imperial posture on the Arabian Peninsula. The British Foreign Office challenged much of Rentz's research, asserting that he misled readers about the nature and extent of control exercised by central Arabian leaders.[45] Meanwhile, Aramco executives played a complicated game in Saudi Arabia as they endeavored to pressure the U.S. government, mollify the British, bolster the Saudi monarchy, and protect its concession. Aramco's selective and deliberate use of the past reveals the degree to which corporate diplomacy extended into state and identity formation on the Saudi frontier in the late 1940s and 1950s.

Numerous actors, all with diverse interests, outlooks, and histories in the region, were pitted against one another. The U.S. and British governments argued from divergent historical vantage points. Britain had a long imperial presence in the Middle East, whereas the United States had no formal historical ties to the region. And while Britain conducted its oil diplomacy through state apparatuses, the Americans relied more on corporate leadership. During the Buraymi dispute, the United States hoped to improve relations with the Middle East and prevent Soviet advancement in the region as the Cold War heated up, whereas Britain hoped to retain its presence in the region and its standing as a world power. The Saudis deeply distrusted the British, who supported rival Arab clans for leadership positions in surrounding nations. In making these new claims, the monarchy, in light of its close ties to the Americans, hoped to dispel any appearance of complicity with Western imperialism in the Middle East, a suspicious relationship in an era of emerging Arab nationalism. For the states involved in the conflict, the issue was less about oil than about international and regional politics.[46] From a corporate perspective, however, it was about oil and power, and

Aramco's actions during the height of the dispute indicate its deep desire to secure its place as the sole exploiter of Saudi oil reserves.

The Buraymi oasis is situated in the east of the Arabian Peninsula near the southern border of the present-day United Arab Emirates and the western border of Oman. To the south and west is the Rub al-Khali, or "empty quarter," as the desert was known in the West. In the 1950s Buraymi consisted of eight villages, about six miles across, circling its water wells. Settled farmers in the area primarily grew dates along with some fruit and other grains, and mainly Bedouin pastoral farmers raised camels, goats, and sheep. The scarcity of vegetation prevented much more economic activity than that. For centuries the oasis served as a strategic outpost and a point of departure for armies staging invasions to the east. While no oil had been found in the region by 1949, expectations remained high.[47]

The Saudi monarchy's move in Buraymi stirred international alarm, and Aramco's executives quickly positioned the company alongside the Saudi Arabian government as a protector of Saudi interests and a potential guarantor of American protection. Saudi soldiers and company surveyors descended on the border regions to the east as early as spring 1949. Accompanying this team were officials from Aramco's Government Relations Organization. The group spent most of its time conducting such operations as geological reconnaissance, water testing, and data compilations on the natural and cultural aspects of the region.[48] These seemingly innocuous activities, however, troubled the British, who on April 21, 1949, dispatched two armed soldiers along with Patrick Stobbart of the Foreign Service, a brother of the sheikh of Abu Dhabi, and an employee of the IPC. Stobbart "rather officiously" announced to Paul Combs, an Aramco driller, that the Saudi-American party was in Abu Dhabi territory and must leave. Combs encouraged him to meet with "company men" and Saudi officials at a nearby base camp, at which point the encounter became heated. Saudi soldiers disarmed the two guards, revealing that the guards were carrying loaded weapons, which heightened tensions even further. Unhappy, Stobbart exclaimed, "This is going to cause a frightful stink!"[49] While British power on the Saudi frontier appeared to be ineffectual, before departing Stobbart handed the Aramco employee Don Holm a note declaring the trespass and advising all parties to leave "before any possible incident occurs between the Saudis and the Subjects of Abu Dhabi."[50] The political problems this could generate would have been quite clear to the Aramco surveyors and relations men, who must have known the recent history of the oasis. As late as 1945 the oasis served as a meeting place for the sheikhs of Trucial Oman and the British government to discuss ongoing wars between the sheikh of Abu Dhabi and the sheikh of Dubai.[51] This encounter would be the opening salvo in a years-long dispute that constantly had the potential to become very violent.

The Saudi Arabian government agreed to enter into negotiations over its eastern boundaries but insisted that the region's historical, social, and economic practices be the basis for talks. The British rejected this stipulation from the start, noting two problems: first, nomadic tribal boundaries made defining territorial boundaries almost impossible; second, contemporary politics heightened the importance of the area. A British subsidiary of IPC, it seems, had already begun explorations in the region, angering the Saudi king.[52] Despite these differences, the parties met in Riyadh on August 30, 1949. The Saudis confirmed the extent of their claims deep within the territory of Abu Dhabi, far too deep for either the sheikh of Abu Dhabi or the British government to accept. Arguments centered on a starting point for negotiations, often on the basis of various British treaties signed over the preceding decades that had established the eastern frontier.[53]

The dispute worried American oil executives, who consistently promoted the Saudi position. Manley Hudson, an Aramco lawyer who served the monarchy in its legal disputes, opined to State Department officials that attempted British intimidation of the Saudis frustrated relations more than anything. The monarchy hoped to negotiate with regional sheikhs, not the British, who the king argued had no legal authority. Many times in 1950 Aramco pushed this line of reasoning, hoping Washington would support the Saudi claims.[54] The following February 'Abd al-Aziz formally requested Aramco's assistance, specifically that of Rentz, in preparing his legal claim on the region. Aramco began planning a fact-finding mission that would include studies of geographical features, tribal considerations, and tax collection.[55] A year earlier Hudson had stated that "tribal allegiances and the extent of their ranges are too conflicting or indefinite to offer a fully reliable basis for judgment," but that was exactly the tack Rentz and his aids took to buttress the Saudi case. Apparently Hudson's position evolved, signaling corporate thinking, as he noted that Saudi tax collection in the contested territory granted sufficient legal right.[56]

This position was an interesting one in light of the historical meaning of tax collection on the Saudi frontier. The first of the Saʿud family to emerge as a regional leader in the eighteenth century, Muhammad ibn Saʿud, employed *zakat,* an Islamic tax paid to the Muslim community's leader, as a way to centralize and consolidate his authority in central Arabia. Originally part of the duty of Muslims as one of the pillars of Islam, zakat eventually became part of permanent administrative governance, and it is a tradition that survived into the mid-twentieth century.[57] A wealthy landowner and local amir, Muhammad ibn Saʿud, boosted commerce financially, and his protection of tribes in the area allowed him both to gain a position of status and to collect tribute, that is, a tax, from residents in the region. To enhance his political standing, he allied with Muhammad ibn ʿAbd al-Wahhab, an Islamic reformer who provided religious legitimacy to Saʿud's political authority. As the Wahhab–Saʿud alliance expanded its control in the mid-eighteenth century, tribes continued to show fealty to the amir through payment of zakat. It was, one historian notes, "a token of political submission."[58] Taxes and Wahhabi religious austerity helped consolidate local authority in an era when borders meant very little. ʿAbd al-Aziz continued this arrangement in the early twentieth century while expanding his reach in central Arabia, and zakat became one of his most valuable revenue sources before the discovery of oil. Since this system of taxation was so crucial to rule in Saudi Arabia, defining allegiance on the Saudi frontier for centuries, it is no wonder it was such a vital part of the Saudi claim on the Buraymi oasis.

Whatever the historical basis for Saudi claims, the monarchy hoped the U.S. government might help coax the British into accepting the Saudi position. In a letter of friendship to ʿAbd al-ʿAziz written in 1950, President Truman, commenting on his satisfaction that American private enterprise was working to develop the kingdom, added that "the United States is interested in the preservation of the independence and territorial integrity of Saudi Arabia. No threat to your Kingdom could occur which would not be a matter of immediate concern to the United States."[59] Nearly three years later the king and his son, Crown Prince Saud, invoked this letter when the new secretary of state, John Foster Dulles, arrived in Riyadh while on a trip in the Near East. They demanded American backing. Dulles assumed an aloof posture, however, averring that he could not dictate to the British and that the disagreement was not existential but a problem of boundaries. Saudi Arabia was not under attack.[60] Washington's position evolved, but the government never exerted the kind of pressure on the British that the monarchy desired.

In this environment, talks between the Saudis and the British proceeded slowly, with tensions often running high. The British called for international arbitration, and the Saudis requested either mediation by the United States or submission of the problem to the United Nations. The Americans shuddered at taking a mediating role between two allies, one with oil and the other a central component of its regional and global security interests. They were anxious too about the dispute's coming before the UN Security Council, where, State Department staff worried, the Soviet Union might score a propaganda victory against Western imperialism. Additionally, the United States had been resistant to arbitration, also seeing it as an opportunity for the Soviets to propagandize. But mediation soon became the most agreeable option.

With no clear end to the struggle in sight, in August 1952 'Abd al-Aziz sent the Saudi amir Turki bin 'Abdullah ibn 'Utayshan with a forty-man occupying force to the Hamasa settlement within the Buraymi oasis, escalating tensions further.[61] The British responded with a blockade, hoping to prevent the resupply of Turki's party, and then began to discuss its military options. 'Abd al-Aziz still held out hope for American intercession, but the United States offered only to ask the British to lift their blockade and discontinue their provocative Royal Air Force overflights. The British agreed to end the flights, but local forces loyal to the sultan of Muscat mobilized soon thereafter, as did more Saudi troops. Meanwhile, Turki, it seemed, had been bribing local tribes since his arrival in August. The British, for their part, played a similar game, reportedly sending a Desert Locust Control Mission to Buraymi from nearby Sharja.[62] While the British continued to push arbitration, the Saudis introduced a new plan: a plebiscite of local residents, which the king believed he would win handily. Britain and Saudi Arabia eventually reached a standstill agreement on October 26, 1952, hoping to ease tensions for a time while a permanent settlement could be reached. But this too caused conflict, as Turki used the less heated atmosphere to continue offering bribes to locals who were willing to prop up Saudi claims in return.[63]

Buraymi's importance to British imperial policy expanded rapidly in the early 1950s. It was the start of a difficult period for the British in the Middle East, one which would end in the surrender of regional hegemony to the United States. The refusal of the Anglo-Iranian Oil Company, which was controlled by the British government, to negotiate a fifty–fifty profit-sharing agreement on oil revenues with the Iranian government, coupled with the rise of Nasser and Arab nationalism in Egypt leading to the Suez crisis, seriously challenged the British position in the Middle East. Buraymi represented the possibility of locking in future oil rights—something the British refused to give up on easily—while maintaining a degree of international prestige.[64]

In defense of its own strategic interests, the U.S. government privately sided with the Saudi monarchy but publicly came to support arbitration as a time-honored—and probably the best—diplomatic solution. Washington's concerns remained divided. Aramco held concessionary rights in Saudi Arabia, but other American oil firms, including two of Aramco's parent companies, held rights through British syndicates, including the IPC, the Bahrain Petroleum Company, Superior Oil Company, and the Kuwait Oil Company.[65] Further, State Department officials were not convinced by Saudi arguments, but they warned U.S. embassy officials not to share this information with the Saudi monarchy.[66]

Saudi Arabia and Great Britain finally agreed to arbitration on July 31, 1954, but tensions did not abate. The agreement called for an arbitration tribunal to define a permanent boundary between Saudi Arabia and Abu Dhabi. The committee was to have five members, one nominated by Britain, one by Saudi Arabia, and three with no ties to either. Both sides agreed to halt expansion of oil operations beyond the Aramco and IPC teams already in place.[67] Additionally, each side was to remove all its forces except for fifteen soldiers.[68] At this point, however, a change in government in London altered the British stance. The new prime minister, Anthony Eden, looked to take a tougher line than his predecessor, Winston Churchill, as British power waned in Iran and Egypt.[69] Thus when arbitration began the next summer, it ended almost immediately when the British delegate resigned from the tribunal in disgust over alleged Saudi tampering. The British charged the Saudis with bribing local leaders, improperly influencing the Pakistani delegate to the tribunal, and plotting a coup in Abu Dhabi. Although the first charge was true and the second likely so, there is scant evidence of the third.[70] In any case, arbitration fell apart, and on October 16, 1955, the British seized the oasis by force, declaring a new border unilaterally.[71]

The military occupation in October only enflamed the dissension, and it frustrated U.S. officials, who had hoped the British would see that American oil interests benefited the entire West. The British had no intention of relinquishing their position, one that Eden viewed as being enormously essential if Britain were to remain a regional power. British actions did not stop the Americans from pressuring Britain to return to arbitration, but events elsewhere in the Middle East soon took precedence for the British, as the Suez crisis heated up. Regardless of their differences on Buraymi, Anglo-American relations before Suez seemed positive, except for one issue. A British policy paper of July 1956 called Aramco "the greatest obstacle to Anglo-American harmony in the Middle East."[72] Anglo–Saudi friction did not lessen for years to come. Saudi assistance given to rebels in Oman in 1957 led to further military incursions by the British; meanwhile, American oil executives assured American and British officials that they were not involved in the affair.[73] Diplomatic relations between the British and the Saudis were restored in 1963, and plans were made to settle the Buraymi dispute once and for all.[74] Over a decade later Saudi Arabia signed a treaty with the United Arab Emirates that defined the eastern borders of Saudi Arabia.[75] Buraymi, in the end, would not be part of the kingdom.

Aramco's role in all of this discord, while seemingly small, speaks volumes about its corporate diplomacy. The company, to be sure, kept its distance from the squabbling early, contending that it simply served at the pleasure of the Saudi monarchy. George Ray, a lawyer for the company, declared that oil explorations conducted on behalf of the king were about pleasing him, not about corporate political interests.[76] If the Saudi government wanted an area explored, the company argued, it was wise to assign Aramco to conduct the exploration. In 1952 Aramco published Rentz's study of the southern and eastern borders of Saudi Arabia. Much as the corporate image making that came before it did, Rentz used history to situate the company as a diplomatic partner, this time through boundary making. Aside from describing the region for readers, Rentz himself stated in 1951, "This study is an attempt to bring to light the truth regarding areas where boundaries on the mainland happen to be in dispute." Further, he hoped it would "be of value to those who are actively engaged in the endeavor to settle the boundary problems that now exist."[77]

Rentz placed the Buraymi oasis well within Saudi authority, warranting that the Trucial sheikhs and therefore the British had no historic stake in the region. Buraymi's link to central Arabia dated as far back, he argued, as 1803, when previous Arab rulers established residence there and collected taxes from area tribes. Throughout the first half of the nineteenth century Buraymi transitioned between periods of independence and periods of control by the rulers of central Arabia. By the twentieth century, Rentz argued, Buraymi was all but independent, if still tied to various rulers along the Trucial Coast. Rentz marshaled evidence from travelers who described the oasis as being independent and from others who suggested the region relied on the Saudi monarchy for protection and paid tribute to Saudi tax collectors into the 1930s. This study by Aramco bolstered 'Abd al-Aziz's boundary claims by asserting a historical foundation of continuing influence in the region, the basis of the Saudi legal contention.[78] Foreign Office officials demurred to much of Rentz's argument, saying he misled observers about the nature and extent of control exercised by central Arabian leaders. In fact, most histories of the region placed the oasis outside Saudi control.[79]

Publicly Aramco executives attempted to distance the company from the dispute, but they maintained their zealous interest in the possibility of ensuring more oil resources. When Britain and Saudi Arabia began working on the organization of an arbitration agreement, it allowed for continued oil exploration by IPC, a stipulation that worried Aramco's executives.[80] Vice President James Terry Duce stated Aramco's position, namely, that these activities actually exacerbated the dispute and that the company had not entered the region since 1949.[81] He continued to assert that the company had no interest in the area and had no intent to search for oil there. The company's holdings, he stated, were "already sufficiently large."[82] But as both American and British diplomats knew, Aramco consistently protected its concession and its role as the sole oil company in Saudi Arabia, neither of which it planned to relinquish easily.[83] Duce told diplomats from both countries what they wanted to hear, even while assuring the Saudi monarchy of his firm's real intention to uphold its claims and produce Saudi oil. When asked about the statements Duce made to the British, Vice President Floyd Ohliger pleaded ignorance. He stated emphatically that Aramco would not surrender any concession rights and, moreover, would be delighted to explore Buraymi for oil.[84]

Aramco's efforts to define the eastern frontiers of Arabia were a result of two of the company's primary interests: extending its concessionary rights and giving diplomatic sanction to the Saudi monarchy. Duce and Ohliger consistently voiced the company's support of Saudi interests to the monarchy. The identity of the company as an independent actor—with

American ties—could not be questioned following the Buraymi dispute. The foundation for this identity was constructed through a complex set of actions and representations, all of which served to establish the company as a partner in Saudi nation building. The boundary dispute and other ongoing quarrels, however, shed light on a looming problem in the Middle East. Colonialism, as Prime Minister Churchill told President Eisenhower in 1954, no longer posed the threat it once had. What had replaced it was "oilism," and Aramco represented one of the most powerful and influential midcentury practitioners of it.[85]

Aramco's diplomatic wrangling in favor of Saudi boundary claims, combined with its rhetorical strategies, forged the company's status as an independent agent in Saudi Arabia.[86] The company's role in bringing development aid would add to its service as a goodwill ambassador to the kingdom. Creating a positive image was a corporate strategy that allowed the company to legitimate its social and moral role.[87] Aramco sought to be much more than a foreign oil enterprise, but its primary objective was always to protect its concession and future profits. To do so, it projected an image to both the world and the Saudi monarchy that it was a partner in Saudi nation building. Aramco marshaled its Government Relations Organization to the king's side in hopes of expanding its resource base. Thriving in this environment, however, required a constant revision of many ideas the Americans had about nation building in the mid-twentieth century.

2

Constructing Balance

To CELEBRATE the opening of the Saudi Government Railroad in October 1951, the American Banknote Company created a postage stamp issued by the Saudi Arabian government in 1954. The stamp showed two men, one astride a camel, the other standing nearby holding the animal's reins, motionless in the desert. Both witnessed the passing of a locomotive pulling cars that receded into the background. The stamp was based on a photograph taken for Aramco in early 1951 by Yarnall Richie and published in the company's glossy magazine, *Aramco World*. It demonstrated Aramco's involvement in the construction of the railroad, which was the kingdom's largest development project at the time. An engineering feat, it traveled from the Dammam port on Saudi Arabia's east coast through new oil towns like Dhahran, the agricultural region of al-Kharj, and the ancient oasis town of Hofuf on its way to the capital, Riyadh. The oil company wanted its supervisory and financial role in the enterprise to be well advertised. Published again in the magazine after the railroad opened that October, the picture contained a caption that affirmed its message: "An ancient form of transportation gives the right of way to a new diesel electric of the Saudi Government Railroad."[1] The image of the train making one of its early journeys from Dammam to Riyadh shows the Bedouin and railroad conductor waving as they cross paths. The dichotomy pictured was entirely intentional. Ancient Arab tradition observed new cultural forms: those that symbolized efficiency, the movement of goods and people, the connection of distant lands to the modern world, and the future of Saudi Arabia.[2] The Bedouin waved to the future as it passed them by, while at the same time they welcomed the technology as a symbol of new opportunities, brought to them by an American corporation.[3]

The railroad, however, faced a cultural obstacle that engineering could not address. Shortly after it opened, a passenger train struck and killed a camel standing on the tracks. Local authorities promptly stopped the train and arrested the American engineer. William Owen, whom Aramco had just named general counsel of the railroad, received a call from the railroad's American president, Jim Gildea, requesting assistance. Owen, along with Thomas Barger from the company's Government Relations Department, arranged a meeting with the local amir who informed the Americans that Sharia, Islamic law, clearly stipulated that the one who struck the camel was at fault. A trip to Riyadh and a meeting with King 'Abd al-Aziz secured the engineer's freedom after the king angrily demanded his release.[4] This particular interaction between economic development and Saudi customs proved difficult but not impossible to manage. Following the Second World War, Saudi society and law dictated adherence to religious principles that often conflicted with contemporary cultural and technological messages coming from the West. In this case, Aramco sent an expert in government–company relations and a lawyer to negotiate with local officials for the release of the American engineer, but to no avail. Saudi tradition held sway. In the end, however, the negotiations were not simply about law; they were about Saudi Arabia's future and how best modernity would overlay those traditions, and which of them might be preserved. The Saudi Government Railroad represented newer and faster modes of transport for men and material. It meant increased wealth for the Saudi monarchy. It symbolized entry into the modern world in the same way that transport on the backs of camels, represented in the postage stamp, symbolized isolation from it. 'Abd al-Aziz knew the local roots of this dispute, but he modified his attitude to fit better his perceived needs regarding Saudi nation building. This conflict exemplifies an ongoing dialogue between corporate interests on the one hand and Saudi customs on the other in the mid-twentieth century.

Modernization discourse held that Islam should be relegated to secondary importance as the Saudi monarchy attended to nation building and economic development. Certainly one would imagine the American collaborators in this partnership might reason this way. Edward Shils, one of modernization theory's leading proponents in the 1950s and 1960s, argued that as societies modernized they cast off religious identity in favor of national identity. Religion held back traditional societies, which had a firmer, more widespread attachment to religion and kinship networks at the expense of civil politics. Moreover, the "responsiveness to the ultimate transcendent powers" and "the devotion to symbols of the past" were often, he added, "resultants of a situation without alternatives. Once alternatives become visible and available, what appeared to be an immobile tradition might yield to a new practice."[5] Many regional experts in the early fifties worried that Islam, like communism, offered what Eisenhower's secretary of state, John Foster Dulles, called an "emotional appeal" for a better future rather than a rational path. But soon it seemed that the religion offered a potential defense against communism.[6] In Saudi Arabia, nation building's relation to religion operated a bit differently, as the monarchy sought not only to breed a new national identity but also to reinforce Saudi Islamic identity and the monarchy's role in protecting it. Religion became central to state building, not an alternative to it. As self-described partners in Saudi nation building, Aramco accepted this arrangement, conceding to certain Saudi religious conventions that appeared essential to the Saudi state while circumscribing and renegotiating those it deemed more superficial. The company occupied a unique position, one in which American cultural traditions, diplomacy, and American law had to conform to a new environment. It did so as business strategy, before the U.S. government turned to religion in the mid-1950s as a way to isolate Nasser and promote Saudi Arabia's King Saud as a regional leader.[7]

American oil executives strived to position the company as the primary diplomatic representative of the United States and as a partner in Saudi Arabia's future. As the historian Matthew Jacobs notes, oil executives imagined their role in the region as that of a tutor: "they believed the theme of transformation offered the most plausible grounds on which the oil companies could make their case." The company positioned itself in the region much as Americans before them had, that is, imagining the American role in the Middle East as instructive.[8] And it did so in the understanding that it was not creating a crisis between tradition and modernity, as many regional experts saw it in the late 1940s and early 1950s, but putting into practice a business strategy that would balance, at least rhetorically, certain local practices with the needs of the corporation.[9] Aramco's public relations arm promoted Saudi interests and demonstrated the company's power in providing for Saudi development. But when the ideas connected to the company's operations clashed with Islam, the centralizing idea of state and society in Saudi Arabia, Aramco and, following it, the U.S. government had to reshape key strategies regarding technical advice and development around practical considerations of diplomacy. While the company worked to shape the future Saudi kingdom through its role as a partner in development, national and regional religious concerns compelled acceptance of certain Saudi norms as the monarchy looked to embolden its authority as the protector of Islam. When Saudi Islamic traditions conflicted with American norms on display in Aramco's American Camp, the company had a different attitude, as it looked to negotiate space for greater American cultural expression, not as a model of modernity but as a corporate policy meant to make oil operations efficient.

To many in the West at midcentury, Islam and modernity occupied polar ends of the development spectrum. The Middle East expert and Arabist William A. Stoltzfus Jr., who served in various diplomatic posts in the Middle East during the 1950s and 1960s, offered his succinct assessment of the interaction between modernity and Islam by saying, "The Moslems don't accept our technology," adding that Americans typically failed to seek out information about other cultures, instead relying on the idea that "we're better off simply because we're more modern."[10] The putatively imminent transfer from tradition to modern framed development theorists' understanding of United States–Middle East relations at precisely the time practitioners worked out these ideas in the field. As Daniel Lerner argued in 1958 in his influential study of modernization in the Middle East, the region in the 1950s was in the midst of a "secular process of social change."[11] He contended that "traditionals," those still wedded to the past, attended mosque regularly, whereas "transitionals," those more receptive to change, acted in far more secular fashion.[12] Secularization was a crucial dividing line within a society faced with change imposed from the outside. Lerner argued that scholars agreed on one thing: "secular enlightenment," or modernization, was something Islam could not resist for long. It would supplant tradition in the Middle East.[13] In many cases development doctrine rejected traditional notions of religion in favor of more enlightened, objective ideas about law and society. The United States, in the eyes of midcentury development theorists, had reached the pinnacle of modernity during the fifties and early sixties, a modernity encompassing what the historian Nils Gilman describes as a "secular, materialist utopia."[14] To many adherents of development theory, modernization represented a faith in and of itself, a universal, rationalist, secular, and democratic order to be imposed on traditional people the world over, the results of which would be the gradual erasure of dominant traits of cultural distinction.[15] In practice, however, Saudi Arabia was a difficult place to sell many of these ideas. A state that emerged in conjunction with the extension of strict observance to Wahhabi Islamic concepts, Saudi Arabia proved unwilling in the mid-twentieth century to accept easily much of the secular models of Western-driven modernization. Even in the early twenty-first century, it remains a difficult society to penetrate, as strict Islamic codes continue to shape social practice.[16]

The unification and consolidation of Saudi Arabia in the early half of the twentieth century inextricably linked Islam and the monarchy. With the annexation of the Hijaz, 'Abd al-Aziz secured control over Mecca and Medina. Today, when Muslims around the world kneel five times a day to pray, they face Saudi Arabia. With this reality come certain responsibilities, which have been well known and widely exploited by the monarchy. The king consciously and conspicuously promoted himself and the Saudi state as the protector of Islam in order to legitimate his continued rule.[17] The monarchy's role in this regard as protector of the two holiest sites of Islam did not go unnoticed by outside observers. Hector St. John B. Philby, the British official and later the king's confidante, observed in 1925 that 'Abd al-Aziz's capture of the Hijaz signified a forceful and improved governance of Mecca.[18] The American mining engineer Karl Twitchell reported to the U.S. State Department in 1941 that 'Abd al-Aziz was "the most important figure in the Moslem world" owing primarily to the location of Mecca within his kingdom, which made the king's influence substantial, stretching from North Africa across to India and into the former Dutch colonies of present-day Indonesia.[19]

One of the king's primary responsibilities became the protection of Muslim pilgrims who, performing the *hajj*, descended on Mecca each year as part of their duty to Islam.[20] In the 1920s the annual pilgrimage brought nearly 120,000 Muslims to Saudi Arabia from regions as close as Egypt and Syria to those at considerable distances, such as Morocco, India, and China. These travelers joined pilgrims from the Arabian Peninsula whose numbers reached almost as high. Pilgrims arrived by camel, on foot, and aboard boats. With the advent of worldwide depression in the 1930s, the numbers declined, fewer than 30,000 traveling from abroad. Muslims arriving by land came from all directions as they made their way to Mecca, while those who came by sea tended to disembark in Jeddah, the southwest

Arabian port city that one Western traveler described in 1924 as "an old, decrepit and dirty little town" in which "a stranger . . . is a sort of prisoner" and "the port to paradise."[21] Once there, pilgrims traveled in groups the fifty miles inland to Mecca.[22] The king's obligations to the hajj could be fulfilled in a variety of ways, and the interaction of 'Abd al-Aziz, Islam, and economic development commenced shortly after the king's annexation of the Hijaz in 1926. American diplomats reported in 1928 that "the tendency toward modernization" with respect to the hajj meant greater security and improved road construction along traditional pilgrimage routes.[23] The king reportedly addressed these improvements to pilgrims in 1931, declaring his intent to "promote the material advance" of the kingdom, which, he said, included the expansion of industry and the exploration of mineral resources. But, he maintained, it did not mean abandoning Islam. He said, "It is not by pandering to western ways that we can gain equality with the west."[24] By the mid-1930s, however, global economic depression, as noted, meant a decrease in pilgrimage traffic and a subsequent decline in tax revenue to the king. Roads were reported to be in disrepair, but sources within Saudi Arabia made sure to promote the monarchy's protection of visitors through continued construction of new roads, lodging facilities, and other improvements intended to comfort travelers.[25] In 1948 the American ambassador to Saudi Arabia, J. Rives Childs, expressed the connection between economic development and the king's religious responsibilities. In a transmission to Washington, he noted that the king's schemes to improve hajj facilities in the region during the late 1940s stemmed from his intent to substantiate his role as the "protector of the Holy Places."[26]

The austere form of Islam the king employed in the consolidation of Arabia from 1902 to 1932 complicated attempts to centralize authority and strengthen control by means of Western-styled development. By 1926 'Abd al-Aziz had incorporated the Hijaz into his realm, gaining control of the Muslim Holy Land. The region's administration, however, remained separate from his base of power in the Najd, the central district of Arabia, with Riyadh at its center, where 'Abd al-Aziz dwelled. These two regions constituted separate spaces, both physically and culturally. From the Najd the desert slopes east to the Persian Gulf, and to the west are the Tuwaiq Mountains, "the backbone of Central Arabia," as they were described. To the south lay desert, the Rub al-Khali, or Empty Quarter, as westerners called it. Riyadh had roughly twelve thousand inhabitants in the early 1920s, most centralized around oases that fed off drainage from the nearby mountains.[27] The majority of Najdis were either Bedouin or settled Arabs who lived in separate, isolated villages and engaged in pastoral farming, some trade, and raiding to sustain life. Many of the king's most loyal followers were religiously austere Najdis.[28]

The Hijaz, the region containing Mecca and Medina, remained almost entirely separate from the Najd and had a very different history. Residents lived a much more settled and urban existence in this region. Pilgrims descended each year to the area from around the Muslim world, and trading centers formed along the coast, giving the Hijaz an international, cosmopolitan texture. By gaining control of this region and ruling Islam's most sacred places, 'Abd al-Aziz hoped to acquire prestige and also the tax revenue from pilgrims and customs duties, all to help offset his loss of revenue when British subsidies dried up following the First World War. Additionally, unlike the Najd, the diversity of the Hijaz meant that no one powerful figure had authority over the various tribal confederations spread throughout the region. The boundaries between desert and city were much more clearly drawn, which, travelers noted, made the region seem less united and more defensive about territory. When 'Abd al-Aziz unified the two regions under his rule, he became saddled with the twin responsibilities of uniting the Hijaz and trying to merge the two regions legally and culturally.[29]

The Hijaz quickly became the administrative center of the nascent Saudi Kingdom, while its religious center remained in the Najd. Complaints about the "cosmopolitan and secular" ideas emanating from the cities of the Hijaz were voiced by the religious factions on the central plateau. These critics hoped for a more rapid transformation to Islamic traditions preached by Central Arabian Wahhabis. Najdi supporters grew unhappy as the Hijaz dominated more of 'Abd al-Aziz's attention. Their complaints also targeted his construction of telegraph and telephone lines in the area, leading to concerns among his Najdi followers that he had lost his way. To them, 'Abd al-Aziz was turning away from the strict Islamic traditions that helped him centralize Arabia under his rule. Most troubling was the power this new technology summoned. The king could now rule the Najd from afar, monitoring his Najdi followers and circumscribing their economic freedom to raid, possibly looking to extract greater taxes from a populace now more closely observed.

The introduction of new technologies did more than damage relations between 'Abd al-Aziz and his religious base in the Najd. It also provided a cautionary tale for how such actions might be embraced in the future. These concerns could not be ignored. As centralization progressed, so too did dissatisfaction among 'Abd al-Aziz's faithful Ikhwan, the religious warriors who initially helped him consolidate his rule.[30] Caution in the implementation of new technology continued to play a role in the kingdom following the Second World War. American officials outlined these preoccupations in the 1940s as they reported on Saudi advancement. Childs stated in 1948 that Saudi Arabia seemed disposed to remain "on the path of modernization," however, he added, 'Abd al-Aziz continued to have difficulties as he "overlay the material advantages of Western civilization upon existing Arab culture without too greatly affecting the spiritual values of a deeply religious people." Childs recognized the difficulty the king faced, not only, it turns out, with his own people but also with "some of the more romantic members of the foreign colony [there], including the British Ambassador" who believed "charm" was being lost in Saudi Arabia.[31]

This interaction between the past and the future is central to twentieth-century Saudi Arabian history. Wahhabi teachings stressed conservative lifestyles and generated objections from many Saudi Muslim leaders about outside trends in contemporary life. The preservation of Saudi Islamic traditions became more salient with the addition of Mecca and Medina to the equation. The historian Madawi Al-Rasheed summarizes the problem fittingly: "The country's transformation in the twentieth century is shaped by this important fact that required a careful and reluctant immersion in modernity."[32] As American oil engineers and geologists stepped onto the sands of the Arabian Desert, the cautious relationship between development and Saudi religious traditions served as an ever-present backdrop always in need of negotiation. American embassy and consular officials recognized how central these religious conventions were in Saudi Arabia, and they often crafted messages to the monarchy's liking.

Americans operating in Saudi Arabia contended with restrictions many deemed to be rather unusual at times, but company officials wanted to maintain a positive relationship with the monarchy. As the U.S. government increased its presence in the kingdom after 1944, it had an interest similar to that of the company in helping the monarchy promote itself as the protector of Islam, a position that stemmed from multiple worries, including the fear of communist advances there. The Saudi monarchy certainly failed to meet American ideals of democratic government, but when it came to Cold War interests in Saudi Arabia, secure access to oil remained the central objective. American embassy and consular officials grasped the unique position of the United States with respect to the Saudi monarchy and therefore worked hard with American propaganda officials to limit Saudi exposure to certain images and ideas that upset the Americans' relationship with the kingdom. Embassy officials reported that the monarchy had an unfavorable reaction to most of the State Department's anticommunist propaganda,[33] which included pamphlets, posters, books, music, movies, newspapers, magazines, cartoons, embassy libraries, exchanges of individuals, and technical cooperation.[34] Much of this material extolled American democracy, freedom, and power as virtues, while at the same time outlining the dangers of communism. The Saudi monarchy disapproved of the messages of democracy and, according to embassy officials, communist influence in Saudi Arabia remained minuscule anyway.[35] The embassy's recommendations instead called for more technical cooperation and exchange that might better serve American interests in Saudi Arabia.[36]

Religion was a decisive theme the U.S. government promoted in the 1950s, consistently stressing its importance in combating Soviet influence.[37] In a letter of June 1951 to State Department officials, Aramco executives, and religious leaders in the United States, the Aramco consultant and CIA employee William Eddy highlighted the necessity of the Christian West and the Muslim Middle East presenting a "common moral front against communism." Eddy claimed that the West consistently placed little value on Muslims but argued that the two religions were united in a "moral alliance." This was a theme discussed both by Arab leaders in the Arab League and by King 'Abd al-Aziz. Moreover, Eddy stressed the key position Saudi Arabia held as the protector of Mecca and Medina, reiterating that the king was the most "influential Muslim in the world today."[38] Within a year this religious partnership against communism constituted a central component of National Security Council thinking.[39] By the end of the 1950s President Eisenhower confirmed this interest in a personal letter, writing, "I never fail in any communication with Arab leaders, oral or written, to stress the importance of the spiritual factor in our relationships. I have argued that belief in God should create between them and us the common purpose of opposing atheistic communism." Eisenhower knew, however, that Israel represented a far more immediate issue for the Saudi monarchy. U.S. troops had just arrived in Lebanon following the announcement in 1958 of the Eisenhower Doctrine, at the same time he wrote these words, but Eisenhower stressed that military power alone "can never insure any nation's security." He added, "The problem then is to create in the United States a true understanding of our proper relations as well as the measures necessary to keep those relationships healthy." The private sector, he emphasized, needed to be involved in promoting these issues.[40]

American leaders through the 1950s worried not about a general war that might bring Soviet troops to the Middle East but instead about communist influence that might upset Western hegemony and threaten access to petroleum. Military power, Eisenhower understood, would not ensure this security, but technical cooperation and the protection and promotion of Islam, he believed, could. To be sure, American diplomats imagined a sort of brotherhood with Muslims nations. As Andrew Rotter has shown, American support for Muslim nations against communist influence or even neutralism transpired in part from a shared sense in monotheism and the strength it conveyed. Religion occupied a central place in American foreign relations in the 1950s, and Christian–Muslim cooperation could serve Americas' needs.[41] Finding the right proportions between Saudi customs and American interests, however, remained a difficult task.

Aramco also looked to create an amicable balance. The company introduced new American employees to Saudi Islamic customs at orientation programs before they traveled overseas. In briefings designed to help employees adapt to life in the kingdom, the company noted that Muslim employees would and should be allowed to pray five times daily. It reminded employees that during the holy month of Ramadan, fasting Muslims were forbidden to eat, drink, and smoke and that engaging in these activities in front of them would be insulting. Additionally, workers were warned against discussing politics and religion with Saudis and advised that political conversations about Israel, open expressions of Christianity, and public consumption of alcohol were not looked on kindly by the kingdom's religious authorities.[42] American staff members entered a politically charged environment, and Aramco wanted them to understand the delicate position of an American company operating in Saudi Arabia.

Confronted with this reality, Americans working in Saudi Arabia faced challenges as they settled into their new lives. Supplanting Islam or the monarchy, or even the indication of such an act, could be costly. Aramco promoted an identity as an agent of progress, yet when possible it made substantial efforts to mediate its position in the kingdom to conform to Islamic law. Specifically, the company worked to ensure the Saudi monarchy's place in Islam as the steward of Mecca and Medina, and it supported the monarchy's practice of forbidding Jews from entering the kingdom. These same restrictions compelled even the U.S. government to alter some of its campaigns in Saudi Arabia. Americans serving in Saudi Arabia felt that the government encouraged a cultural and religious separation of Americans, one fully supported by the religious establishment.[43] This division allowed the American employees living in their separate colonies to worship in their own way and celebrate their own holidays, although quietly. A culture of cocktail parties and social drinking flourished in the American enclaves, but once these prohibited activities made their way into the Arab community, the Saudi government swiftly shut them down.

By the beginning of the 1960s, after Egyptian-backed nationalists rose against the monarchy in neighboring Yemen, prompting the Saudis to send aid to the Yemeni government, Crown Prince Faisal had announced a ten-point domestic reform program, one that blended the monarchy's interests in modernization and in Islam. Faisal freed Saudi slaves, organized new legal councils, and established local governments, all in an effort to update state governance. While many of the reforms never materialized fully, successful aspects of the program included the extension of Islamic propaganda and the restating of Saudi Arabia's commitment to Islam.[44] As the kingdom conducted its own modernization schemes, it had to take account of its religious identity.

Long before Faisal reaffirmed it in the early 1960s, Aramco's American personnel clearly understood Saudi Arabia's connection to Islam. American workers sensed stark contrasts between their own culture and what they witnessed when they arrived. As one American described the scene, "The oil camp itself was a world within a world, an outpost of Californio-Texan culture set down in the last redoubt of Islamic Puritanism."[45] This juxtaposition remained visible throughout Aramco's concession. Despite company rhetoric to the contrary, Saudi Arabian officials often complained to corporate officials about its sometimes callous attitude regarding Islam, ranging from company busses picking up Saudi employees during prayer to Americans forbidding prayer at work and recreational "Christian" swimmers failing to keep quiet while Muslims prayed.[46] These grievances call into question the narrative Aramco constructed about its easy adaptation to and careful negotiation with Saudi religious traditions. But it also speaks to the increasing difficulty of maintaining an American enterprise and colony in a burgeoning nation-state immersed in a religious piety unlike anything most American employees knew. While this balance proved challenging throughout the concession, the company strove to promote its comfort with Islam and to distance itself from the disruptive forces that worked to challenge the position of the monarchy or the role of Islam in the kingdom.

Uncertainties over the balance between Western, secular traditions and Saudi Arabia's position on religious issues extended beyond hiring and the company's backing of Saudi Arabian policy and into the kingdom's domestic public sphere. Company operations in Saudi Arabia ultimately were subject to Saudi Arabia's laws and the king's rulings. Taken literally, this subjection would mean a complete ban on alcohol, the exclusion of Christianity, and stringent codes regarding gender and other social practices. In reality, however, the company worked to meet American employees' needs and desires while observing the kingdom's social and legal proscriptions. Aramco recognized that rules applied to Saudi Arabs, and it worked to contain American culture within a defined corporate American environment. The balance required a certain respect for Islamic traditions, which often simply meant, for many Americans, recognizing them. The company officially observed the Muslim Sabbath of Friday, and work operations often revolved around Islamic law but not without some protest from American supervisors. As noted, Saudi officials complained of disruptions to religious observance, but Aramco's American staff complained as well. Conflict arose more than once regarding work during Ramadan, for instance. As early as 1942 the monarchy faced work stoppages but settled them not by shortening workdays during the month but by imprisoning and beating leaders of the strike. A second strike by Aramco workers led the monarchy to try to reduce the workday during Ramadan for oil company employees to six hours. The monarchy issued a royal decree to resolve work schedules, but the company soon relaxed a few of the new restrictions through negotiation.[47] Dress at work also generated conflict. One American noted that the company faced difficulty in securing a relaxation in Saudi dress so that Saudi Arabian employees could wear helmets and goggles rather than headscarves in dangerous work areas.[48] Protective headgear could certainly prevent certain types of injury, yet working long hours while fasting seemed not to raise similar issues. Oil production always took precedence over the safeguarding of Saudi religious practice.

Saudi Arabia insisted that Americans accept Saudi governance in most social relations, although in American enclaves authority typically fell to the company. Outside these areas, Saudi authorities gave little latitude when upholding Islamic law.[49] American employees tended to have the most trouble when facing the kingdom's restriction on alcohol. Until the early 1950s Americans who wanted to drink generally had no problems as long as the alcohol they consumed was restricted to the American enclaves.[50] This arrangement lasted until 1952, when a Saudi prince was involved in an alcohol-related shooting after leaving the British embassy, an episode that infuriated the king and led to his issuing of Royal Decree #79 banning the transport and sale of all liquor. Aramco's management at first refused to believe it, but its inability to import a three-month supply of beer waiting on a ship in the Netherlands confirmed the decree's reality. The company's Government Relations Organization asked Prince Faisal if this meant alcohol could be manufactured and consumed. The prince reportedly replied that such a permit could be added to the decree "in three seconds."[51] The implication seemed to be that the company could make alcohol, but it must be contained within the American compounds. By the late 1950s copies of the "Blue Flame," a company pamphlet instructing American employees on how best to distill alcohol at home, were available to any who wanted them.[52] Drinking that once took place at large parties in the American enclaves soon occurred only at smaller gatherings. Violations could lead to jail, fines, and deportation.[53] Saudi Arabians faced lashings if they were caught with alcohol. The Government Relations Organization's local division, charged in part with ensuring that "government regulations and customs are observed," quickly descended on scenes of trouble, but given that personal stills had been set up by American employees, managing alcohol use appeared to be a more realistic approach than enforcing its ban. This strategy, however, necessitated quick action by the company, and it mattered where exactly the infraction took place. At a private party in the oil town of al-Khobar in February 1962 alcohol was reportedly being consumed, compelling the local Public Morality Committee to intervene. Tests of bottles and party attendees (a "sniff test") came back negative, and all charges were dropped. Such leniency failed to materialize a month later when William Cowan, a staff member, arrived at Saudi customs on his return flight from Bahrain. He was said to be "under the influence of alcohol," and he had a bottle of liquor in his baggage. Cowan paid a small fine and was sent home. A hearing in June 1962 held that he had violated the Royal Decree banning the transportation of alcohol. His sentence: two years in prison, which could be commuted to a fine of five Saudi riyals for each day sentenced, and deportation. Whereas the company intervened successfully when it came to the private party, Cowan's public violation led to a far stiffer penalty, one that Aramco could not get commuted.[54]

The former Aramco executive Baldo Marinovic remarked that the company's independence within the American compounds began to disintegrate in the late 1970s, after the Iranian Revolution. He surmised, "The Saudi government became quite concerned about being out-maneuvered by the Iranians." But he knew for sure that life inside the American compound from that point forward became far more stringent as Saudi officials policed American religious ceremonies and social behavior.[55]

While fitting an American community into Saudi Arabia caused headaches for the company, it faced further problems as it endeavored to make new technologies comport with Saudi laws, a challenge Saudi officials shared. When in the early 1950s Crown Prince Saud began to worry that his succession might be in jeopardy owing to periodic public insults levied against him by his father, he sought to shore up his support among the tribes by instituting a large-scale news apparatus. He ordered press equipment and set in motion a print shop to produce a newspaper and a news magazine. The print shop began by publishing religious tracts in order to retain the support of religious authorities in the kingdom, and one of the first publications Saud planned was the Koran, which had never been published in Saudi Arabia. Saud went even further, however. He called on Aramco to secure radio equipment so that he could broadcast from Riyadh. Again, the plan was to begin with broadcasts of religious material. This could have a twofold impact. First, he hoped it would introduce new listeners to an unfamiliar medium with familiar texts, and, second, like the publication of religious tracts, it would please religious authorities, who might worry about the use of such technology.[56] Just as important, it could champion the Saudi monarchy's parallel project of nation building by bringing the Saudi community together through communications advancements.

Similar frictions surfaced earlier in Aramco's relationship with the monarchy, but these related not to radio but to the showing of movies. American employees enjoyed recreation facilities that included space for showing films. Saudi Arabian employees, on the other hand, living in General Camp, had no such facilities, primarily because of government restrictions on such activities.[57] The public showing of movies could, and did, lead to conflicts. Raymond Hare, the U.S. consul general, reported a case in which a movie with an attached newsreel about Israel was shown by U.S. military personnel at the Dhahran airbase in 1951. When a Saudi Arabian military officer in attendance objected to the newsreel the film was stopped, and an apology made in order to dilute the insult. A similar incident, Hare recalled, occurred during an Aramco viewing. In the context of apprehensions about violence expressed in the media in the United States, one movie depicted a villain who shot a lock off of a door with a shotgun. This behavior appeared to be mimicked soon after by a Saudi viewer who tragically shot and killed a man who was behind the door of a locked dressing room.[58] Public showings of movies in the country were mostly forbidden, but private ones were common, particularly among members of the royal family. By the end of the fifties, the Saudi monarchy was importing documentaries, French films, and even some less wholesome productions to royal palaces.[59] Aiming to relax certain regulations, Faisal promised in 1964 to open a few public movie houses and to establish a Saudi television network.[60]

Such moves certainly would have satisfied American modernization theorists, who emphasized the transformative possibilities of mass media. Walt Rostow, a leading modernization theorist and former adviser to Presidents Kennedy and Johnson, was said by those who were tired of his constant refrain regarding these ideas to have imagined "a TV set in every thatched hut." A joke for sure but a telling indication of the impact Rostow and other like-minded modernizers supposed this technology would have.[61] Lerner, for instance, explained how powerful television could be in bridging social gaps. Mass communication, he argued, created a "mediated experience" that expanded one's world in much the same way that travel did during the age of discovery. To emphasize this point, he quoted an Iranian bureaucrat who said, "The movies are like a teacher to us, who tells us what to do and what not." Tradition, Lerner maintained, would be overtaken as people began to "imagine how life is organized in different lands and under different codes than their own."[62] Saud hoped, however, that new media could bring new modes of living to Saudi Arabia while also sustaining Saudi customs.

Television created some unrest among the general population of Saudi Arabia when it arrived. Many complaints about the medium in Saudi Arabia dated back to Aramco's Channel 2, which originally intended to run programming for employees and their families and which observed strict adherence to the cultural restrictions placed on such media in Saudi Arabia. It began airing on September 16, 1957, with many of its shows coming from the United States. At the time, about two hundred television sets existed in Arab homes, but within five years the number had climbed to over twelve thousand, and Aramco began to pattern its programming to meet the preferences of Arab viewers in the Eastern Province. Programmers avoided content with any conspicuous political agenda, opting instead to run Arabic language films, American films with Arabic sound tracks, weekly sports telecasts, and such favorite American shows as *Father Knows Best* and *Perry Mason*. Almost 40 percent of airtime was dedicated to programs aimed at children, shows that were largely educational in nature. Language lessons, in both Arabic and English, were the most popular offering of this nature, but other programs dealt with safe driving, new agricultural techniques, and science and nature.[63] As in the case of radio, television generated opposition among religious leaders in Saudi Arabia. Faisal's new Saudi network, launched in 1965, ignited a ferocious religious backlash. A resurgent Ikhwan movement led by Faisal's nephew Prince Khalid attempted to attack the station. Eventually Khalid was shot and killed in a scuffle with police, leading to a supposed pledge of revenge by his younger brother, who would indeed eventually assassinate his uncle King Faisal in 1975.[64]

Americans in Saudi Arabia faced a challenge even larger than the one presented by new technologies, however, and that revolved around the kingdom's policies vis-à-vis Israel. Aramco faced an early, long-lasting obstacle to protecting its oil interests from 1941 until 1948, when the new president, Truman, decided, against the advice of almost every Middle East expert in the U.S. government, to support Jewish interests in Palestine. President Roosevelt's assurances of March 1945 to King ʿAbd al-Aziz that the United States would consult with him and other Arab leaders before making any decision about the future of Palestine died when the president himself died a month later.[65] Truman had made no such promises. As noted, he supported Jewish refugees' immigration to Palestine in 1946 and later backed the United Nations partition plan. In 1948 Truman recognized Israel only minutes after it declared independence in the wake of British troop withdrawals.[66] The American relationship with Israel factored into Aramco's relationship with the Saudi Arabian government throughout the remainder of the concession, and it sparked the unraveling of the concession after public outcry by Arabs following the Arab–Israeli war of 1967. To protect its interests, the company looked to distance itself from Truman's decision, one most Middle East experts within the government loathed. Loy Henderson, one of the State Department's most famous diplomats and Arabists, informed Secretary of State George Marshall in late 1947 that the "overwhelming majority of non-Jewish Americans who are intimately acquainted with the situation in the Near East" opposed the creation of a Jewish state. Henderson indicated that such a decision would damage Americans' relations with Muslims across the globe.[67] Marshall himself famously informed Truman that if the president recognized Israel in 1948, he would not have Marshall's vote that November.[68] Many diplomats worried, as Truman's next secretary of state, Dean Acheson, did, that American interests in the region would be endangered by such an act.[69]

For Aramco, the decision presented a conflict between its identity as an *American* oil company and its *independent* connection to the Saudi monarchy. While Truman opted to recognize Israel, evidence suggests that Aramco actively worked against U.S. government interests. When Arab League representatives identified oil as the best and only weapon to fight the Americans' support of Israel, company leaders certainly had reason to worry.[70] Fred Davies, a vice president at Aramco, reported to the State Department in late May 1948 that the Saudi king "indicated that he might be compelled, in certain circumstances, to apply sanctions against the American oil concessions."[71] The warning implied that continued American encouragement of Jewish fighters might damage the country's oil interests in the kingdom.[72] To combat possible sanctions, Aramco took an active role in promoting Saudi positions to the United States and the world. For example, there is evidence that the company funded Saudi officials' trips to meetings of the United Nations in 1947 to debate the Palestine issue. When this assistance became public, however, some on the company's board threatened to remove Vice President James Terry Duce, who wrote a letter to William Moore, the president of Aramco, outlining the company's adversarial position.[73] In the letter, Duce stated that he had promised Arab leaders that "they could count upon the active support of the oil companies and of the United States Government experts in their opposition to the Jewish State, and, second, to kill partition by advising the State Dept. of its dangers and reporting the views and proposals of the Arab leaders."[74] In 1948 the company supplied vehicles, fuel, and other materials to aid in the movements of Saudi troops against Israel. Aramco's opposition to Israel would have been very clear to the monarchy, but the Saudi government also was aware that sanctions could be disastrous to the monarchy. A State Department study showed that Saudi oil at the time constituted only a fraction of world development, yet it represented the king's principal source of income. 'Abd al-Aziz chose, for the time being, to distinguish between Aramco and the U.S. government.[75] To ensure further that the king appreciated Aramco's independence from U.S. policy, the company moved to relocate the proposed Trans Arabian Pipeline so that it avoided Israel, carrying oil instead from Saudi Arabia to the Mediterranean Sea through Syria and Lebanon.[76]

The company's efforts to cater to Saudi customs and political positions remained difficult as it was confronted with the kingdom's opposition to a Jewish state, but corporate executives believed they needed to continue to advance Saudi interests whenever possible. Domestically, the king forbade visas not only to Israelis but to all Jews—a policy Aramco also endorsed. This act meant that no Jewish U.S. government personnel or private company employees could serve in Saudi Arabia, a practice that led to a series of complaints in the United States regarding religious discrimination at Aramco. In 1950 the company, which identified religion as a "bona fide occupational qualification," enjoyed the full approval of the State Department in its religious discrimination in hiring. Diplomats argued that American–Saudi relations required equilibrium between American ideals and Saudi demands, and American courts without fail upheld this discriminatory position.[77]

Controversy continued when, in 1956, Samuel J. Ravitch answered an Aramco job advertisement for a physician. The company discouraged his employment because of his Jewish faith, noting that his presence in Saudi Arabia might put him at risk. Correspondence with the Saudi Arabian embassy only served to harden Aramco's position on the matter. The lawyer at the U.S. embassy seconded the company's position, arguing that Ravitch would be "ill-advised to attempt either to pursue employment with Aramco in Saudi Arabia or to attempt to hide his background."[78] That same year a parallel dispute compelled the American Jewish Congress (AJC) to bring suit against Aramco's personnel office in New York through the New York

State Commission Against Discrimination (SCAD). Aramco countered that it had to "abide by the laws and practices" of Saudi Arabia, and because Saudi Arabia recognized a state of war with Israel, the king refused visas to Jews, who he believed might be "working as Zionists in behalf of Israel."[79] The AJC charged that New York state law forbade discrimination based on religion and that Aramco engaged in this very practice even by asking potential employees about their religious background. The investigating commissioner, Elmer A. Carter, dismissed the case, but that did not end the case.[80] The AJC appealed the decision, more than once, until finally, in 1959, Justice Henry Epstein heard the complaint and ordered SCAD to reconsider its decision.[81] Epstein stated, "The film of oil which blurs the vision of Aramco has apparently affected the commission in this case." If Aramco could not comply with New York state law, he urged it to "go elsewhere to serve [its] Arab master."[82] Carter appealed Epstein's decision on Aramco's behalf. The company's lawyers continued to hold that, owing to its relationship with the Saudi Arabian government, Aramco had received a court exemption from following state discrimination laws after the 1950 ruling. In the end, the courts upheld Epstein's order, and Aramco faced a SCAD commission in early 1962 that would settle the question for good.[83]

The question was not whether Saudi Arabia could allow Jews access to the kingdom. Aramco's illegal practice of discriminating against Jews incensed the AJC, but in addition Aramco seemed to serve the Saudi Arabian government blindly rather than comply with American law.[84] Aramco's position conformed well to the way the company interacted with the Saudi monarchy over religious issues. It considered the monarchy's anti-Jewish policies existential, central to Saudi Arabia's foreign policy and its identity as an Islamic kingdom. In September of that year, however, the newly named New York State Commission for Human Rights ruled that Aramco could no longer question applicants regarding their religious background or affiliation. In the order, the commission agreed with the AJC, protesting that Aramco "acts in this regard as an agent of a foreign power, implementing a policy inimical to our democratic principles, contrary to our law."[85] Aramco in 1962 was not only being charged with discrimination, owing to its self-perceived need to uphold Saudi standards, but also depicted as a servant of the Saudi Arabian government. In contrast, Aramco continued to hold the position that it weighed American law and Saudi sensitivities equally. In the end, the company did hire a few Jews, but by that point the king had relaxed his demands on the company.[86] Aramco's endorsement of the monarchy's position on Israel, however, never changed. As late as 1977 the company had prepared a series of talking points about its acquiescence to the long-standing Saudi Arabian boycott of Israel and of companies doing business with Israel. Aramco officials were encouraged to highlight the significant long-term benefits of good American–Saudi relations in contrast to "short-run support for Israel." In testimony before Congress on antiboycott legislation, company lawyers coached witnesses to "show that support for legislation derives from 'selfish' interests of those who would spoil present opportunities for creating stability in [the] Middle East."[87] Aramco's continued defense of the Saudi position on Israel was never in question.

By building these relationships with the Saudi monarchy, the company tried to establish itself as a partner in Saudi nation building. Nasser's promotion of Arab nationalism, secularism, and Cold War neutrality concerned policymakers in the United States, who worried about communist encroachment in the region. Nasser flirted with the Soviet Union, offered diplomatic recognition to Communist China, and balked at negotiations with Israel. American backing of King Saud was problematic, as he failed to live up to the ideals of a so-called good Muslim himself and had few friends outside Saudi Arabia. His opulent spending exposed him as a less-than-devout Muslim, making him an unlikely leader of Muslims worldwide. And often, as historians have shown, Saud's determined defense of Mecca and Medina led to problems in his relations with the United States, such as the claims he made in 1957 that Israeli use of the Straits of Tiran threatened the annual pilgrimage. Aramco's actions were driven more by fealty to the monarchy than by global politics.[88] Demonstrating that loyalty even as they exploited the kingdom, however, called for more than diplomatic support. It required constant work on the ground, putting Saudi nation building needs into a development framework that supported corporate goals.

3

Curing Antiquity

WHEN Ivor Morgan arrived in Dhahran in late 1952 to work as an obstetrician and gynecologist in Aramco's medical services, he found himself on a cultural frontier. He spoke almost no Arabic aside from what he had learned in the brief language course offered by the company, and he knew very little of Saudi culture beyond his orientation classes. On arriving, he received a tour of the facilities, a description of his duties, and an introduction to what he later referred to as the "primitive culture of most of the local populace."[1] While Morgan handled, with little difficulty, common ob-gyn cases among the American senior staff, the skilled craftsmen, and their families, he confronted unfamiliar clinical complications when attending to local patients. These patients had had no prior prenatal care, and even taking their histories required multiple levels of translation. Besides the language barrier, the female patients remained veiled and often followed a custom that dictated that all communications go through the husband, who generally accompanied the patient. Not only an Arabic translator was necessary but also someone to act as the filter of a local male authority. Not surprisingly, these cultural divides created a number of difficulties in the doctor–patient relationship. Taking a patient's history, for instance, often proved challenging, and Morgan expressed a great deal of frustration about doing so. "Facial expressions and body movements," he said, helped doctors recognize symptoms, and "tak[ing] a history of a veiled Arab female was much the same as trying to communicate with a tent . . . a futile exercise."[2] To overcome what he believed was an unnecessary cultural obstacle to proper medical care, he hoped the husband could convince his wife to remove the veil. When such a concession could be achieved, it often led, in Morgan's opinion, to a more comfortable patient–doctor relationship. Lifting the veil, however, did not remove the primary challenges to treating what he called "the problems peculiar to the more primitive culture of the Middle East and Saudi Arabia" at that time.[3] He recalled, for instance, asking a man to give blood in order to save his wife's life. The man refused. Another, he stated, insisted that tomato juice—also a red liquid—could substitute.

The Saudi national body, and perhaps the racial body of the Saudi Arab, constituted patients through which Aramco's medical practitioners and corporate officials exercised authority over the nation and its people.[4] More practically, Western medicine became, by the mid-twentieth century, an almost obligatory tenet of modernization. It seemed important, asserts the historian Ashis Nandy, for modern medicine to be "taken out of the dominion of folk wisdom, domestic remedies and non-modern healers."[5] Medicine gave the oil company a means to regulate Saudi Arabian hygiene, agricultural practices, water supplies, maternal and child health, nutrition, waste disposal, and modes of life, purportedly on behalf of the general public more than for corporate gain. To Aramco, medicine was a central instrument for defining, categorizing, and acting on Saudi Arabia in an attempt to enmesh itself more inextricably in the future of the kingdom and, more important, of its oil.

Technology's optimistic postwar context suffused the Aramco physicians' mission. The proliferation of technology and the desire to spread and measure American notions of progress were central objectives of Aramco as it constructed its medical programs in Saudi Arabia. The eminent historian Arnold Toynbee reported to Aramco in 1958 about an ongoing confrontation between "traditionalists" and "modernisers" in Saudi Arabia, arguing that "modernization means the mastery of modern technology."[6] Medicine was one vehicle by which Aramco looked to export modernization to Saudi Arabia. Western visitors to the company's domestic camps, Toynbee continued, stumbled on "an American city that has been shipped to Arabia on a magic carpet." Within the walls of these magical imports Aramco constructed and maintained clinical facilities where they employed and mastered technology and measured their own progress against a backdrop many Aramco medical professionals would call backward. The possession of the latest medical equipment came to signify the company's modern, progressive capabilities. When the Saudi Ministry of Health began constructing hospitals, the accumulation of the latest equipment there came to represent the kingdom's entry into the modern world.

In the eyes of many Aramco physicians arriving in Saudi Arabia, as Morgan's experience illustrates, Arab customs bred ignorance. The firm's Medical Department embarked on a decades-long mission to supplant local nostrums with American medical technology and standards, to teach Saudis Western hygienic standards and practices in order to rid the Eastern Province of centuries-old diseases, and to construct facilities to house new medical technologies. These technologies not only supplanted local cures but also spread American ideas about progress throughout the kingdom and worked to cure the Saudi body of the vestiges of antiquity that many of Aramco's officials believed continued to linger far into the twentieth century. Yet these programs did not emerge out of a civilizing mission. Instead, they evolved as the company's presence grew, and while some executives were reluctant to expand medical care, others understood the practical role of medicine and its impact on the relationship with the Saudi monarchy. Aramco conceived its programs, in part, as antidotes for the restrictive forces of antiquity that held sway in the Saudi nation and among its people, but, more important, it hoped to prove that the company brought progress rather than exploitation. Many Americans in Saudi Arabia believed that the ancient past maintained a powerful grip on the region well into the twentieth century and that the corporation, through the expansion of American medicine and technology, could reverse this trend and bring the kingdom into the modern age.

Aramco's American employees represented Saudi Arabia as ancient and narrated their own presence as modernizers through the use of Western medicine. They defined, observed, shaped, and controlled Saudi citizens, demonstrating corporate goodwill and fashioning corporate authority. As the previous chapter highlights, the corporation supported the Saudi monarchy's attempts to legitimate its authority as protector of the two holiest Muslim sites, Mecca and Medina. By the twentieth century, medicine constituted the center of a new physician–patient relationship, one in which the unwell body became the object on which authority was constructed.[7] The construction of various medical facilities by the corporation, private Saudi citizens, and, later, the Saudi Arabian government illustrates how Aramco promoted its influence in the kingdom through the postwar decades. Not coincidentally, the monarchy's adoption of these medical technologies and practices and the cultural forces they embodied enabled the Ministry of Health to construct state systems that extended the reach of governmental authority through an assertion of sovereignty over health matters within Saudi borders. That step was yet another attempt by the monarchy to establish itself as the caretaker of the kingdom and defender of the Muslim holy sites.[8]

To achieve the company's goals, many of its medical practitioners looked to address what they called folk medicine.[9] As Morgan's experience with Saudi female patients implies, the Medical Department immediately confronted a culture with traditions that very few company doctors understood. They firmly believed that the application of American technology would bring about monumental changes in the standard of living of many in this supposedly backward civilization. Medical practitioners were convinced that so-called folk beliefs, beliefs in the supernatural, and ritual "naturally decrease as Western scientific education expands."[10] The Medical Department, in this regard, saw its role in Saudi Arabia as to some degree that of an interlocutor in the discourse of modernization that the company initiated. As the company physician and medical director Julius Taylor put it, Aramco's transportation and modeling of Western technologies and practices allowed Saudi medical practices to enter "the next phase of medical practice."[11]

Taylor arrived in Saudi Arabia in the early 1950s and immediately observed that the indigenous populations in many communities relied on local healers, who employed hot wooden sticks to cauterize the chest skin in order to relieve the abdominal pain of pregnant women and to treat tuberculosis.[12] Morgan speculated that these techniques, or "primitive treatment modes," as he called them, which were sometimes self-administered, were employed to distract the patient from the original pain.[13] While generally ineffective against tuberculosis, locating cautery scars often allowed for a quick diagnosis. It "suggested that local medical healers had attempted to alleviate the patient's pain with that technique."[14] Another Aramco physician observed that cautery appeared to be a Saudi cultural tradition in medicine equivalent to acupuncture in China. It had been used to treat all sorts of bodily pain from jaundice to headaches.[15] There is evidence, however, that local indigenous practices, including cautery, proved useful in some instances and also served as models for American doctors, particularly mission doctors during the first half of the twentieth century.[16]

Aramco's doctors found that many of the indigenous remedies could create serious problems. For one thing, merchants with little or no medical training tended to be the ones who supplied them. Certain illnesses treated with medications sold by street vendors could lead to what the company physician Robert Oertley referred to as "interesting kinds of interconnecting problems," problems that manifested themselves once Aramco's medical staff saw the patients.[17] In one instance, an infant arrived at an Aramco clinic with signs of lead poisoning. Finding the source of lead proved difficult but not impossible. As Oertley explained, "It turned out the mother had cracked nipples earlier on, and she'd gone to a local nostrum dealer. She gave her complaint to him—and he was not a certified druggist or anything of that sort—and he gave her this paste, which she was to put on her nipples as a healing ointment."[18] He suspected that the ointment was the cause and convinced the mother to quit using it. After testing it in Aramco's labs, he found that the ointment was concocted from "pure lead paste." Oertley passed this information on to the regional medical director, and the authorities quickly arrested the ointment dealer and put him in prison. Dissatisfied, Oertley pressed the medical director in the region, avowing that more education about the dangers of these types of products would be more effective than putting one purveyor out of business. Soon after, he began sending the company's Arabic-speaking physicians into the provinces to inform residents about such dangers.[19] Aramco's medical staff eventually saw fewer and fewer problems related to local remedies. The Medical Department, in combination with the spread of a private and governmental clinical presence, led to a reduction in the use of local healers, and Western medical science became the normative approach to most health problems.[20] This transition, although progressing slowly over time, elevated the company as the primary medical authority in the Eastern Province.

In the early years of the Aramco concession, the company's doctors served American employees, helping to ensure a healthy labor force that was capable of opening new territories for exploitation. As the company's role expanded throughout the Eastern Province, so too did its medical mission. Company officials began to define their role through the metaphors of disease and therapy. Expanded medical programs served corporate needs but at the same time enhanced the company's prestige. Corporate officials working in the kingdom often imagined themselves to be much like European colonial administrators; they spoke in terms colonial propagandists would recognize. While motives varied, protecting the concession and potential future profits dominated Aramco's interests. Several American officials even went so far as to aver that health initiatives blocked incursions from communist forces by offering examples of democratic values at work.

Yet most Americans operating in Saudi Arabia knew that displays of democracy were neither necessary to prevent communism nor advisable given the authoritarian nature of the monarchical regime.[21] Western medicine signified power, and it served as a central instrument in colonial control during the nineteenth century, but traditionally the transmission of Western medicine across the globe was not dominated by the nation-state. Aside from missionary work that often preceded the existence of nations, private foundations developed an interest in the extension of medical modernization in the twentieth century, the most prominent being the Rockefeller Foundation. Many of these programs helped establish national public health structures and eventually became subsumed into them. One can see the interplay between European cultural heritages and indigenous cultures as nations looked to science and medicine to guarantee progress.[22]

Along similar lines, Aramco quickly developed a corporate medical tradition of its own in Saudi Arabia. Diplomacy demanded that the company do more than exploit the desert for its riches. Accordingly, American oilmen engaged in numerous transfers of technology to Saudi Arabia that worked to alter Saudi life. This was neither a new role for an oil company operating in foreign territory nor specific to Aramco. American oil giants operating throughout the world promised similar benefits to their local employees, and Aramco's pursuits were no different.[23] Medical programs were a tool of corporate diplomacy. Business decisions often compelled greater emphasis on the health of employees. The investment required a healthy workforce free of the ravages of malaria, trachoma, and other diseases common in tropical climates. Many Aramco medical practitioners, however, fashioned their role in the Eastern Province as a labor that went beyond the traditional functions of an oil company, one that could bring the kingdom into the modern world. Aramco constructed facilities near company housing settlements, and, much like medical practitioners operating in colonies throughout the world, they operated under the assumption that a narrow focus on specific diseases could heal the populace and generate economic development.[24]

Many residents of the Eastern Province encountered Americans for the first time long before geologists began gathering near present-day Dhahran in the 1930s. They had a history of turning to American medical personnel, and by the 1920s the Sa'ud family knew firsthand the benefits of Western medicine. The early twentieth-century Reformed Church of America maintained a mission on the nearby island of Bahrain, part of an Arabian Mission organized in 1889 in present-day Iraq. The very first Americans most eastern Arabs met were missionary doctors who traveled around the Eastern Province during the first half of the twentieth century furnishing medical care to local Arabs, including the Sa'ud family. 'Abd al-Aziz had turned to the American medical mission after contracting a severe infection that threatened his life in late 1923 and again when his son and daughters needed medical attention. As one mission doctor expressed it, "Medically, the prestige of the mission is high. We are thanked cordially for what we do, by merchant, priest, prince and pauper."[25] Another doctor remembered oil company executives later observing aloud that the medical mission facilitated corporate relationships in the kingdom.[26] When Aramco physicians arrived, people in the Eastern Province who remembered American doctors already had a model of positive engagement. Taylor certainly felt appreciated, stating, "The Arabs hold American medical practice in very high esteem."[27] Many other Saudi Arabs still had no experience with westerners or their medicine, however, and, as Morgan's story attests, Aramco faced new challenges as it aimed to span the cultural divide in the 1950s.

Aramco initiated its medical programs in Saudi Arabia after commencement of drilling operations in 1936. Thomas Barger, one of the company's early geologists, wrote to his wife in 1938 to illustrate the local understanding of medicine, pointing to a lack of understanding of Western practices. "Pills have to be doled out in single doses," he stated, "as the Bedu are confirmed in the belief that if one is good, six would be better."[28] In these early days, a solitary doctor, T. C. Alexander, served the first American employees in the field, mainly treating common communicable diseases in the area like malaria, small pox, trachoma, and tuberculosis. He referred more critical cases to localities better suited to handle them, such as London or New York. As the American corporate presence grew, its medical mission expanded as well. More medical practitioners arrived, and programs commenced to train Saudi men to become nurses, dental hygienists, and medical technicians. By the close of the Second World War, the oil company's presence swelled, and it soon began to construct and operate clinics throughout the Eastern Province.[29]

Many of Aramco's medical staff looked back on their time in Saudi Arabia with excitement, remembering their work as an adventure that served the needs of an undeveloped society. There memories fit well within the larger company narrative. The former company physician and administrator Armand Gelpi, for instance, remembered Saudi Arabia as a "medical frontier. . . . A society being propelled rapidly into the twentieth century—a change taking place in a matter of years, rather than centuries." This "extraordinary cultural change," as another medical practitioner put it, originated in the corporation's medical policy, which stated, "The Company will provide medical service to its employees and their designated dependents through facilities established or designated by the Company. It will encourage and promote the development of public and private medical services and facilities in the area of the Company's operations. Consistent with this development, it will allocate a reasonable part of its medical service to the care of the general public. It will arrange for appropriate programs of preventive medicine, health education, industrial hygiene, and medical research."[30]

To this end, Aramco began by treating its American employees. As operations expanded, Arab employees and then their dependents were offered medical care in company facilities. Company caregivers had to accommodate an unfamiliar model of dependents. A Saudi Arabian dependent included the employee's multiple wives, his children, and any other family member living in his home. Because management believed the rewards came in goodwill and found the extra costs of dependents minimal, they made adjustments, extending coverage to the general public. There were few local medical facilities in Saudi Arabia until the early 1950s, when an expansion began to alter locals' perceptions of clinical spaces in Saudi Arabia. At first Saudis avoided Aramco's clinics, seeing them as "the place to die, like the old times in this country," but this perception changed rapidly.[31] Company doctors believed that an infusion of American medical technology and a reconfiguration of the Saudi relationship to Western medicine could have encouraging effects. The medical staff worked tirelessly to make their presence relevant by making the clinical experience as comfortable as possible and an essential part of contemporary Arab life.[32]

The corporate narrative proposes enlightenment as the key to Aramco's medical expansion, but government guidelines played a notable role also.

In 1942 Saudi Arabia imposed labor regulations that compelled Aramco to "provide the worker, free of charge, all necessary treatment which he may require." It also required that the corporation work to "do all that may be deemed necessary for the preservation of the workers' health and comfort." In 1947 new directives required free services, "whether during or outside working hours," and included workers' families.[33]

While the company guidelines and Saudi labor regulations dictated much of how this treatment occurred as Saudi medical capabilities incorporated American forms, Aramco management also assumed it would be "politically ill-advised," as one medical director stated, to turn the general public away.[34] The extension of medical services to the local population resulted from corporate foreign policy as much as from the practical expansion of operations. As the medical policy stated, the company needed to mobilize resources for the general public. Assisting Saudi citizens was polite and helpful, but Aramco officials and medical practitioners believed that the Medical Department created diplomatic goodwill for the company in Saudi Arabia. As one medical official described it some years later, "The Medical Department was . . . a public relations" tool for the company, meant to show "altruistic involvement."[35] There are, however, some indications of management dragging its feet on the medical front. Taylor complained that management pushed back on the hiring of specialists to the point that it "slowed down the progress that," he claimed, "should have been made." Corporate records on other development programs show a similar reluctance to invest heavily, the hesitation deriving from a desire to avoid creating a local dependence on the company and thereby dissuade the general populace from taking advantage of the company's tutelage.[36] If one looks through a widened lens, it is clear that although Aramco continued to dispense prompt care to Americans, medical access for Saudis emerged more slowly than the company claimed. Diplomatic goodwill, some feared, could be a double-edged scalpel.

A nuanced reading of Abdelrahman Munif's novel *Cities of Salt* (1987) illustrates the complicated relationship between company medical personnel and local populations.[37] The story captures the early moments of exchange between Arabs and the West through an analysis of the first few decades of oil expansion. It is a history from below, as Saudi Arabs experienced it, rather than the official narrative supported by the Saudi monarchy and Aramco. A central episode late in the novel explores the interaction between Western and indigenous medicine, demonstrating the disruptive force of the West and the varied response in Saudi Arabia. A new doctor, trained in Western Europe, enters the company-controlled town and initiates a campaign to expel the local doctor. Through displays of his advanced equipment, he befriends local leaders and uses his assistant as a cultural translator to convince patients of his skills. Bedouin continue to see the traditional doctor, however, because of his effectiveness and affordability. The company hospital, like the new doctor, is seen as exclusive, open only in limited ways to local citizens. This account of Western medicine hints at a certain suspicion and distrust of Aramco medical personnel among Saudis.[38]

More practically, the construction of a large-scale medical program stemmed from concerns regarding the cost of labor. According to WHO in 1948, the health of the workforce had very real economic consequences.[39] To these ends, Alberto Missiroli of Italy remarked at a WHO meeting that year that "Africa cannot be fully exploited because of the danger of flies and mosquitoes; if we can control them the prosperity of Europe will be enhanced."[40] C. E. A. Winslow, an advocate of public health and a consultant to WHO, asserted in 1951 that the economic uplift that a healthy community might enjoy from a public health program could be immense. While cure of disease might be beneficial, prevention, he argued, cost far less.[41] These ideals and objectives were not lost on Aramco, this giant of the oil industry. Its Medical Department quickly expanded its obligations in the late 1940s, contending that "an expanded program of preventive medicine and public health . . . is a most important factor in labor costs."[42] Morale and efficiency combined with fewer lost work hours, fewer accidents, and reduced medical costs resulting from sickness and injury would reduce overhead related to labor. According to Aramco's physicians, it was "not only justifiable for the protection of those employed but contribute[d] toward a definite financial saving as well."[43] Aramco imagined its employees much like equipment that might require preventive maintenance; they noted that in this field, upkeep "applied to men instead of machines" and would, doctors said, forestall "eventual breakdown with necessary replacement, or repair, accompanied by many losses and delays."[44] One health official put it succinctly: "You don't get good work out of people until you find that they're healthy."[45] The company's preventive program combined research, education, and training related to various environmental issues, including hygiene and insect control, in part to organize the labor pool. It was in the area of clinical medicine where Aramco first expanded.

Regardless of the company's reasoning or the local population's suspicion, Aramco comprehended the significance of supplying good medical care to both its Arab employees and the general public, but it often failed to live up to its stated achievements. As early as 1944 an Aramco planning committee declared that treating the general public was "one of the greatest services we can offer the country."[46] But the hospital facilities for non-Americans in the mid-1940s were squalid. An American consular official noted that the hospital in 1945 was "a disgrace to the company and indirectly to Americans in general. . . . A well run hospital and a fine school are worth more than a hundred banquets and eloquent speeches voicing their good will."[47] Executives knew the diplomatic power of development, and with the Second World War finally over, it hoped to remedy these problems.[48]

Satisfying non-American employees' complaints about poor medical facilities proved difficult, but by the end of the decade Aramco had made some strides in improving medical facilities. Yet in the summer of 1947 a U.S. diplomat in Jeddah commented that the facilities for non-Americans continued to be "a disgrace to American foreign enterprise and the American medical profession. . . . [I]t is depressing to walk from bed to bed, covered with soiled sheets, to gaze upon sick bodies." He suggested that this reality injured the company's relations with Saudi Arabia, and, in a statement of the importance the U.S. government placed on the corporation, he noted that in addition it failed to "popularize the foreign policy of the United States government."[49] A year later, however, American diplomats visiting the newly opened and relatively modest medical facilities in Dhahran proclaimed them "very modern and spotlessly clean."[50] A change was occurring in short order as the company worked to incorporate new technologies and medical infrastructures in Saudi Arabia.

By the 1950s Aramco had upgraded its medical facilities and continued its implementation of new technologies. Opened in 1956, the Dhahran Health Center (DHC), described as being modest by Aramco's physicians, was characterized by other American observers as being the place where "American medical science can . . . arrest the centuries-old tide of communicable diseases in the Middle East."[51] Containing two operating rooms, the latest in medical equipment, and air-conditioning, the Dhahran hospital was to many Americans a beacon of modernity in an ancient and vital oil oasis. Throughout the next decade the company expanded its clinical facilities and encouraged the construction of private clinics in towns and villages in the Eastern Province and eventually of facilities administered by the Ministry of Health. Aramco began construction on the new hospital in the early 1950s around the existing modest structure. DHC "developed slowly . . . along the lines of current American medical care," one Aramco physician recalled and, when finished, resembled new hospitals in the United States.[52] After it opened in 1956, company physicians no longer had to contend with old equipment and operate on patients in sand-filled, oppressively hot, excessively sunny operating rooms.[53] The company effectively conquered the desert environment by constructing a new facility that kept the heat and the elements at bay. By early the next year, the hospital received accreditation from the Joint Commission on Accreditation of Hospitals (JCAH), located in the United States.

Accreditation of the DHC indicated very little about the quality of care directly, but it served as a symbol of modernity and created a measurement of Aramco's medical modernization in Saudi Arabia. Better facilities and consistent record keeping could certainly improve care, but not guarantee good care. To gain accreditation of the hospital by JCAH, Aramco first had to request and pay for it.[54] Once the assessors arrived, the company needed to demonstrate that its facilities and methods of record keeping conformed to American standards of medical organization and operation. The building needed to be safe, which required such things as the proper number and placement of fire extinguishers, the possession of an emergency generator, and the appropriate placement of smoke detectors and fire hoses. Further, proper ventilation and use of air-conditioning to prevent cross-contamination between wards had to be shown conclusively. DHC was able to meet each of these requirements with no more than minor structural and organizational changes.[55] In addition, JCAH inspectors verified that administrators had organized the proper committees and kept the proper statistics.[56] Record keeping seemed to consume the investigators' time. Rather than explore the type of care provided for particular ailments, the investigators selected cases at random and reviewed the patient charts to make sure that practitioners recorded each and every aspect of the patient's history, diagnosis, exam, and progress, if any. The comprehensiveness and organization of the chart were the essential aspects of the accreditation review process.[57] In the end, DHC continued to receive JCAH accreditation, maintaining its status for years as one of only two American hospitals outside the United States with such status, the other being located at the American University of Beirut.[58] Accreditation defined Aramco's medical program by means of American medical standards.

In addition to DHC, the company built and operated two smaller clinics in its oil producing centers of Ras Tanura and Abqaiq, but the Dhahran facility continued to serve as the focal point of the Medical Department. The medical footprint of these facilities proved substantial in the Eastern Province. All told, nearly eight hundred doctors, nurses, and staff members worked for Aramco in these facilities, the costs of which grew steadily, running almost $7 million in 1955 and growing to almost $13 million by the end of 1970. Many local residents used the facilities in 1956, the high point of such use, numbering roughly 29 percent of out-patient services and 48 percent of in-patient services. Most of the services were free. The estimated costs remained bearable, about $79,000 in 1953 before a substantial jump in 1954 to $424,000 and another in 1956 to $1.1 million until dropping to just over $300,000 in 1970. These costs were comparatively low considering the total amount of money expended in medical programs.[59] Expansion guaranteed that modern American medical culture would continue to resonate throughout Saudi Arabia, but it required the continued financial endorsement of the company.

The decline in costs beginning in the early 1960 was the result of the emergence of the Saudi Ministry of Health and various local medical facilities. The company worked with the Saudi Arabian government and private medical contractors to extend new clinical facilities and practice beyond Dhahran in what were known as contract facilities. By instituting new technologies and new management techniques and overseeing practices, Aramco broadened its medical compass and thereby widened its authority within the kingdom while decreasing its financial obligations. Aramco granted about $227,000 in initial loans to private interests that organized the ash-Sharq Hospital in al-Khobar, one of Aramco's oil boomtowns, and it guaranteed another $786,000. The company also contracted for beds for these hospitals, ensuring space for local employees and their families while also affording the hospitals a steady income. These contract facilities consisted of hospitals and clinics owned and operated by Saudi Arabians and other Middle Easterners, all selected by Aramco. Company doctors supervised the facilities, made rounds, evaluated standards and care, and ensured that the facilities kept proper records.[60] The firm's records and its medical practitioners advance the notion that, in part, altruism drove this expansion but corporate needs mattered too.

Aramco enjoyed continued control and supervision over these contract facilities beginning with the initiation of the very first contract hospital. In the mid-1950s the company reached an agreement with the local contractor Sayyid-Muhammad al-Dosari to build a private, eighty-five-bed hospital in the Saudi Arabian residential community of al-Khobar, just outside Dhahran. Aramco drew up plans for the facility and guaranteed it a daily income of 90 riyals by contracting to use sixty-five of its beds for ten years. This assurance persuaded a group of apprehensive Lebanese doctors to enter the agreement as well. Dosari was to build the facility with loans obtained by Aramco, and he was to rent it to the private doctors. He built the hospital, but he had the rental contract with Lebanese doctors annulled in sharia court, most likely owing to a personal affront he believed he had suffered at a social engagement with one of the doctors.[61] Dosari essentially held the facility ransom, making payments on the loan but refusing to come to terms with the Lebanese doctors or sell the facility outright. This forced Aramco to soften the deal a bit by agreeing to an increase in its sixty-five-bed guarantee from 90 to 121 riyals a day, roughly $6.3 million.[62] In the end, Aramco got what it wanted, an extension of its medical influence in the Eastern Province through hospitals owned and operated by noncompany personnel. While Aramco saw contract hospitals as a largely trouble-free way to impose standard procedures with little involvement, it failed to turn out that way. What the contract facilities did was shift only some of the workload away from Aramco-owned facilities while maintaining the company's standards and supervision.[63]

The contract hospitals were a start, but they were by no means the final step in spreading American medical authority throughout the kingdom. As late as 1959 many Aramco physicians still regarded government hospitals as being primitive. With the eventual construction of new government medical facilities, the Saudi government brought about medical modernization through similar uses of technologies, standards, and continued American supervision.[64] The facilities that did exist in the Eastern Province numbered only a few, one in Dammam close to oil production, one in Hofuf located within the largest oasis in the Eastern Province, and one in Riyadh. Saudi Arabia finally came into its own with the construction of the King Faisal Specialty Hospital (KFSH) in Riyadh in the early 1970s, making it one of the most technologically up-to-date hospital facilities in the world.

Taylor said of KFSH, "They put everything in that hospital that you could think of in the way of monitors, computer systems and equipment. They had all kinds of modern x-ray equipment, as modern as you could get in those days. . . . The very latest thing in hospitals."[65] The hospital was immense, covering several city blocks and containing over three hundred beds. It had its own nursing school and a cancer therapy center, something even the Aramco hospitals lacked. Although the government built the hospital, Americans managed it. Retired chiefs of surgery and other prominent, accomplished Americans moved to Saudi Arabia, working for the Hospital Corporation of America, a for-profit hospital management company. Aramco organized the staff, salaries, benefits, and schedules and met with hospital management periodically. Taylor recommended specific equipment and the organization of the operating room. Aramco's medical staff worked alongside Saudi personnel and continued its hands-on relationship with the administration of the facilities. This continued reliance on the oil company resulted primarily from early problems in the hospital's staffing. The government stocked the hospital with the latest equipment but had trouble finding enough qualified staff to operate it. Eventually, even Aramco sent patients to KFSH for treatments and procedures that could not be performed in Dhahran.[66] If new equipment and American standards were the measurement of modernization in Saudi Arabia, the nation achieved a new level of capabilities with the construction of KFSH, albeit with continued American corporate supervision.

With the extension of American medical culture into, first, the contract hospitals and soon afterward hospitals operated by the Ministry of Health, Aramco achieved the ability to manage Saudis from a distance. The company established the organization, provided the equipment, and stepped in when the general public or even the royal family needed medical assistance. Western medicine helped instill a scientific mindset as Saudi Arabia expanded its own medical infrastructure, but it did so not only to promote development. The use of Western technology and expertise was a primary means by which Saudi Arabia pursued nation building and in the process fortified the monarchy's position in the Islamic world. Development, in this case, helped protect religious tradition and autocratic rule.[67]

One can see the impact of Western models in the monarchy's employment of medical technology and organization to impose its sovereignty over matters related to the annual pilgrimage to Mecca and Medina. WHO announced at a meeting in May 1956 that medical regulations regarding the hajj would be removed beginning January 1, 1957. The construction of a new quarantine station by the Ministry of Health brought about this change. For years the Saudi government had complained about regulations designed by WHO and previous international health regimes to prevent the spread of contagious disease, calling them an insult to the monarchy and to Muslims.[68] It was not the offense of international regulations within Saudi borders that prompted the shift, however; it was the kingdom's newfound ability to promote itself as a purveyor of health and sanitation through the construction of a new quarantine station for arriving pilgrims, one that integrated the latest technology, organization, and expertise. The Saudi king's solidification as protector of the two holy places could not occur without more complete authority over the hajj, and medical modernization helped bring that about.

During the Fourth World Health Assembly in 1951, WHO agreed to international sanitary regulations consistent with its mission of advancing public health and its efforts to reduce the spread of disease. Implementing these regulations required that sanitary facilities be installed in high human traffic areas where "disinfecting, disinsecting, deratting and other sanitary operations" would be performed.[69] WHO also mandated suitable quarantine facilities and other measures, such as proof of inoculations, to deal with diseases like the plague, cholera, yellow fever, smallpox, typhus, and relapsing fever. With respect to the hajj, WHO drafted a series of special provisions referred to as Annex A.[70] These regulations dated to the hajj stipulations formulated by an international sanitary agreement reached in Paris in 1926. The ministry argued that these rules, against which it protested many times, had "always been a source of irritation."[71] Indeed, the Saudis objected to the imposition of these regulations from the outset, declaring that the singling out of the Muslim pilgrimage specifically constituted an affront to Islam.[72] But Saudi Arabia complied nonetheless. WHO agreed to lift these specific regulations "when the Saudi kingdom would have an adequate hygienic system for controlling the pilgrims and for providing them with the essential health services."[73] Basically, WHO told the government that an insult was not a good enough reason to lift restrictions.

The government still needed to meet international hygienic standards. A new $3-million facility was built off the coast of Jeddah as a result of this agreement. The facility conformed to WHO standards and opened the way for the Saudi monarchy to assume a new legitimacy authorized by Western medical technology.

Hygiene during the hajj had always been a preoccupation of health officials. Dating back to the nineteenth century, when health statistics began to be collected, it was clear that the gathering of large numbers of people in close quarters brought potential health risks. As early as 1865 a major epidemic of cholera during the hajj not only killed upward of one-quarter of the pilgrims but also spread via the worshipers who traveled back to their homes in Egypt, Europe, and the United States. Western nations met the next year and organized a quarantine system in hopes of reducing future epidemics and, specifically, of protecting the West. Yet cholera continued to pose problems. Western doctors complained about the health facilities in Jeddah, reporting that they were, by all measures, inadequate. A series of temporary quarantine stations were erected at port facilities and along the pilgrimage routes, and by 1926 an International Health Convention took charge of health and sanitation issues related to the hajj.[74]

Problems persisted, however, as pilgrims continued to face the threat of contracting communicable disease. A WHO report in 1956 described the cleanliness of Jeddah to be very poor and "always deficient owing to the bad habits of pilgrims." Many pilgrims disregarded the sleeping quarters erected for their use, preferring to sleep outdoors "in the streets and waste land around the city." The number of quarters available to pilgrims also failed to meet the need, and overcrowding led to further sanitation problems. Clean water was hard to come by, and human waste, which could not be dealt with hygienically in pilgrim campgrounds, attracted flies and increased the possibility that pilgrims would contract fly-borne diseases like dysentery and enteritis.[75]

To promote the new quarantine station and expand its sovereignty over matters of health inside Saudi borders, the Ministry of Health, a month before WHO's meeting of May 1956, published a booklet that described the facilities. The booklet opens a window into the ways in which the ministry incorporated technology, experts, and other tropes of development discourse into their representation of the facility. It advertises that the new facility "stands there, fully equipped by the most up-to-date technical means," including electric generators, water purifiers, and disinfecting machines. The buildings were furnished with "bath-rooms, water closets, kitchens and washing quarters. They are all lit up by electricity." Readers are inundated with images of these devices in their appropriate settings. Most photographs show electric equipment and laboratory facilities in a static, clean environment. Some depict men standing beside the equipment. The booklet reports, "In the laboratory building all apparatus and machines are well chosen by experts. They are of the latest type." Presumably, the men next to the equipment, who are wearing Western dress and white lab coats, are the very experts who chose and use the equipment. The ministry makes no reference in their literature to the fact that the U.S. government furnished a great deal of the technical equipment put to use in the quarantine station.[76] No doubt it, too, understood the importance of the king's authority over the hajj.

The brochure juxtaposes the old quarantine station with the new one, highlighting the Saudi entry into modernity. In a two-page spread the old and the new sit beside one another. The old quarantine station appears to have been haphazardly designed: the buildings are crumbling, the grounds are dusty and rundown and covered with brush. On the facing page, readers see the new facilities: clean buildings painted white and arranged in long, straight rows and surrounded by gardens with plants arranged symmetrically. The Ministry of Health declared that it could accommodate 192 patients in its first-class wards, 320 in its second-class wards, and 1,600 in its third-class wards. The isolation hospital could treat 100 patients, the internal disease section another 100, and the general hospital another 40, bringing the total patient capabilities to 2,352. Modernity seemed to be quantified in bed counts.

There should have been no doubt when looking at the new quarantine station that the ministry had improved its ability to control disease and care for the health of its citizens and the pilgrims of the hajj.[77] The reconfiguration of Saudi medicine to include the latest in Western medicine allowed the government and therefore the monarchy to organize governmental structures in such a way that it could more easily gain independence to control the hajj. By establishing clearly the modern, technical nature of the new facilities, the monarchy reclaimed control over health and sanitation from WHO and announced to the world that through the maintenance of its own medical resources it occupied the role of sole protector of the Muslim holy sites.

The Saudi Arabian government recognized the power medical technology conferred, and so did Aramco. One former company medical director suggested that an insistence on "the American Way" in medicine allowed Saudi Arabia to stand alongside modern nations of the world.[78] The Saudi government acculturated American medical technology and met international standards of health and hygiene through the construction of the quarantine station at Jeddah. With the promotion of Western medical technology and expert advice, the Saudi monarchy used medicine to promote its fitness to govern Saudi Arabia and its ability to maintain its religious authority as protector of Mecca and Medina. Aramco's promotion of Western medical culture through its own Medical Department highlights the extent to which these technologies transformed Saudi culture and made Aramco's presence in Saudi Arabia essential.

4
Man-Made Disease

In the early 1950s the Saudi monarchy requested a unique form of assistance from an oil company. It invited Aramco's chief malaria expert and head of its malaria control program, Richard Daggy, to come to Riyadh and bring his spray teams along with him. Located in the desert interior of the kingdom, Riyadh was not known to have a malaria problem. But it was not the malarial mosquito the king worried about. He wanted to see if DDT could reduce the number of flies in his palaces. Corporate diplomacy seemed to drive the application of the latest malaria control techniques as much as the science of the disease. Daggy, an entomologist with experience fighting malaria in the Pacific during the Second World War and the American South after the war, had difficulty believing that most Saudis understood the connection between the mosquito and malaria, but he was certain they recognized that the spray kept their homes free of flies, ticks, and scorpions. He assumed many appreciated it.[1] World health officials observed this phenomenon as well, noting that aid "can be more easily enlisted for residual spraying than for naturalistic measures, because the people realize immediately the benefits of the spraying."[2] The amir of Hofuf, the administrative center of the al-Hasa oasis near the company's oil fields, wanted these benefits too, so he requested that his stables be sprayed with DDT, hoping to remove the ticks that had infested his camels. Aramco not only offered protection from the malarial mosquito but also served the monarchy as an exterminator.

Aramco's work in this regard is telling. Its preventive medicine programs combined development with diplomacy, as the company understood its own and the kingdom's needs. Disease prevention was another way for the company to connect Western medical technologies to the Saudi monarchy and to the people of Saudi Arabia. Aramco engaged in a number of preventive campaigns, but malaria and to a smaller extent trachoma constituted the Medical Department's broadest operations in the Eastern Province. In Saudi Arabia corporate officials merged everyday operations with broader notions of development, erecting a corporate modernization framework built on technical aid and service to the Saudi monarchy. While public health might seem to be outside an oil firm's area of concern, it served as a central component of Aramco's larger engagement with the Saudi monarchy. These programs were an excellent source of ideas about development, public health, and diplomacy enacted by a transnational corporation.[3] To Aramco, malaria control was less an altruistic deed than a function of business policy related to labor expansion and corporate goodwill. Public health and development became business strategy and diplomacy. Similarly, trachoma research emanated from the company's unique positioning in the kingdom, offering a laboratory to tropical medicine specialists.

Aramco coordinated its malaria control program within a larger context of control offered by American scientists in the 1940s and 1950s, but when Saudi officials assumed leadership of the program, they proceeded differently. Obliged to combat the mosquito by the Saudi king, who, as the opening story highlights, seemed more interested in pest control and technological support, Aramco attacked the mosquito with the latest chemicals, hoping to protect its indigenous labor force, despite its own research that social and economic factors dictated an alternative strategy. Daggy's studies for the company defined malaria as a symptom of underdevelopment rather than an endemic problem, yet at the start the company largely neglected socioeconomic solutions. When the Saudi Ministry of Health and WHO assumed control of the program from the company in 1956, they too connected the disease to economic stagnation and its control to economic growth, but they offered a combination of approaches that finally reduced the incidence of malaria in Eastern Arabia.

Shortly after the Second World War, Aramco predicted that its newly discovered oil fields in the Eastern Province would bring the company staff into greater contact with the residents of the al-Hasa oasis nearby. Not only would materials and support services originate from the area but also local government relations with the company would increase. Most important, however, were the potential workers from the area. George Rentz, who headed the company's Research Division, emphasized the necessity of conducting research on the tribes and villages of the area in order to facilitate the entrance of field parties and other operations into the area.[4] By 1950 the division was studying the nearby oases to evaluate what the company's anthropologist Federico Vidal later described as "the readiness or reluctance" of local populations "to accept employment with the Company, on their choice of living sites, on their preferences and suitability for one type of work or another, and other important points." An opportunity to collect and analyze data presented itself when Aramco's medical team established the malaria control program in the al-Hasa and neighboring Qatif oases, a program that resulted from three years of company surveys in the Eastern Province beginning in 1947.[5] Daggy made the corporate objectives of the program clear, noting that "malaria is a very real threat to future economic development and industrial progress in the Eastern Province."[6]

The notion that tropical disease breeds underdevelopment remained strong among world health officials after the Second World War. At a conference on malaria sponsored by WHO in 1956, the participants argued that the disease restrained nations' potential and kept them from progressing. Early postwar malaria programs sponsored by the UN Relief and Rehabilitation Administration and the Rockefeller Foundation looked to previously successful programs as models for how to ensure a healthy labor supply, gaining knowledge of eradication efforts that could be copied throughout the tropics. In 1951, for instance, world health officials reported that they had proved that malaria control increased crop yields and decreased "the man hours of labor which have to be expended per acre" in East Bengal. Since it was well understood and accepted, according to a WHO report of 1948, that the health of the workforce had real economic consequences, it made sense for Aramco to construct a large-scale medical program in the late forties that addressed malaria.[7]

The postwar logic that malaria slowed or impeded economic development drove many malaria control efforts, but this thinking often rested more on faith than on data, and it frequently prevented other economic analyses and potential modernization schemes.[8] Accordingly, strategies to combat malaria became separated from the socioeconomic context.[9] Alternative ways of understanding the relationship between development and malaria existed. In early twentieth-century India, for instance, British programs increased agricultural production but exacerbated public health problems. Engineers and agricultural specialists irrigated more and more land, which led to improper runoff, increased flooding, and the creation of perfect breeding grounds for malarial mosquitoes.[10] Malaria eradication attempts in postwar Sardinia and Sri Lanka increased agricultural yields, but increases in population stalled economic growth.[11] These examples notwithstanding, the perceived connection between malaria control and economic growth persisted. Soon a new method of malaria control arose, and it became linked to nation building.[12]

In the early twentieth century the Rockefeller Foundation promoted what became known as the American way of managing malaria: vector control through the use of chemicals and new organizational techniques.[13] In 1902 Walter Reed effectively eradicated both malaria and yellow fever from Havana, Cuba, by using these methods.[14] A few years later in Panama, William Crawford Gorgas drained swamps, cleared weeds, spread various chemical mixtures, and provided screens and nets to keep mosquitoes at bay. Within three years his teams had reduced the incidence of infection by half, with a steady decline in subsequent years.[15] These experiences encouraged technological solutions to insect-borne disease, and though social methods continued, American scientists privileged vector control to improve living standards.[16]

Shortly after the First World War a serious debate raged over the best way to contain malaria. Some backed vector control, believing that by eliminating the mosquito they could eradicate malaria entirely. Others promoted a combination of economic development, such as agricultural improvements and sanitary reforms, and treatment with prophylactic drugs, such as quinine. The resulting debate deeply divided world health officials and led to a report by the League of Nations Malaria Commission in 1927.[17] The commission concluded that treatment of those infected was of primary concern, but it also called for a focus on "general schemes of bonification which aim at improving the economic and social condition of the people and their general well-being and standard of life." Agricultural reforms, the commission stated, could lead to measurable improvements. Greater economic prosperity would lead to more funding for treatment, hospitals, and wastewater systems and to an overall improved quality of life.[18] Flexibility within local settings in using the above approaches was the commission's primary recommendation. In general, vector control through the use of chemicals was thought to be of secondary importance.[19]

Vector control, however, continued to be the most widely practiced mode of attacking malaria among American practitioners. The Rockefeller Foundation, in conjunction with the U.S. Public Health Service, began an antimalaria campaign in the American South after the First World War. Malaria was actually on the decline in the region, mainly owing to improvements in agricultural development and standards of living, two key issues stressed by the League of Nations report. Through this program, the government helped improve production and develop a healthier labor force at low cost.[20] The enthusiasm for widespread eradication through vector control, however, was generated primarily by the success of Fred Soper and the Rockefeller Foundation in northern Brazil in 1938, an achievement which later led to similar campaigns in Italy and Egypt. Soper's victory in spite of complicating environmental factors and the promotion of his techniques reinforced technological eradication methods.[21] The subsequent discovery of an even newer and more potent chemical, DDT, verified the supremacy of the vector control approach for many malariologists, particularly after its success during the Second World War. The Italian malariologist L. W. Hackett started to refer to DDT as the American solution, and malaria started to be conceived of as "an entomological rather than a social problem."[22] By the end of the war, it was clear that there was a new weapon in the ongoing battle against malaria.[23] When WHO initiated its worldwide campaign against the disease in 1955, many believed DDT would bring success.[24] In Saudi Arabia environmental factors also explain the unique endemic nature of malaria in desert oases, and the history of control in such places hints that officials there had a similar faith in the new insecticide, although when DDT's effectiveness ultimately waned, success was achieved through an integrated social and economic plan.

As we have seen, it made sense for Aramco to promote Western medicine as a strategic part of its presence in Saudi Arabia. And here, too, Aramco's malaria control efforts conformed to programs constructed earlier by European empires. Historically, Western attempts to control malaria expanded medical services in the colonies, eventually to the benefit of indigenous workers. European physicians working in colonial outposts before the twentieth century treated westerners with prophylactic drugs, predominantly quinine. Sanitary reforms were enacted to "cleanse" the environment of suspected malarial agents.[25] As the historian Margaret Jones notes, colonizers viewed medicine as "an agent of progress and improvement" that put undeveloped civilizations on the right path to modernity. This so-called civilizing mission became a way to legitimate rule.[26] Situating colonial medical practice in the political, economic, and social environment of colonies highlights the complicated interplay between colonial powers and their subjects.[27] Aramco's linkage of diplomacy and medicine took place early, and preventive medicine had a role to play. The company's Medical Department quickly broadened its obligations in the late 1940s, claiming that public health programs could substantially reduce labor costs.[28]

The renewed energies expended in medical initiatives originated primarily during the company's postwar expansion, and the malaria control program provided it with statistics used to evaluate whether local Arabs could work for the company, a common concern being the strength and health of the labor pool.[29] The company had sponsored an early program from 1941 to 1947, one which attacked malaria in northeast coastal areas where oil facilities were located, but a broader, more extensive scheme in outlying areas had not been put in place.[30] Still somewhat doubtful of the extent of the malaria problem, Daggy soon realized that he faced severe difficulties.[31] Aramco's American employees lived in homogeneous compounds located far from malarial oases. Those cordoned off in American enclaves in Dhahran, Ras Tanura, and Abqaiq had little to worry about. The air-conditioned, single-family homes of these employees reduced their exposure to the elements. As Robert Vitalis has shown, the segregation had a major impact on employee relations, but geography and climate dictated malaria infection as much as anything.[32] These isolated communities remained separated from malarious regions by a large swath of desert, and the mosquito that carried malaria in the Eastern Province had a very short flight range.[33] Many of Aramco's current and potentially future Arab employees, however, lived in these oases, and, Daggy states, malaria lived with them "from time immemorial to the present."[34] Tropical disease, in this formulation, was an indigenous problem.[35]

Malaria indeed constituted a serious concern in the Eastern Province. Not long after the program ended, Daggy wrote that "so many were stricken, that Aramco didn't have enough hospital beds for even its own employees."[36] Its American workers stayed healthy, but its indigenous workers, along with their dependents and neighbors, continued to suffer. Daggy estimated that over 90 percent of residents in some areas carried the disease.[37] WHO numbers were slightly lower, but the fact remained, regardless of the precise percentage, that residents suffered high infection rates.[38] The prevalence of malaria among Saudi employees meant lost work time, which, Daggy worried, could result in reduced efficiency. He was also troubled about the fact that employee direction was likely to suffer among the Arab workforce if a Saudi employee in a leadership position contracted the disease.[39]

The parasite that causes malaria, plasmodium, travels through the mosquito's saliva while it feeds on blood. Sufferers develop headaches, drowsiness, and fevers followed by, in severe instances, confusion. After about four days the symptoms diminish, only to return again if not treated. Westerners used drugs to treat the disease, but in the Middle East and elsewhere indigenes employed local cures to attack the often-unknown fever. Some carried or wore beads, charms, and other objects that might be used to defend against the disease. Indigenous healers sometimes employed cautery, herbal teas, and bloodletting to relieve fever.[40] But these local nostrums were what Aramco was trying to supplant.

Unlike many international health officials who saw malaria as a cause of underdevelopment, Daggy believed the reverse was true. He determined that along with climate and topography, underdevelopment—inefficient agriculture, poor living conditions, and a general lack of education—triggered malaria's pervasiveness in the Eastern Province. He argued that in Saudi Arabia malaria was "man-made."[41] Daggy's perception echoes an alternative framework for understanding this malaria–development link. Constructed by public health officials as far back as the 1920s, it became more common after the Second World War. Justin M. Andrews, a specialist in communicable diseases, wrote in 1947 that experts widely agreed that malaria eradication in many parts of the American South derived from socioeconomic progress and economic improvements. A few years later he avowed that the malaria outbreak of 1936 in the United States was directly related to the Great Depression, and he and other malariologists worried about a similar postwar depression and outbreak in 1945.[42]

Both the malaria problem and the level of development in the Eastern Province were difficult to measure, but the company initiated a widespread program in 1947 to chart the disease and devise mechanisms to contain it. Earlier studies conducted by the British in early 1938 and by the Americans in 1941 had tracked cases of contagious diseases contracted by oil workers, many of which were incidences of malaria. Both indicated high rates of infection in Eastern Arabia, but no official record of the populations at risk existed.[43] Daggy pricked fingers to obtain blood samples and checked for enlarged spleens in an endeavor to collect data that might help him classify diverse aspects of the population and gauge the risk and rate of infection.[44] Through this study medical personnel hoped to gain control of the disease and reduce the incidence of malaria among the company's indigenous employees and their families and neighbors.

Eastern Province malaria, they discovered, seemed limited "to island-like cultivated areas in a sea of sand."[45] The Arab lifestyle, Daggy held, exacerbated the problem. The al-Hasa oasis, located roughly forty miles from the Persian Gulf, south of Dhahran, and the Qatif oasis, located about fifteen miles north of Dhahran, were the primary breeding grounds for the area's chief carrier of the disease, *Anopheles Stephensi*.[46] The dense population of these oases compelled man, mosquito, and malaria to live in close proximity. The largest oasis in Saudi Arabia, al-Hasa had roughly 160,000 people living in 165 square miles, a highly dense population. Qatif had roughly the same population and density. Prior to the institution of Aramco's malaria program, many Saudis understood that fever overran the oases at certain times of the year. Nomadic Bedouin tended to avoid the areas at these times.[47] Health in the Eastern Province, as an American surveyor who contracted malaria there in 1942 opined, was "among the worst, if not the worst, to be found in Saudi Arabia."[48]

Daggy concluded that Saudi living arrangements and agricultural practices contributed heavily to this problem. Most residents lived in *barastis,* huts constructed of palm trunk and palm thatch, or in buildings made of limestone and mud. Few, if any, contained windows or screens. Many residents, eager to escape the heat, slept outside, a practice that lent itself to greater exposure to mosquitoes. Further, irrigation practices, drainage ditches, and the management of natural springs gave the mosquito an ideal breeding environment. Daggy found "miles of unnecessary ditches, and many improperly constructed," which resulted in leaks and seepage and led to several areas of standing water in low-lying areas.[49] After years spent studying malaria in the Eastern Province, he declared that the disease was "directly connected with the local practice of agriculture." An agriculture survey conducted by the U.S. government in 1942 indicated similar problems, underlining drainage issues and open water as impediments to effective mosquito abatement.[50] The most common method practiced involved channeling free-flowing water until it pooled and became stagnant.

Investigations by Aramco resolved that while very little water accumulated in the hot, dry summer months, these pools developed into lakes in the cooler months, perfect locations for mosquito larvae to mature.[51] The initial British study of malaria in the area in 1938 presumed a similar source.[52]

The climate of the Eastern Province contributed to the spread of malaria but also meant that control might be more achievable. Rainfall was meager during the summer, and a band of high humidity stretched across the western shores of the Persian Gulf every autumn.[53] These months of high humidity in the Eastern Province brought about the highest incidence of infection. Humidity allowed for sustained breeding conditions, but they reached elevated levels only once each year. The human assault on the mosquito could be confined in time as well as space. Here we witness a shift in Daggy's thinking. His own assessment of the problem theorized that malaria had its origin in agricultural practices, education, and living conditions, but climate, experience, and a powerful malaria control discourse pushed him to direct his attention away from social and economic improvements and toward the vector.

After all the investigative work to determine the broad social and economic origins of oasis malaria, in 1948 Daggy initiated a program of residual spraying of DDT, dispersing sixty thousand gallons that first autumn.[54] From 1948 to 1956, after which the Saudi Arabian government exercised complete authority over the program, Saudi spray teams, trained and supervised by Aramco, attacked oasis mosquitoes.[55] The process involved spraying the insides of buildings every autumn with the chemical. Since Saudi Arabia was so arid most of the year, a layer of DDT applied immediately before the humid period often sufficed for an entire year. Mosquitoes flew into the buildings through open windows and doors and landed on the walls and ceilings, where they rested and absorbed the poison that killed them within days. While some objected to having their homes sprayed, the Saudi government mandated the campaign, leaving citizens with little choice but to welcome Aramco's teams.

The program provided an opportunity for corporate diplomacy and company research.[56] It gave Aramco an opening to touch the lives of thousands of Saudis in the region as it collected blood samples and performed numerous physical examinations. American spray canisters filled with DDT circulated through the villages, demonstrating the power of American technology.[57] As Aramco displayed its value to the kingdom, it catalogued the populations of the region, data that were valuable to Aramco's Research Department as the company expanded into new oil fields. The census gave impetus to a five-year study of the al-Hasa oasis aimed at indexing potential employees.[58] While Aramco physicians remember the public relations value of control, it fit evolving business strategies as well. Much of the research conducted during the program contributed to further medical research, as Saudi Arabia's Eastern Province became a laboratory for inquiries into tropical medicine.[59]

As the above story of corporate exterminators indicates, the monarchy seemed only partially committed to malaria control throughout the early stages of the program. Aramco began its research at the request of the king, who reportedly had heard of the legendary qualities of DDT and who sought health improvements in his kingdom.[60] He called on Aramco for help, but he occasionally refused to fund the program. Some corporate officials firmly believed in 1948 that public health was the primary responsibility of the government, not the company, regardless of the benefits Aramco might accrue. So the spraying stopped when payments stopped. The company's narrative of altruism came up against costs, and costs prevailed. Only two years after the residual spray program began, the Saudi government failed to approve and fund the campaign. Daggy and his spray teams made no general application of DDT that autumn, although they did experiment in two small villages at the company's expense. The results proved powerful. Malaria infections dropped in the two sprayed locations but rose in the untreated areas. Similar problems occurred in 1952 when payment negotiations delayed the program until after the high humidity of autumn had set in. Malaria infection increased once more. The delay was the culprit, as there was another short drop in infections in December after DDT application. This disjointed method actually served the company's interests in the end. Aramco's experts could apply bottled health from a DDT spray canister, but it was now clear they could withhold that health as well. Daggy referred to the increases in morbidity caused by delay as "a lesson in timing," one presumably meant for those organizing the campaign, himself included, but one certainly not lost on Aramco's Saudi hosts. Payment issues never again plagued the company's malaria control efforts.[61]

While perhaps an effective tool of corporate diplomacy, DDT proved ineffective for the long-term control of malaria. Spray teams in the Eastern Province applied the insecticide successfully until 1953, when studies began to show an increase in malaria infections in the region. From a 2 percent parasite rate in 1952, surveys recorded a rise to 19 percent the next year, followed by 31 percent in 1954. Once-a-year spraying no longer sufficed. By 1954 mosquitoes returned to DDT-sprayed dwellings within months of application.[62] For assistance, Daggy contacted officials at WHO, which in 1955 confirmed that the mosquito had adapted.[63] A new insecticide, Dieldrin, tested well and replaced DDT, bringing declines in infection. When the Saudi Arabian government took over the program the next year, it too employed Dieldrin to good effect.[64]

Following Daggy's early belief that underdevelopment caused malaria epidemics, Aramco mixed other techniques but not extensively. To reduce stagnant water in irrigation ditches, teams worked to ensure a steady flow and prevent seepage. They also encouraged local populations to empty pools of standing water. Daggy even introduced fish that ate mosquito larvae, a tactic he had used during the Second World War.[65] As the 1950s progressed, malaria lay at the heart of Aramco's public health campaign. Educational materials produced by the company included the film *The Battle Against Malaria,* pamphlets, and posters, all encouraging Saudi Arabians to "Kill the Mosquito before it kills you." Officials cautioned Saudis to drain pools of stagnant water, to "drain and dry water jugs once a week," and, using the company's own product as preventive medicine, to "put oil on stagnant pools."[66] A curriculum was prepared for use in elementary schools, and Saudi schoolchildren were encouraged to take the lessons they learned home. In school, they watched movies about malaria and other health dangers and received numerous educational pamphlets.[67] The company and the government promoted these efforts through schools, on television, and in broader public health initiatives.[68]

Aramco's Medical Department turned the management of its efforts over to the government and its nascent Ministry of Health in 1956. Aramco had always maintained that malaria control should be the government's responsibility. By 1956, Saudi Arabia, with WHO assistance, had organized a National Malaria Service to supervise malaria control directly.[69] While control efforts in the Eastern Province consisted of a variety of approaches, Daggy's reconfiguration of the causal relationship between the disease and development had failed to alter the company's primary approach. American experts had pursued a frontal assault on the mosquito, suppressing broader economic approaches that were later employed by WHO and the government. Daggy's training as an entomologist and his earlier experience in malaria control, the enthusiasm surrounding DDT, and the unique climate of the oases pushed him to favor vector control. The educational and agricultural measures remained a small part of Aramco's program. The government turned to WHO as early as 1951 for technical assistance in finally eradicating malaria in the kingdom, but the Eastern Province remained Aramco's realm, and WHO accepted responsibility for programs in the western and central regions of the country.[70] WHO would gradually become more involved in eastern Arabia by the mid-1960s.[71] In 1959 the Saudi program experienced another increase in malaria infection in the east, mainly because mosquitoes were developing resistance to Dieldrin. At this point the government abandoned insecticides and turned to older larvicides like Paris Green and various prophylactic drugs.[72] The government signed an agreement with WHO in January 1963 for renewed outside assistance in the Eastern Province.[73]

Experts at WHO also characterized the nature of malaria in Saudi Arabia as man-made. In 1965, after working to establish a demonstration project in the Eastern Province oasis of Qatif to "strengthen and develop the technical, administrative, and operational setup in Saudi Arabia for a long-term eradication program," WHO turned the focus again to water usage.[74] H. R. Rafatjah, like Daggy before him, stated without equivocation that malaria was man-made in the country owing to improper irrigation in agriculture, and he recommended a "reduction of man-made mosquito producing sources."[75] WHO representatives, rather than promote eradication with insecticides, demonstrated new techniques for control and began to retrain Saudi personnel.[76] Combined with the extension of clinical facilities throughout the Eastern Province during this same period, Saudi medical officials began taking more curative and preventive measures. Increased educational programs, including films, pamphlets, posters, and an elementary school curriculum expanded during the late fifties and into the sixties. With the addition of further advances in irrigation, Saudi Arabia began to experience, once again, a reduction in malaria infection. By the early 1970s malaria no longer posed a substantial threat to the populations of the Eastern Province. For all intents and purposes, the region saw few incidents of malaria after 1979.[77]

While the malaria control program put Aramco's public health mechanisms to work for the Saudi monarchy, a joint research program with the

Harvard School of Public Health (HSPH) allowed Aramco's medical staff to reach beyond clinical experiences in other ways, specifically in attempting to alter personal and public hygiene habits. The company's sanitation efforts included events like clean-up days in conjunction with Saudi health officials.[78] After attempting unsuccessfully to secure Rockefeller Foundation funding, the company turned to HSPH, and together they began using Saudi Arabia as a laboratory in which to search for a cure for trachoma, the primary cause of blindness in the developing world at that time, especially in Saudi Arabia. The company vice president James Terry Duce, after meeting with King 'Abd al-Aziz in the summer of 1946 and discussing the "prevalence of blindness" in Saudi Arabia with the Medical Department, found that nearly 85 percent of those undergoing company physicals showed some symptoms of the disease.[79]

Funded by the company and conducted jointly, the trachoma research program got under way after a meeting of the Gulf Medical Society in Dhahran in 1953. Aramco's chairman of the board, Fred Davies, toured the company's medical facilities with the Harvard microbiologist John C. Snyder, who had made the trip to fill in for a colleague. Davies inquired as to how Snyder thought Aramco's lab space might be best used. Snyder responded by saying that "local health problems should have high priority."[80] Snyder's previous work in the Middle East and his knowledge of common ailments there (many of the papers read at the meeting were about local health problems) obliged him to suggest that Harvard and Aramco work together to find the causes of trachoma and possibly develop a cure or vaccine. Given that close to 90 percent of Aramco's Saudi employees had, at one time or another, suffered from the effects of trachoma, Davies endorsed Snyder's proposal.[81] After an agreement by which Aramco would finance the operation was hammered out, work began the following year.

The first priority was to determine the cause of trachoma in people who lived in the al-Hasa and Qatif oases in the Eastern Province. The trachoma research program received a five-year, $500,000 grant from the company followed by a second five-year grant in 1959 of $585,000.[82] By 1970 the company had spent close to $2 million on the program.[83] A team of Harvard scientists, joined by Aramco's medical staff, set up their equipment in the newly erected company hospital in Dhahran. They brought with them the latest in technological research needs and spread out across the second floor.

Trachoma, an infection of the conjunctiva, the thin layer of tissue between the eyelid and the cornea, is thought by many to be one of the most ancient diseases in existence. If left untreated, trachoma can not only spread easily to other people but also leave sufferers with permanent cloudy or blurry vision, scars on the eyeballs, constant itching, and blindness. Earlier, researchers had maintained that through this project they could cure the kingdom of this affliction entirely with medication. While they sought that end, this kind of infection received only scant attention prior to the 1950s. Doctors determined the cause of trachoma only in the mid-1950s, but they did not fully understand the implications of their discovery. They hoped, however, that an inoculation might be possible, but that prospect would be realized only if the specific pathogens could be studied clinically and tested effectively.[84]

The research team began collecting scrapings from patients' eyes, both from people who traveled to one of the company's hospitals and from villagers in the Eastern Province. Eye scrapings were used to isolate individual cultures for study. While they found the primary etiology of trachoma, they concluded that the spread and extent of the disease were related primarily to lifestyle and traditional medical practices. A change in both of these areas, the researchers judged, would most likely reduce the incidence of trachoma as well as bring about greater health in the region.[85] The widespread use of medicine, delivered by injections and topical ointments, resulted in decreased cases of trachoma. In time, Saudi Arabs readily accepted these cures. As the research team conjectured, "hostility decrease[d] and suspicions relaxed," changes that improved the health of the inhabitants of the Eastern Province.[86]

Despite the widely held belief that the acceptance of Western medicine could rid the kingdom of trachoma, related data suggested that medicine alone was not the solution; rather, as one observer noted, "It's almost faster to raise the standard of living."[87] As in the case of malaria, this argument implies that poor health was a symptom of a lack of economic development, not, as WHO and other experts contended, the other way around. The research team identified three types of villages in its study: rural villages with few conveniences like running water and proper sewage, town sites that had indoor plumbing and updated housing construction, and towns in which some dwellings had these facilities and some did not.[88]

As a result of this enlarged research agenda, the oil company was able to help the nation implement meaningful changes in public health. Aside from the introduction of Western medicine, the kingdom saw new, improved water, sewage, and electricity facilities, waste disposal programs, and health education, measures that constituted essential aspects of managing diseases like trachoma. Elinor Nichols, the wife of the Aramco physician who headed the trachoma research program from 1956 to 1963, remembered the difficulty in treating the disease only with medicine. She insisted that the reinfection rate was 100 percent if changes in lifestyle did not occur, adding that trachoma existed only in countries where "the standard of personal hygiene is low."[89] Infected Saudi Arabians used and reused towels to clean the infected eyes of multiple children, they slept in close proximity, and in many cases they had little access to soap and running water. As the researchers soon concluded, "Additional socioeconomic improvements, such as which have occurred in the 'townsite' communities in Arabia [meaning communities built by Aramco], will be required before the impact is apparent in the health of the eyes of this population."[90] In the communities built by Aramco, people could wash their clothes more easily and more often, and soap and running water were readably available. A lower incidence of infection resulted in these areas.[91]

An analysis of the trachoma research program further illuminates the ways in which Aramco medical officials categorized and defined Saudi Arabia as a nation in need of social and economic improvements if it was to achieve greater health. In the battle against trachoma, as in the one against malaria, researchers determined that Western medicine was crucial, but a reduction in the spread of the disease required a change in lifestyle, particularly education about hygiene. While it might seem obvious that better health comes from better hygiene, it is also important to understand that the initiatives taken to eradicate trachoma from the Eastern Province fit the company's established pattern regarding medical care. The company needed healthy employees, and campaigns to increase hygiene in the villages led to a greater interest in the development of town sites, which meant more changes in Saudis' living arrangements. As a company health official, Dottie McComb of the trachoma research program, said of public health and hygiene, "You don't get good work out of people until you find that they're healthy."[92] The health of workers, their dependents, and their neighbors, the Medical Department found, required not only the introduction of Western medicine, but also changes in Saudi Arabia to help dampen local susceptibility to certain "ancient" diseases. Development led to better health, and better health to better work. Promotion of better hygiene helped expand corporate exploitation.

In the trachoma project Aramco engaged in a broader health education program throughout the Eastern Province that consisted of pamphlets, books, movies, and a curriculum for Aramco schools that company representatives presented, first to their Saudi Arab employees and then to the public. Aramco regarded these programs as efforts at corporate diplomacy. Armand Gelpi, an internist for the Medical Department in the 1960s, spoke of the public heath program in much broader terms, saying that the company's "outreach activities" provided "a model for corporations abroad, and for developing countries."[93] A proper public health infrastructure became a primary concern. The lack of sewers, for instance, meant high contamination of drinking water, and so preventive medicine programs included the construction of sewer systems to clear the streets of human excrement.[94] Good food could be provided in part by ending the practice of using nightsoil, or human feces, as fertilizer. A common procedure for Aramco surgeons included the removal of worms from the digestive system of Saudi adolescents, a problem the doctors attributed to nightsoil.[95] The company's outreach included posters meant to advertise the importance of health. One poster, titled "Health in Arabia," defined public health as a primary concern of any modern nation. Photographs and captions identified the role Aramco played in these endeavors: "Dental Care, Vaccination, Medical Care, Fly Control, Malaria Control, Good Food, Water, Exercise, and Cleanliness."[96] These were all interconnected issues, and by calling attention to its involvement, the company inflated its story of accomplishment. The story of malaria control is a success story, but one that must account for varying interests and approaches—social, economic, and entomological—that developed on the ground in Saudi Arabia. Corporate interests drove Aramco's efforts, and although the company initiated the control program, the Saudi Arabian government and WHO brought an end to the inevitability that people in the Eastern Province would contract malaria. Aramco's story says as much about malaria control as it does about the role of transnational corporations and their impact on world affairs in the early Cold War. The company's malaria control program and trachoma research program centered as much on concrete issues of public health as they did on defining and managing the Saudi countryside and its populace for profit and diplomacy. Aramco's exceptionalist claims mask the company's exploitation on one level, but, more important, they illustrate the role of public health and preventive medicine in Cold War–era development discourse and the significance of transnational corporations in mid-twentieth century world affairs. Globally, practitioners continued to shape eradication and control programs around the belief that tropical medicine constituted an obstacle to modernization. The oil giant carved out its role as one centered on goodwill and service to the monarchy, and this, when combined with the expansion of its clinical presence and agricultural aid, helped establish an American corporate presence for decades after.

5

Aramco's Eden

GROVER BROWN, an America soil specialist who worked for the U.S. Department of Agriculture, and 'Abd Allah al-'Arfaj, a Saudi merchant turned farmer who leased a ten-acre plot of land in the al-Hasa oasis, seemed an unlikely pair, but Aramco brought them together in the early 1950s as part of its ongoing agricultural experiment in Saudi Arabia. 'Abd Allah did not plant dates on his land, as was traditional in the Eastern Province, but instead grew a variety of produce, including alfalfa, pumpkins, eggplant, tomatoes, and pomegranate trees. His saw limited success, however, since fruit flies, worms, locusts, and aphids invaded his farm before he harvested his crops. This is when Brown arrived, at Aramco's invitation, to provide technical assistance to area farmers. The assortment of foods the company imported to Saudi Arabia cost a great deal, and farms in the area produced mainly dates, which were of little use to the Americans, who preferred fresh fruits and vegetables, eggs, and poultry. Brown offered 'Abd Allah a deal. Brown would take just one acre of 'Abd Allah's land and supply hybrid seeds, chemical fertilizers, insecticides, and advice for growing crops on it, while 'Abd Allah would provide the water and the labor. Brown planned to demonstrate the efficiency and effectiveness of American agricultural technology and expertise. Instead of alfalfa and pumpkins, Brown planted lettuce, tomatoes, carrots, and cauliflower, which yielded more produce on his one acre than 'Abd Allah was able to grow on his nine. 'Abd Allah soon made sure that all ten acres resembled Brown's one. He had a ready market in Aramco, which happily purchased his harvest. The merchant-turned-farmer found success as a businessman, working his land to the benefit of the company. But soon he was producing more goods than Aramco could readily purchase, so the company's medical staff began holding public classes to introduce unfamiliar foods to Saudis and offer instruction on how to prepare them. A market was created where none had existed. Aramco continued to purchase a percentage of 'Abd Allah's harvest, and he sold the remainder to local Arabs. It was not long before other Saudi farmers sought Brown's aid. Later, Brown not only helped 'Abd Allah build a poultry farm but also aided in the training of local agricultural specialists. By the mid-1950s Brown had become an indispensable actor in the agriculture of the Eastern Province.[1]

The oil company, the U.S. government, and the Saudi monarchy believed agriculture could create new classes of settled citizens, entrepreneurs, middlemen, and laborers. The government contended in 1942 that the promotion of sharecropping would make for "better citizens" and "at the same time result in actual profit to the government."[2] In the case of 'Abd Allah, it resulted in profit to the company, but one could imagine the benefit increased agricultural production might bring to the Saudi monarchy. After visiting Saudi Arabia in 1955, S. W. Edgecombe, the dean of the School of Agriculture at the American University of Beirut, reported on the achievements of the Saudi Arabia–Aramco demonstration farms at al-Kharj, highlighting the creation of settlers who supplied labor to government farms.[3] In just over a decade, sharecropping had been transplanted from the American South to the deserts of Saudi Arabia under the guise of modernization. The Saudi monarchy hoped these settlements might bring food independence and improve national security. Agriculture became a primary means by which Saudi Arabia looked to achieve such security, as the kingdom could create citizens who would be loyal to the monarchy, a type of civic participation favored by the royal family. For this new nation, consolidating power among a largely tribal, nomadic population was essential and therefore a primary concern of the Saudi Arabian government.[4]

Saudi Arabian agricultural needs in turn provided the fertile ground Aramco needed to cultivate corporate interests and promote itself to the monarchy as a partner in the kingdom's future. The company engaged in transfers of technology and technical advice in the deserts of Arabia, first, through a complex, multipartner agricultural project at al-Kharj and then through similar experiments in the Eastern Province. The demonstration farm at al-Kharj, located roughly sixty miles south of the Saudi Arabian capital of Riyadh, publicized the company's good standing and served as an illustration of Aramco's usefulness, regardless of the farm's successes or the actual extent of Aramco's involvement. While Aramco embellished its involvement at times and often participated only reluctantly in Saudi agricultural plans, to ignore the company's role is to disregard the meaningful attempts the company made at enacting corporate diplomacy.[5]

Postwar agricultural development in Saudi Arabia drew in three distinct actors: the oil company, the U.S. government, and the Saudi monarchy. The ultimate goal of each served to reinforce that of the other two but not always as intended. Aramco's interests resembled those of a colonial power, but corporate imperialism was not what the company was practicing. Oil was the raw material of value, not cotton, rice, or some other cash crop. Agricultural production, to Aramco, was about service to the monarchy, cultivation of workers through capitalist social and economic reorganization, and the creation of self-sustaining agricultural models that could serve the company by supplying food and allowing the company to focus on oil exploitation. Aramco's endeavors were unique in this regard. Colonial powers worked to alter their colonies' social and economic structures for the profit of the metropole by substituting local products and farming practices, ones that served local needs, with cash crops, up-to-date techniques, and new technologies.[6] Aramco effected a similar transformation in the Eastern Province, but one with very different motives. Aramco did not aim to feed the industrial West through agricultural development, a nineteenth-century European interest, or to spur industrial growth locally, an intent of Americans during the Cold War.[7] In Saudi Arabia, it was more about service, practicality, and, the company hoped, long-term stability. Aramco's primary interest was corporate development, and agricultural improvements were employed to serve that end. The U.S. government worked alongside the oil company in promoting American agriculture in the hope, first, of securing rights to construct military airfields and, later, of maintaining friendly relations with the monarchy as well as access to airbases and oil. For its part, the monarchy desired to consolidate authority over the kingdom, become a food-independent nation, and generate national and international prestige as a caretaker of the land.

Aramco's first agricultural venture, al-Kharj, was located at the confluence of a series of underground water reservoirs fed by runoff from the nearby Tuwaiq Mountains, nearly two hundred miles west of the region. Temperatures in the area ranged from almost 120 degrees Fahrenheit during the day in the summer to as low as 35 degrees at night during the cooler months. The recorded humidity reached as low as 5 percent, and in spring and summer winds blew sand and dust across the region, causing frequent summer dust storms.[8] These were harsh conditions, for sure, but the area had been described by one traveler in Arabia as "the only desirable part of southern Nejd."[9] Philby, the king's British friend, noted in 1918 that the area served as an oasis for nomadic Arabs and that stories of al-Kharj's majestic yet tragic history abounded in the region. Once known as a prosperous region of Arabia, it had villages and oases built in close proximity. Philby wrote, "In those days, the story goes, God visited his wrath upon His people in the shape of a double scourge of locusts and plague, from whose effects the stricken land has never recovered."[10] The revitalization of al-Kharj spawned by the demonstration farms represented a central component of Aramco's modernization program in Saudi Arabia, and in annual reports intended for American investors and the Saudi monarchy the company promoted these efforts as "Services on Behalf of Saudi Arab Government."[11] In 1950, just over a decade after cultivation at al-Kharj began, reports described the new land under development, the machines and commercial fertilizers being used, and the scientific irrigation the company helped establish to replace traditional agricultural practices.[12]

By the end of the 1950s annual reports were citing the company's continued studies of insect pests and supervision of agricultural development.[13] Excerpts from Wallace Stegner's book *Discovery!,* which Aramco funded, highlighted for an American audience the early role the company's geologists played in surveying available water resources that could be used for expanded land cultivation. Stegner boldly—and somewhat mistakenly—proclaimed that an agricultural mission organized by the U.S. government was actually part of the company's early philanthropic efforts.[14] Americans had read of these programs long before Stegner's account; journalists and other visitors to Saudi Arabia reported on their journeys to the "Man-Made Oasis" that Aramco supervised at al-Kharj, where "acres of desert wasteland" were being "reclaimed" through American expertise.[15] Aramco, a headline in the *New York Herald Tribune* read in 1948, was "Creating Modern 'Eden.'"[16] There could not have been much doubt about Aramco's service to the Saudi monarchy. The transformation worked by the company at al-Kharj, Aramco's publications maintained, established it as "a good 'citizen' of the country and as a friend."[17]

More than a story of corporate mythmaking, however, al-Kharj symbolized the transmission of American technical expertise to a government the company described as having "not yet developed an engineering and technical organization of its own."[18] Aramco's work at al-Kharj showed American corporate participation in development activity in Saudi Arabia that resembled similar work conducted for over a century in European empires. As European states in the nineteenth century sought to rework colonial economies and societies to suit their own needs, agricultural development favored monocropping, or the growing of single crops, mainly for markets outside the colony. This practice, carried out with no thought of the impact it had on colonial society, allowed European powers to connect their colonies to global markets. This ideology persisted through the Green Revolution of the 1960s. But in Saudi Arabia, Aramco cultivated oil first; agricultural development actually served the company better through a diversity of corps. In the end, however, Saudi Arabian traditions and social structures underwent major alterations as internal trading patterns centered on date cultivation and livestock herding broke down, replaced by the oil industry.[19]

Saudi Arabia, while hot and arid, is not the flat, lifeless desert it is often imagined to be. The northwestern portions of the kingdom are filled with mountain peaks that reach eight thousand feet and get nearly four inches of rain a year. In the southwest, elevations can reach as high as nine thousand feet, and rainfall can amount to three times the annual average in the kingdom. In the Eastern Province, where Aramco operated, the land is rocky and sandy and rainfall averages about four inches a year. The Najd, the central portion of the kingdom that includes Riyadh and al-Kharj, is dominated by deserts, the Nafud in the north and the Rub al-Khali in the south. Rainfall there is sparse, but the grazing of herds is possible in the summer months in the east.[20] The large natural water reservoirs, or pits, as they were called, that could be drawn on for irrigation made al-Kharj a prime location for agricultural development projects. When American experts arrived in Arabia, much of the irrigation water was pumped not by mechanical means but by men and animals. The *saih*, or flowing, irrigation used in the Eastern Province in the 1950s worked well in that region, but in al-Kharj the water needed to be drawn from underground pits through what was called *murakkab* irrigation. The water was tapped by using donkeys or, in the more remote interior of the kingdom and at al-Kharj, camels to lift skin buckets filled with water. A rope was tied to a wheel set in a wooden frame with one end secured to the animal. On the other end, a bucket or bag made from animal hide was tied to another rope that dangled into the pits. When the animal walked forward, often down an incline, the wheel turned and the water rose to the surface. A second rope tied to the bottom of the container emptied the water into an irrigation canal. When the animal reversed direction, the bags dropped back into the pits.[21] Early efforts would be directed toward improving this process.

Although the company took substantial credit for them, the experimental farms at al-Kharj initiated exclusively from Saudi interests. Finance Minister Abdullah Suleiman, King 'Abd al-Aziz, and other leading Saudi officials sought an economic freedom they believed only agricultural independence could bring. The Great Depression and the Second World War precipitated a combination of problems in the nation, including a decrease in pilgrimage to Mecca, meaning less tax revenue, and a decline in agricultural yields owing to locust infestations. The king, taking into consideration his recent consolidation of power and the future stability of his rule, sought to improve and expand agriculture in order to secure the independence and authority that sufficient domestic food production might allow. In negotiations with the U.S. government for lend-lease aid during 1943, another objective emerged. 'Abd al-Aziz sought to transform Saudi Arabia from a Bedouin society to a settled agricultural economy.[22] Bedouin settlement helped him consolidate control of the kingdom in the 1920s, as formerly belligerent tribes had been settled in order to alleviate conflict between them and to shift tribal allegiances toward a centralized government. Newly settled Bedouin were thus enabled to serve the monarchy as an army and be united under Wahhabi traditions that spread to new settlements through special religious instructors.[23] In postwar Arabia, demonstration farms could be examples of settled agriculture and help promote this transformation further.

Owing to its Saudi origins, the al-Kharj farm was established before American aid started to arrive. Suleiman, with the king's approval, began devising plans for the project in the 1930s, and the first major construction began in 1937 when pumps and Iraqi agricultural experts arrived. A Dutch diplomat who served in Arabia at the time recalled Suleiman's conviction that modern technology would make al-Kharj the center of agricultural advancement.[24] In 1941 Egyptian experts replaced the Iraqis, and at about the same time the oil company sold six tractors to the government for the project.[25] Through 1941 Egyptian agricultural engineers supervised the installation of water pumps and began operating the new machinery purchased from Aramco.[26] The company also furnished the monarchy with soil and water surveys conducted by the company geologists Thomas Barger and Archie Perry and the company engineers R. A. Bramkamp and L. M. Snyder. Water was an indispensable part of oil-drilling operations as well, and more wells meant less transportation of water to new oil sites. These men recommended the installation of further irrigation projects, which helped define the future of agriculture in Saudi Arabia for years to come.[27] The oil company's report further indicated that more and better irrigation would reduce the need for food imports and afford employment opportunities.[28]

The choice of al-Kharj for the construction of experimental farms originated from two equally important geographic realities: proximity to Riyadh and favorable geologic and climatic conditions. Although the king spoke of his desire to attain food independence throughout the nation, the produce grown at al-Kharj in fact supplied the royal family in Riyadh, not the population as a whole. Probably of greater centrality to the success of the project was the relative abundance of water in the area as well as the comparatively favorable weather conditions. Three enormous natural springs, or *ain*, served the farm. Two of these, Ain Semha and Ain Dhila, were described by one geologist as being "each about a hundred yards across and containing water perhaps 450 feet deep." The third, Ain Umm Khisa, was much smaller and located over a mile from the others. Smaller water sources existed, but these three pits were the most bountiful water sources in the region. Company officials reported to the monarchy in 1941 that Ain Semha and Ain Dhila were the best possible source of water for irrigation, but also that the amount of water to be had was limited by rainfall.[29] While the climate in Saudi Arabia generally prevented substantial cultivation, rain did fall in the al-Kharj region, though, as noted, only some four inches a year. These conditions were not ideal, but experts believed that with proper irrigation they could enhance agricultural production in the region. Eventually, both the oil company and the U.S. government allotted substantial resources to Saudi agricultural development in central Arabia. Aramco saw its funding as a gift to the monarchy, one symbolizing its fealty.[30] The U.S. government, however, had strategic plans in mind. The Second World War hastened America's entrance into the interior of Arabia, where it hoped to win the right to build an airbase in Dhahran, thereby giving the U.S. military a base from which to attack Japanese troops in the Pacific.[31]

The United States Agricultural Mission arrived in Saudi Arabia on May 10, 1942. At the king's request three of the members of the mission, Albert L. Wathen, James G. Hamilton, and Karl S. Twitchell, began to study the soil, water, and climate of the region.[32] Clear in the agricultural mission, however, was an agenda hidden from the king. Secretary of State Cordell Hull had emphatically apprised both Twitchell and State Department officials in the Middle East of the department's desire for "a suitable *quid pro quo.*" Hull hoped positive relationships could "be carefully cultivated" to smooth the way for the Army Air Corps to construct one or more airbases in Saudi Arabia.[33] The alleged gift of technical assistance in agriculture was thought to be a valuable token of the Americans' appreciation and aid the king could not refuse.[34] President Roosevelt, in a message to 'Abd al-Aziz delivered by the mission, chose not to mention America's designs; rather he underlined the king's interest in increasing agricultural yields, emphasizing that the "bonds of civilization" united the two nations. Continued support of American war aims, he added, would help bring about "freedom, security, and progress." Roosevelt understood the exchange implicit in the mission, and he subtly let 'Abd al-Aziz know that he expected something in return.[35] No doubt now part of American interests in securing airbases for the War Department, the agricultural mission began its work as a diplomatic mission engaged in technical assistance and public diplomacy. Twitchell, long acquainted with Saudi Arabia and King 'Abd al-Aziz, represented for the State Department a primary instrument of U.S. wartime diplomacy in Saudi Arabia.[36]

As an unofficial diplomat, Twitchell had considerable experience in Arabia. An American mining and hydraulic engineer, he arrived there first in 1931 in the employ of the philanthropist and entrepreneur Charles Crane, whom 'Abd al-Aziz had charged with exploring the Saudi deserts for water. At the time, Twitchell had been working in Yemen, and thereafter he began a journey across the Arabian deserts to conduct his work. When he arrived in the southwestern city of Jeddah in April 1931 he informed officials that no large cache of water existed, so the king sent him back to the United States to drum up possible interest in oil exploration. He returned with Lloyd Hamilton, who represented Socal, to negotiate the oil concession that marked the beginning of American oil exploration in the kingdom.[37] Twitchell himself would rightly say in 1947, "I have probably been longer and more closely associated with King ibn-Saud [as 'Abd al-Aziz was commonly known in the West] and his country than any other American."[38]

As early as 1940, before Saudi Arabia formally requested U.S. government assistance, the king told Twitchell of his interest in securing expert aid in future agricultural advancements in Saudi Arabia through the introduction of new drilling and pumping equipment. Twitchell proposed that 'Abd al-Aziz allow U.S. government representatives to conduct a survey that could help him develop the kingdom's agricultural future.[39] Clearly the right man for the job, Twitchell was the expert to whom the U.S. government turned to lead this mission.

The mission's reliance on Aramco was obvious from the start. When Twitchell and his team arrived in Saudi Arabia in May 1942, representatives from Aramco escorted them. These men had been living and working in the country for nearly a decade, whereas the U.S. State Department had only recently established an official legation in Saudi Arabia, located in Jeddah.[40] Aramco's well-established ties to the monarchy provided the agricultural mission with the connections it needed to begin its work. When Twitchell, his team of agricultural experts, and the new U.S. minister to Saudi Arabia, Alexander Kirk, made their way to Saudi Arabia—after a stop in Bahrain, where they were guests of the Bahrain Petroleum Company, a subsidiary of Aramco's parent company Socal—Floyd Oligher, the general manager at Aramco, and Max Steinike, Aramco's chief geologist, accompanied them on their flight to meet 'Abd al-Aziz. They landed at an airfield constructed by Bert Perry and Merle Holbard, two engineers who worked for the company. Aramco personnel were in charge of transport, acted as guides, constructed the runway where the party landed, and officially introduced the American legation to the king. Kirk then presented himself to the king and introduced the agricultural mission.[41]

Within days the party began its work at al-Kharj, surveying the farms and ongoing activities, including Aramco's earlier irrigation work.[42] New American equipment, much of it ordered earlier by the company, began to arrive by early 1943, and petroleum engineers soon began digging irrigation ditches and installing new pumps.[43] The agricultural mission's primary charge—aside from stimulating goodwill that might translate into permission to build American landing fields in the kingdom—was to conduct a survey and make recommendations for the agricultural project already under way.[44] With this in mind, Twitchell and his team left al-Kharj, and ultimately traveled over ten thousand miles by car, boat, and camel in order to record the soil, water, and climate conditions of the country.[45] In the end

Twitchell said the Saudi water supply was "of suitable quality" and adequate, but alternatively he indicated that the biggest hurdle to agricultural development in Saudi Arabia remained the inadequate supply of quality water.[46] Apparently what he meant was that arable land existed in some locations, but water scarcity prevented large-scale farming in most regions. Irrigation was difficult, and substantial amounts of water, overused in irrigation, needed to be recovered in order to bring about more efficient water use. With the right intervention, he believed, it could happen.

Twitchell's report anticipated a bright future for Saudi agriculture. He maintained that agriculture in Saudi Arabia could develop over the years to come through efficient national planning and application of technical solutions. New infrastructure could speed up advancement in the field, and chemical fertilizers could increase yields, although like Aramco's specialists before him Twitchell counseled greater rotation of high-nitrogen crops, a cheaper option than fertilizer. Along with his advice on improving irrigation, Twitchell proposed introducing bees to Saudi Arabia. In such hot, dry climates, flowers tended to open only briefly, and thus very little pollination occurred. Consequently, the numbers of bees in the region were quite small. Recognizing the reasons for the scarcity of bees, the report advised that special hives be constructed to protect the insects from the harsh climate. The report even generated a qualitative measurement for success that redefined the economics of such a plan to justify the costs proposed: "If a project results in raising the standard of living of a group of people it is economically sound."[47]

Measuring success in this way implied that American agriculture conveyed new values. Agricultural development, in Twitchell's view, shaped new economic and social relations and produced better citizens. By advocating sharecropping, the report indicated, farmers could make a profit for the government while being employed in government works programs such as constructing irrigation systems. It helped situate the government, through development funding, at the center of Saudi Arabian social and economic arrangements, spreading agricultural profits—in food and money—throughout the kingdom more evenly, an outcome that served to "increase the standard of living of the greatest number of people."[48] Twitchell thought the most urgent need was for the U.S. government to supply a group of agricultural experts to work in Saudi Arabia for two years in order to assist with the expansion already under way. Soon, the U.S. Department of Agriculture sent David Rogers and a team of specialists to direct the construction of new irrigation and drainage systems similar to those used in the American Southwest. Working for the War Relocation Authority, Rogers had been managing farms in the Japanese internment camps in Rivers, Arizona, with much success.[49] "It was hoped," Twitchell said, "that this . . . project will eventually become the center of an efficient [Saudi Arabian] Department of Agriculture and serve as a working example to teach the most modern practices to landowners and farmers from all parts of the Kingdom."[50] To the Saudi monarchy, al-Kharj was the primary place where the nation's agricultural future would be realized. A sanguine Twitchell remarked, "The future is promising."[51]

To organize a properly working farm, Twitchell recommended that new irrigation practices be introduced to ensure a greater, more consistent flow of water. Saudis had engaged in irrigation for centuries before the arrival of American experts, but Twitchell asserted that fertile areas could eventually become useless unless the farmers adopted the latest practices. First, enough quality water needed to be secured. Here, cost, quantity, and quality had to be balanced. In addition, new irrigation systems needed to be constructed to recapture drainage water. These additions, Twitchell predicted, might generate 25 percent more water to irrigate new lands and would prevent water from being wasted. Improper drainage and runoff water collected into large pools of standing water, which attracted mosquitoes and contributed to the malaria epidemic in the Eastern Province. Second, water quality depended on the accumulation of mineral deposits, some good and some bad. Throughout Saudi Arabia salt proved highly troublesome, as it remained in the soil when water evaporated into the dry desert air, thereby poisoning it and making it unsuitable for most agriculture. At al-Kharj, where the land was higher than the water, flowing irrigation from natural wells was impossible, necessitating the addition of costly pumps.[52] The reorganizing of natural resource use constituted a central method of national planning, and Twitchell believed that natural resources could be marshaled toward these ends through mechanization and scientifically planned irrigation schemes.[53]

Rogers's agricultural mission helped coordinate the construction of new irrigation systems and installation of new pumping equipment. The team consisted of a groundwater expert, two crop specialists, a mechanic, and a livestock expert. Each of these men had experience believed to be essential to the mission, and each also had worked in arid regions of Arizona, which suggested that a direct experiential component might be transferred from the United States to Saudi Arabia.[54] The men dug ditches for irrigation and drainage and worked with Saudi officials to determine the right kind of crops to cultivate at al-Kharj and in other regions.[55] The specific construction projects initiated were still important, but Twitchell hoped al-Kharj could serve as a model for Saudi cultivators, albeit one difficult to imitate. Rogers remarked, for instance, that Arab laborers were shocked when the Americans spaced date palms farther apart than was customary. The locals, he said, "thought we were crazy." But he hoped they would see that "our way is better than their helter-skelter style of planning." Successful modeling led to a certain excitement over what the American agricultural specialists might accomplish. Rogers predicted, "If our trees produce better dates than their own, we will have taught this country a valuable lesson."[56] The lesson was twofold: on the one hand, Saudis had an example of new and potentially valuable agricultural practices, and on the other hand, they could come to trust and perhaps rely on the United States.

For the Americans at al-Kharj, the demonstration farms served to set an example of the ways in which agriculture could be practiced throughout the kingdom. Officials at the American legation also saw value in the farms, reporting that they embodied a new form of cooperation that gained the "emphatic . . . praise" of the king, who benefited from them because they symbolized his role as caretaker. 'Abd al-Aziz revealed to American officials that "the Mission at al Kharj sets the pattern he wants: an enterprise of the Saudi Government, sponsored and protected by the King, with personnel ultimately responsible to him."[57] The American mission stayed in the country until early 1946, all the while augmenting the al-Kharj project. Unfortunately, much of the planned yields never materialized, as another of nature's enemies, locusts, attacked the farms with unexpected vigor. Funding cuts in the United States brought the mission to an end and put the future of al-Kharj in question. Aramco, as it did between the Twitchell and Rogers missions, eventually returned to managing the project.[58]

The American mission was meant to engender a positive psychological effect on local residents, but those very same people seemed to Americans only to get in the way. The general sense among Americans was that their presence was useful and that the mission had succeeded, notwithstanding the specific complaints about the seriousness of the project that lingered among the Saudi monarchy. Two months before leaving, Rogers wrote, "The combination of wind, sand, isolation and Arabs creates a working condition which is most difficult." Arabs, or "coolies," as they were known to the Americans working there, became, in his assessment, another obstacle, a continuing nuisance through much of the mission's work. The monarchy's demands for higher yields in fruits, vegetables, and feed for livestock contrasted with its actions, which often included borrowing trucks and fuel for hunting expeditions, thereby complicating the work. Moreover, Rogers complained that certain Arab employees refused to work alongside members of rival tribes, a work strike that added to his "continual source of irritation."[59] American diplomats in Saudi Arabia, however, valued American technical assistance for its potential to promote better relations with Saudi Arabia.[60] One especially encouraging sign came when American diplomats visited the farms in early 1945. 'Abd al-Aziz told them of his displeasure with Egyptian agriculturalists managing nearby projects and requested that American experts replace them. "I have confidence in you," he told Rogers. The king wanted the entire region to be under the supervision of American specialists. He reportedly told them, "Anything America undertakes cannot fail." Increased crop yields were thus only one purpose of the farms. In the context of these assurances by the monarchy, the question of building an airfield near Riyadh was broached, an enterprise the king approved, albeit reluctantly.[61]

When the second American agricultural mission finally left Saudi Arabia in 1946, the monarchy once again turned to Aramco.[62] 'Abd al-Aziz provided the funding and asked Aramco to hire American experts. Lend-lease materials that had been promised earlier continued to arrive and support the Aramco mission there.[63] Kenneth J. Edwards and, after him, Frank Brookshier worked diligently with a small cadre of American farmers to enlarge the al-Kharj operation in the years after 1946. These men brought more tractors, combines, and other equipment and attempted to demonstrate the efficiencies this equipment promised, even in regions with extremely low labor costs. Tests indicated that plowing the land by hand cost nearly twice as much per acre as using the latest technology, and mechanical plows broke up the earth more consistently and dug deeper trenches.[64] The tractors and combines used to work the land suggested only one form of modeling on these demonstration farms. One observer noted how much better Saudi Arabians ate as a result of the farm's production, implying that the company had reached one of its goals, namely, of improving living standards. In reality, however, most of the watermelons, tomatoes, onions, and peas grown there satisfied the appetites not of the public at large but of the occupants of the royal palaces in Riyadh.[65] Regardless, Aramco's experts continued to boast of the improvements to Saudis' living conditions. Workers purchased what food remained at a reduced rate, and new housing was constructed for some of the highly paid Arab employees. So that the results would not be lost on others, members of the monarchy toured the farms often, sometimes with visitors. On one occasion the king displayed his "modern farms" to the sheikh of Kuwait, who returned home with a plane full of melons and an interest in initiating an agricultural project of his own.[66]

The American farmers Aramco hired in 1946 were on the Saudi payroll, but their dependence on the company persisted. Company planes ferried individuals between al-Kharj and Dhahran, equipment came to the farms through company channels, and when the farms required additional work, the monarchy's first phone call was made to the company. During a visit by 'Abd al-Aziz in the summer of 1947, a visit that included an entourage of some size, Aramco's malaria control teams composed the king's advance team. They applied a coating of DDT to palace residences in the area, exterminating all flies, ticks, and other insect pests before the king's arrival. During the king's stay, a daily convoy of Aramco delivery trucks supplied all the water and ice required. When the king's refrigerator failed, Aramco received an emergency, late-night call requesting a replacement.[67] These episodes indicate some important points. Although Aramco did not officially manage al-Kharj, it continued to influence markedly how the farms operated and how they continued to be perceived by the Saudi monarchy. According to the company, a strong Saudi Arabian governmental agency should have been founded to operate the farms, but the distribution of supplies continued to be directed in large part by Aramco, which could then claim credit for any agricultural gains.

At the beginning of 1950 the monarchy, hoping for even greater yields, asked the company to take fuller control of al-Kharj.[68] A near doubling of production of select crops occurred in 1951, the most productive year up to that point.[69] This increase, boasted Mildred Montgomery Logan, the wife of Aramco's point man at al-Kharj, was "a marvelous thing," especially in that the destination of the large majority of produce was Riyadh, a place where "all around," she stated, "are signs of biblical times." A general sense of fulfillment, she continued, was felt when American technical expertise was shown to abate the "dirt, filth, and ignorance that exists [*sic*] among the Bedouin people."[70] Americans imported D-8 Caterpillar tractors, International planters, and other mechanical equipment to turn soil and build irrigation canals; commercial chemical fertilizers were introduced to improve the high-saline soil in the area that made crops difficult to grow. Logan contended that American patience and know-how made it possible for the Arab to make the adjustment "from the camel's back right into the driver's seat of a truck, tractor, or other mechanized implements." Such narratives emanating from Saudi Arabia declared Aramco's agricultural stewardship a success. The company's training of locals enabled them to live a better life.[71] What Aramco failed to communicate in its narrative of progress, however, was evidence the company had of other water resources in the kingdom. While Aramco hoped to show fealty to the king, it also wanted to limit its involvement with him. Company officials were sure the king would call on them to exploit other resources if they were shown to be available.[72] Aramco gave up its direct administration of al-Kharj in 1952 but managed the farm indirectly once again, from 1957 to 1959, when the farm's new director, the businessman Mohammed Bin Laden, took control. King Faisal hoped Bin Laden would assume all the costs of operating the farms, and he did. But in short order he began to neglect the project, cutting off supplies to the farm to save money. He soon forced out all the remaining Americans. Bin Laden most likely assumed responsibility for al-Kharj only as part of a larger deal that included road construction contracts.[73]

Corporate executives continued to debate the usefulness of Aramco's participation in the al-Kharj demonstration project. In contrast to the stories Aramco told, an audit of the program in 1954 determined the farms to be inefficient, unprofitable, and wasteful in both capital and natural resources as well as habitually mismanaged. Aramco's control was sloppy, its specific "obligations and responsibilities" poorly identified.[74] Executives understood that the company was to increase production "at the least cost through scientific mechanized farm practices." In fact, a field audit found a twofold increase in production from 1950 to 1953. But a full accounting of specific costs proved difficult to arrive at. All accounts intimated that cost increases at least mirrored those of production. Multiple employees seemed responsible for budgetary and accounting procedures, Saudi approval of budgets often failed to materialize, and Aramco's managers furnished no details of capital improvements when requested. Production increases also tended to be overstated, as standard units of measurement were not maintained, and consistent supervisory control of procedures did not exist. The company adopted a policy, for instance, of using the Saudi Arabian *wazn* to weigh certain commodities. The company held that a *wazn* weighed between 3.54 and 3.90 pounds. This wide range widened further when auditors discovered that in Riyadh it converted to nearly 4 pounds. In the end, the company increased production but failed to keep costs down. While one might argue that Aramco's careless administration pointed to a lack of interest, the company certainly delivered substantially more produce to the monarchy through mechanized agriculture. From the company's perspective, the specific operating costs—since it was not funding the program—were far less consequential than increased production, which brought with it political value.[75] Aramco's interests in al-Kharj turned out to be similar to those of Mohammad Bin Laden.

The somewhat symbolic enterprise at al-Kharj extended much further, as agricultural projects also comprised a template for the resettlement of the Bedouin population. 'Abd al-Aziz announced that he wanted to transform his new country from a heavily nomadic society into a settled, agricultural one. The Bedouin, a pastoral people who migrated seasonally across Arabia's deserts following water and grazing land, epitomized for many what was truly unique about the region. The king, known to some as the Bedouin king because of his roots in Bedouin society, epitomized to Western audiences an Arabian masculinity. His admirers in the West fashioned the king as a warrior, a leader of men, a powerful figure who embodied quiet strength and courage while at the same time being steadily loyal to his people and a reasonable, enlightened monarch.[76] The Arabic word for Bedouin not only identifies a people but also means tough and straightforward, the exact qualities westerners attributed to the king.[77] As he consolidated power in the early part of the century, 'Abd al-Aziz relied on Bedouin allies to help secure the interior of the peninsula. This alliance, however, crumbled as state building replaced conquest and Bedouin warriors became a potential threat. The new Saudi Arabia sought to integrate various populations that traditional tribal confederacies could not govern effectively. Consolidating state control also meant securing the borders and centralizing decision making.[78] 'Abd al-Aziz reportedly said to American agricultural experts at al-Kharj, "If there were enough farms like this in Saudi Arabia, the Bedouin would stop their wandering and settle down in green pastures."[79]

Settling the Bedouin in agricultural communities was an early strategy of Saudi nation building, and 'Abd al-Aziz had extensive knowledge of the process. He achieved his expansion and consolidation in the 1910s and 1920s with the aid of the Ikhwan, Bedouin whom he later helped settle in agricultural colonies. These former Bedouin, often referred to as religious fanatics and warriors loyal to the king, personified 'Abd al-Aziz's attempt to alter the way of life in Arabia through his rule. While not all Ikhwan lived completely sedentary lives, 'Abd al-Aziz referred to those who had been settled as *hadar,* or civilized.[80] Curbing violence among various Bedouin tribes became essential to state formation in the years of expansion and consolidation. Once the king's rule over the peninsula had been established, the unsettled Ikhwan came to symbolize not centralization, but factionalism; they challenged his rule until they were militarily defeated shortly before his self-appointment as ruler of the Kingdom of Saudi Arabia in 1932.

More broadly, these new kinds of communities were a means by which states challenged established patterns of life and fixed individuals within new state structures.[81] Given that over half the population of Saudi Arabia was nomadic—for reasons as much ecological as cultural in the mid-twentieth century—the shifts in patterns of land use occurred in small increments.[82] But changes occurred quickly in the date groves of the Eastern Province and in animal husbandry among the Bedouin. The relationship between people who lived in the desert and those who lived in the oasis villages underwent substantial changes after the Second World War. Aramco, in combination with the new market economy that arose in Saudi Arabia, compelled certain economic and cultural adjustments that served to modify preexisting social and ecological arrangements. Many Bedouin were working for the company just as agricultural and industrial development brought Saudi production into the global marketplace. Settlement became not merely a government-sponsored plan; it became a necessary adjustment to new conditions created by the oil industry.

The Saudi Arabian government continued to hope that Bedouin settlement would lead to national unity. The former deputy minister of agriculture A. S. Helaissi advocated settlement in 1959, stating in clear terms that the Bedouin "must be persuaded" to live in homes and make a living in sedentary agriculture. Bedouin, he stressed, did not recognize national borders. They "keep moving between their own and neighboring countries, recognizing no territorial limits but those of their grazing lands." With the successes in reducing tribal warfare after the unification of the kingdom, he argued, Bedouin no longer needed to keep moving. Nomadism retarded economic development in Saudi Arabia, he argued, "because of the virtual failure of the Bedouins to make any real contribution" to the national economy. Fixed habitation lent permanence and assured new rights to Bedouin as citizens of Saudi Arabia.[83]

Settlement, however, rarely resulted from state policy, more often coming from Bedouins' reactions to changing conditions in Saudi Arabia. Since the early 1940s Bedouin groups had applied to the government for land grants near oil company water wells and started to build sedentary communities. The government helped coordinate these formal settlements, but people's choosing to live in them was purely voluntary. After a severe drought in northern Arabia in 1959, the government undertook a program to induce settlement more systematically. This relief effort turned into an agricultural settlement as the Saudi Arabian government encouraged Bedouin to move to individual plots of land irrigated by wells dug on the property. The project failed to persuade many, however, owing to a combination of poor planning, insufficient infrastructure, and Bedouin conventions. An official in the Ministry of Agriculture averred that once water became available to Bedouin outside the settlement, they left, which, he wrote, "confirms in full the dominance of Bedouin customs and age-long traditions in the conduct of people."[84] Settlement programs came and went in various forms in the three decades after the Second World War, most never getting beyond the planning stage.[85] Although formal settlement projects rarely ended in the formation of new Bedouin villages, economic conditions led to many of the cultural changes the Saudi Arabian government desired.

The oil company created new environmental, social, and economic conditions in the deserts and oasis villages of the Eastern Province. Before Aramco's arrival, Bedouin in the area survived by raising sheep and camels, which could be traded or sold for dates and other foods. By midcentury this relationship changed, as the oil industry brought new wealth and ever-expanding cities and towns to the once sparsely populated deserts. The anthropologist Donald P. Cole, who lived with and studied the Bedouin of southeastern Arabia for years, has written that many government officials in the postwar Middle East began to define nomadism as "an evolutionary state that preceded sedentary life."[86] Helaissi, sounding much like the modernization theorist Daniel Lerner, had postulated the same idea in explaining that Saudi Arabia and its neighbors were in the midst of "passing through a transitional stage, which includes the evolution of the Bedouins."[87] The arrival and expansion of the oil industry brought changes in Bedouins' living patterns. Aramco employed Bedouin as unskilled labor and guides and later trained them to drive and fix trucks. The expansion of oil facilities led to new and deeper water wells in new locations. Bedouin migrations shifted, and the new wells centralized many tribes that previously had had little contact. Small settlements formed in these areas and also in the north along the Trans Arabian Pipeline (Tapline), an oil pipeline from the Persian Gulf to the Mediterranean Sea, near railway stops, and at intersections of major roads.[88] By the mid-1950s many Bedouin were camped near Aramco's Gas Oil Separation Plants, which required a steady supply of water. These plants were located throughout the company's expansive Ghawar oil field in the Eastern Province. Company officials were aware that water and the availability of grazing lands dictated the Bedouins' movements, but they still appeared to be unable to identify what combinations of each encouraged which migrations and in what numbers. What they did know, however, was that by 1956 they had what they called a "Bedouin Problem" developing near pipeline facilities.[89] Since the nomads' diet in the Eastern Province consisted almost entirely of livestock they raised and produce traded for in nearby villages, it was obvious that the two societies, while seemingly separate, actually were joined in a centuries' old symbiosis that allowed each to prosper in harsh climates.[90]

Life in the Eastern Province changed for the settled populations and the Bedouin alike in the face of agricultural development projects. Since life as a desert nomad required adapting to the environmental conditions, after the Second World War the Bedouin had to conform to new social and economic conditions. In the Eastern Province, Bedouin who owned large herds of camels held high social status, but this began to change. The introduction of trucks, many purchased secondhand from Aramco, set the scene for new patterns. Sheepherding, which in the past had signaled poverty, became, except in the remote areas of the desert where camel raising persisted, the primary wealth-producing activity among the Bedouin in the Eastern Province. Growing towns in the East increased the demand for mutton, making sheepherding profitable. It was now cheaper and easier to raise sheep, as trucks allowed for simpler and faster herding and could deliver water to remote herds. Over time, more women and children worked as herders, leaving men available to serve in the newly constituted Saudi National Guard or to seek employment in the oil industry. Camel herding came to be viewed by many as an activity connected to the past.[91] Aramco observed this trend but believed that the pace of Bedouin settlement urged by government policy, if achieved, would be so slow that it would have minimal impact on company operations. If anything, Aramco leaned toward less rather than more settlement. Few jobs existed for newly settled Bedouin, and even the government predicted growing instability among some living in urban areas.[92]

Still, the government made various large-scale attempts to settle the Bedouin, the largest and most publicized plan being the Haradh Project. While searching for oil in the late fifties and early sixties, Aramco discovered large pools of water in the Wadi Saba area southeast of Riyadh. The government approved a settlement program in the area in August 1963. Given the government's contention that "nomadism creates an obstacle to development," Aramco backed the project, even championed it.[93] Its involvement likely stemmed not from a need for greater agricultural production but, again, from an interest in showing loyalty to the king and limiting its actual commitments.[94] The government wished to link settled agriculture with national citizenship and allegiance among the Bedouin. The company contributed $400,000, much of it for drilling water wells and paying for technical agricultural advice. Aramco hoped the grant would forestall emergency calls from the government to aid in the completion of the project. Officials hoped the government might "take enough pride in the scheme as a prestige project" and "keep it self-sufficient in most services." And even if the scheme failed, the company held the position that the "project will not go to waste." It anticipated that "for every Bedouin who may give up trying, there will be five Qatifis or Hasawis eager to have their own land and to share in the potential profits." The project could demonstrate to Saudi Arabs once again how to reclaim desert land and bring about new cultivation.[95]

Aramco reacted to Bedouin settlement in unexpected ways. As the self-proclaimed partner in progress in Saudi Arabia, the company, one might assume, would have done more to support settlement. Aramco, however, remained less than enthusiastic, although not publicly. Company officials worried about the practical application of such programs on the company's operation, believing, as they had in the 1940s when they withheld water resource data, that the monarchy would rely on the company to support these projects. Aramco's concession agreement had no specific language in it that required support for the Bedouin, but their pipeline agreement did. The company was obligated to provide water and construct hospitals for Bedouin in need near Tapline facilities. Official reports indicate that the company's interaction with the Bedouin was not substantial, but recently settled Bedouin used company social services in sizable numbers. Aramco's reaction to what one report described as "parasitic villages" suggested that the cost of dealing with the Bedouin in the Eastern Province consisted of many livestock claims, as animals often wandered into oil sumps or pipes. While the final claim costs remained low—only $375 between 1962 and 1965, for example—the time expended researching these tiny claims proved to be higher than desired.[96]

Aramco's research yielded mixed messages regarding how settlement might affect the company. On the one hand, there was support for the larger principle dominant among Middle East governments of "fitting Bedouin society into the standard compartment of modern national life." Aramco's study of settlement in 1965 highlighted Middle East governments' attempts at Bedouin settlement. One Iraqi writer noted, "Once the Bedouins understand that their traditions are obsolete, the causes of their unhappiness will be eradicated." The message Aramco heard here was that many in the Middle East saw the Bedouin as backward and as something "that must be eradicated as a bar to progress." Furthermore, the settled populations sometimes believed the Bedouin to be unproductive, the symbiosis between them notwithstanding.[97] Although Aramco contended that the governments of the Middle East had good reason to pursue settlement plans, company officials realized the positive impact it could have on oil operations, as it could mean an "increased availability of labor."[98] On the other hand, these same reports warned of the problems the company might face. In 1956 company research posited that "increases in the 'Bedu Camp' [shantytown] type of semi-permanently settled areas" might produce "increased requests for local services: wood, fire-fighting, medical care and the like." The corporation expressed its worries over the Bedouins' dependence on company water, their likely crowding of the company's and settlement's roads and other facilities, and the possible increase in violence over water rights.[99] Aramco's Tapline facilities faced problems annually because of water disputes that included gunfights, stabbings, and riots that damaged equipment. By 1966 Aramco perceived many of Saudi Arabia's settlement programs to be, "in a social sense . . . radical," but few believed that much would be accomplished very quickly.[100]

While these changes occurred, the Saudi Arabian government lamented its own inability to encourage settlement more broadly. Helaissi pointed to the Bedouin as a reason for Saudi Arabia's slow advancement toward greater national economic success.[101] Ultimately, Aramco's impact, with its new technologies, roads, railroads, and water wells, allowed some degree of settlement to emerge. American officials who promoted modernization did so in the firm belief that people first needed to be categorized, counted, measured, and guided. "Symbols of progress" needed to be erected as signposts of development.[102] The Saudi Arabian government had made various attempts to settle the Bedouin in hopes of bringing rapid development to the kingdom. But Aramco's research pointed to the actual, on-the-ground trend of what it referred to as "present natural settlement modes. . . . The general trend in Aramco's area of operations has been for Bedouins to join urban populations and to take less strenuous jobs as drivers and mechanics." Attempting to move the Bedouin to cities, a company report of 1965 noted, "would be impractical on a large scale." So while governments in the Middle East wrangled about the need to settle nomadic peoples in order to promote development more rapidly, in the case of the Bedouin in the Eastern Province, these "natural settlement modes," not government policy, gave rise to a settled population. With all the confusion surrounding the problem of how to induce nomadic tribes to remain in fixed locations, new agricultural initiatives in the Eastern Province not only served as an example of economic activity that brought desired cultural changes but also demonstrated another way settlement might be encouraged.

The extension of development aid to Saudi Arabia through the al-Kharj demonstration farms contributed heavily to Aramco's self-identification as the agent of positive change in Saudi Arabia. But al-Kharj was only the first and most substantial of the kingdom's postwar agricultural projects, and many of the exemplary aspects of the program went unobserved since most of the produce was bound for the royal family in Riyadh.[103] When the company introduced new agricultural practices in the East, the symbiosis that had formed in the face of the severe limitations placed on desert farming underwent permanent transformation. Experimental farms emerged in the

Eastern Province, particularly in the Qatif and al-Hasa oases. In al-Hasa, one of the largest oases in Saudi Arabia, conditions were more favorable to cultivation owing to the availability of water. Local agriculture, however, rendered less than adequate food supplies for the oases, and nearly 90 percent of cultivation was in dates.[104] In 1949 the Saudi monarchy initiated the Hofuf Agricultural Project in al-Hasa, which brought American farmers from al-Kharj to the East in order to introduce the latest farming techniques. In short order the Americans were able to produce, as one observer put it, "admiring stares from Arab farmers," which was said to be "a definite achievement." Americans cleared the land, built irrigation ditches and bridges, and introduced area farmers to mechanized farming and new crops, including alfalfa, limes, peaches, onions, pumpkins, figs, wheat, eggplants, and tomatoes, among others.[105]

One purpose of the American program in the Eastern Province was to illustrate to local Arabs the potential of increased mechanization in farming. To this end, many date palms were removed so that tractors could navigate the fields and harvest the dates more easily, which increased the output of each tree. The introduction of machines meant that farmers in the area needed to be educated to operate, maintain, and repair equipment. Where laborers climbed trees, picking dates by hand and placing them in sacks, machines mattered much less. To demonstrate the positive outcomes of reorganization, the groves needed to generate higher yields. New technology meant an increased need for water, and as new lands were cultivated ground water resources decreased.[106]

By 1955 Aramco still reported that much of al-Hasa oasis suffered from poorly constructed, poorly maintained ditch complexes and wasteful regulation of water flow. Ongoing agriculture in al-Hasa required dependence on ever-increasing amounts of chemical fertilizer as well. In the end, Aramco discovered that altering the "cultural elements of a non-technological kind," meaning better regulation of water, would be more effective in the short term for increasing agricultural production.[107] Machines perhaps could be the impetus for cultural change, as much for their demonstrative impact as anything, but technology could accomplish only so much. More important, according to Aramco's study of the region, there seemed to be a need to produce changes that would allow for greater production as well as self-sufficiency. To investigate some of these changes Aramco, in conjunction with Saudi Arabian agricultural specialists, initiated a study of drainage in the Qatif oasis. The hope was to propose better irrigation practices that included recommendations for the proper construction of ditch complexes.[108] Major changes were slower and more complicated than the company anticipated, but mechanization had a more dramatic effect. It meant a special reorganization of date groves, which in turn had a social impact.

Aramco's corporate interests and its huge social footprint in the Eastern Province influenced agriculture dramatically. Date farming no longer produced the same return it had decades before, and Aramco was now the primary employer in the region.[109] As of 1955 reports circulating inside the company hinted that agriculture in Saudi Arabia might be worse off than before the company arrived. Decreased demand for dates and fewer people employed in date cultivation reduced prices for that commodity considerably. Profits from an acre of dates fell nearly tenfold in thirty years. Work in the oil industry now counterbalanced agricultural wage discrepancies.[110] Labor costs alone accounted for substantial increases in growing costs.[111] S. W. Edgecombe of the American University of Beirut visited Saudi Arabia and felt compelled to offer advice to the company after his tour. A primary impediment to agricultural development, he asserted, was that "Aramco technicians have done the job instead of assisting the local people to do it themselves." A more diverse agricultural project, he argued, with higher yields in the Eastern Province could benefit the company by reducing the costs of produce that had to be imported for company consumption.[112] So Aramco would become a larger buyer of locally grown produce. As technical aid in agriculture evolved, so too did the purpose of the farms. Food independence was a central issue of the Saudi monarchy, but company officials hoped to begin benefiting financially from increased production.

More than just economic change motivated Aramco's agricultural specialists. Agricultural aid was an instrument for changing social relations in Saudi Arabia. The company altered the social structure in the Eastern Province, making it less centered on the date and more connected to advancements in technology and linked to the broadening agricultural market economy. Change took place in the date groves but also in the long-established social and economic patterns of the region. Date palm cultivation in the al-Hasa and Qatif oases of the Eastern Province traditionally supplied food for humans and animals, wood for home construction, and a commodity for use in trade with the Bedouin. After the consolidation of the kingdom in 1932, the Saudi government attempted to create a surplus of dates artificially in order to benefit the Bedouin, who relied heavily on them for food. The export of dates was therefore forbidden, a situation which lowered their price markedly. The date, then, as a commodity in trade, meant far less and by the mid-1950s no longer generated the same economic return. As a result, many date farmers turned to Aramco and began working in the oil industry.[113]

The economic aspect of date cultivation is only part of the story, however, as date groves occupied a crucial cultural space in oasis life. They served as the primary place of business and social interaction for the upper echelons of oasis society and a source of wage labor and class interaction among workers. The groves were shady and offered relief during hot days, and the water used in irrigation helped cool the air. Additionally, date groves conferred social status on their owners. Size didn't matter, ownership did. The cultural aspects of date cultivation thus entailed not merely the simple pleasures of oasis life but also the site of social and cultural interaction.[114] And while Aramco boasted that its impact through the development of oil in the Eastern Province brought "a higher standard of living," agricultural experts recognized too that this accomplishment came "at the expense of owners of farm land."[115] Prices for produce continued to drop, and population increases began putting greater strain on the date groves, land that Aramco's experts knew residents had no desire to abandon.[116] Land continued to represent status, regardless of how the company understood its impact on living standards. As it did before the arrival of the oil industry, land continued to allow for civic participation.

Aramco's attempts to bring about cultural change, therefore, targeted more than farming techniques. Encouragement to move away from mono-cropping and a focus on cash crops, while inconsistent with larger global efforts to improve agriculture in the global south, fit Aramco's larger agenda, elucidated in its own study of the oasis of al-Hasa: to generate "reliable information on the Hasawis' readiness or reluctance to accept employment with the Company."[117] Instead, as on the demonstration farms of al-Kharj, American specialists tried to increase the number of crops produced in the region both to reenergize the sagging economy and to generate a more diverse selection of products to market for sale to the company. A review of the company's agricultural programs in the Eastern Province in 1955 pointed to the general demand for fruits and vegetables in the area, implying that the company encourage fewer date groves and more citrus fruit cultivation, which commanded higher prices.[118]

Despite centuries of expansion in cultivation in the Eastern Province, the company saw diversification and technical, economic, and cultural change as the future of agriculture in the region. Oasis life, company experts stated, needed to change in order to connect the residents to new demands in the kingdom, a project that required expanding the types of produce grown and introducing low-cost alternatives to the generally high wages required in date cultivation. Aramco's chief agricultural adviser, James Hamilton, said upon his retirement in 1955 that although Aramco is a "competitive commercial enterprise" it "would seem to have an economic interest in the promotion of a sound agricultural economy in the area from the standpoints of food supply and health of its employees." Aramco's interests mirrored enterprises undertaken in the United States during the Cold War to spur industrial growth in the global south, but the company's ultimate ends related to profit. Mechanical tractors and chemical fertilizers were part of the shift. Internal reports predicted the high yields that could result from these technologies but held that sharing costly equipment might better serve the needs of all farmers. Hamilton noted that "the basis for sound agriculture," meaning diversified crops, lower growing costs, and improved standards of living, "does exist if it is given adequate technical guidance and financial support."[119]

The U.S. government continued to grant agricultural aid to Saudi Arabia as long as it was allowed to do so. In the 1950s representatives of the Technical Cooperation Administration conducted surveys of water resources and irrigation and other agricultural practices as part of President Truman's Point Four initiative. The U.S. government and the Saudi monarchy signed a general agreement on technical assistance in January 1951 and a more specific agreement on technical cooperation in agriculture in November 1952. The U.S. government dispatched agricultural specialists to the kingdom to work alongside Saudi agricultural officials and to train select officials in the United States and provide any equipment the Saudi government needed but could not acquire itself.[120] While the monarchy said it continued to be pleased with the work stemming from this agreement, in June 1954 Crown Prince Faisal reported that the monarchy had decided to terminate Point Four activities "because of the new policy of Saudi Arabia not to bother the U.S. Government." There were some complaints related to the size of the program, but it was the government's inability to intercede more forcefully in the British–Saudi Arabian border disputes that seems to have annoyed the monarchy more than anything else.[121]

Traditionally, agriculture in Saudi Arabia was labor intensive, but mechanized cultivation freed Arabs to seek employment in the oil industry. The results of Aramco's efforts were mixed, but agricultural aid continued to function as a gesture of goodwill. Hamilton argued that, regardless of the progress made, "a great deal of good has been done." He stated that the company had generated a "friendly and understanding relationship" with many of the major date farmers in the Eastern Province. These were relationships that could be cultivated as the company expanded oil operations in the region, surveyed the population for its "readiness" for employment, and explored the area for entry into the more diverse market economy that continued to develop.[122]

Aramco reshaped notions of how agricultural advancements might emerge in the deserts of Arabia. While the company served as steward to the monarchy's agricultural interests at al-Kharj, it promoted crop diversity and dramatic cultural changes in the Eastern Province to better fit the social and economic changes the oil industry produced. When it came to finding a place for Bedouin pastoral farmers in new settlements, the company charted a more cautious path than the one many advocated. With agricultural reform, Aramco continued to promote its identity as a partner in progress. Through its role in the demonstration farms and displays of scientific management and technical prowess, the company sought to promote its goodwill to the monarchy. The Saudi Arabian deserts never bloomed in the way agricultural planning and technology promised. Saudi agricultural self-sufficiency has also proved to be tenuous and most likely a waste of precious resources.

'Abd al-Aziz's original goal of making Saudi Arabia self-sufficient in agriculture came to fruition, but not in the way one might imagine. By the mid-1980s wheat production had risen dramatically, making the kingdom a net exporter of the product. Given that consumption of wheat in Saudi Arabia remains low, the crop serves a symbolic role. As agricultural scientists know, food is water: that is, every bushel of wheat shipped out of Saudi Arabia takes with it the water required to grow it, and given that water in the deserts is scarce, national security is threatened, not protected, by wheat cultivation. Variety too presents various dilemmas. Alfalfa, for instance, needs six times the water that wheat requires.[123] Saudi farms even grow rice, which would have stunned William Owen, whose job for Aramco in the mid-1950s was to evaluate the company's various programs. When asked decades later, while boasting of Aramco's success in helping the kingdom become self-sufficient in food production, if Saudi Arabia grows its own rice, he said, "I wouldn't think so. It requires so much water and swampland."[124] Meat, fruits, and vegetables also require large amounts of water, but Saudi Arabia continues to export many of these products. The food-equals-water equation finally led to a ban on alfalfa exports in 2000, but the future looks bleak. Saudi cities face severe water shortages every day, but all the while water is being consumed by desert agriculture meant for export.

The meteoric rise of Saudi Arabian agriculture in the last quarter of the twentieth century resulted less from agricultural aid and the introduction of new technologies than from disproportionate government subsidies. Oil wealth turned into price supports, subsidies, interest-free loans, and grants that went to support more mining for water, landownership consolidation, hobby farms, and foreign agribusiness. Businessmen started to replace farmers, and much of the land originally set aside for settled, established places to live became part of larger corporate enterprises. Agricultural development has not led to greater national security, and ultimately it might compromise it. The flow of water in Saudi Arabia might stop even before the flow of oil.[125]

Conclusion

THE SOCIOLOGIST Thomas O'Dea, in a study commissioned by Aramco in the early 1960s, wrote, "Saudi Arabia today is a country in that state of transition in which a 'take off' into modest development in agriculture and light processing industries would be entirely possible." The nation has capital, he argued, to move in that direction, but a few issues concerned him. Saudi Arabia was a new nation, and, as the report suggests, it "is emerging from traditional forms of life, in government and administration, in business, and in the structure of family and personal relationships, and experiencing the inevitable ambiguities and confusions of such transitions."[1] In a few sentences O'Dea touched on a number of key developments in both Aramco's relationship to Saudi Arabia in the first few decades after the Second World War and an overarching, persistent development discourse, which by 1963 had come to dominate analyses of America's overseas activities. O'Dea writes of Saudi Arabia's place within Walt Rostow's taxonomy of stages, positing that "take-off" was just around the corner. It was no longer a "traditional society," according to Rostow's stage theory, one burdened by low production capacity, ignorance, and provincialism. Now it was in the "preconditions for take-off," as modern science and new technologies had been applied. These "transitionals," as Daniel Lerner referred to them, had made considerable headway. Families changed, government administration expanded, and social hierarchies underwent the stresses associated with the processes of modernized life.[2]

This confidential study in 1963 cited the oil company as a key component of Saudi Arabia's apparent successes but also of its tensions. The company brought a "modern large-scale western enterprise" to "a hitherto traditional and undeveloped society." It brought money to the monarchy and wages to the people, and it allowed Saudi Arabia to become a modern state and join the world community. This success, however, came at a price. As O'Dea implied, the transition brought confusion. Saudi Arabs, he said, are "undergoing what is often called a 'revolution of rising expectations,' and developing political concerns." This shift threatened Aramco's role as the country's partner. It "is no longer a modern western corporation introducing new methods and ways of life into a relatively undisturbed traditional society. It is today a foreign enterprise operating in a society which stands unsteadily and ambivalently on the verge of a modest 'take-off.'"[3]

This stage gap between the United States and Saudi Arabia, according to O'Dea, indicated a psychological imbalance. These were "people in transition" who were "at different stages of development with respect to modern standards of life and work." O'Dea suggested that a growing Saudi resentment toward the United States and Aramco stemmed primarily from this reality: "When old cultural values are altered, when old frames of reference become inadequate, when new and positionally superior groups introduce new values and new models of life, confusion, frustration, and resentment are inevitable consequences." The oil concession required continued engagement with Saudi development, but the company began to backtrack, and O'Dea perhaps provided some justification. How could the company maintain its "legal obligations" under the concession agreement while at the same time not "alienating advanced opinion and thereby worsening its own popular image"?[4]

Aramco's position in Saudi Arabia became strained for a number of reasons, including, as O'Dea pointed out, ties to the monarchy that were closer than its ties to the Saudi populace. Many in the Middle East began to hold increasingly negative views of U.S. policy, and that began to affect the company. Corporate diplomacy dictated support for the monarchy, but that support had an impact on the firm's relationship with workers. This phenomenon was not new, but it was starting to change the nature of the company's relationship to the monarchy. It was not just company policy that doomed Aramco.[5] More and more, internal Saudi politics and U.S. foreign policy altered the ability of Western oil firms to retain their privileged positions. Political and economic concerns took priority over the kingdom's relationship with the company, as increasing pressure from various segments inside and outside Saudi Arabia required greater Saudi social and economic autonomy. Falling oil prices and the resultant reduction of royalties to the Saudi monarchy by the late 1950s strained relations between Aramco and Saudi Arabia. New sources of oil and the rise of independent oil firms operating worldwide brought a sudden decrease in the wealth of producing states, leading in 1960 to the creation of the Organization of Petroleum Exporting Countries (OPEC), which hoped to put production and pricing more in the hands of those who owned the resources. Nationalization of Aramco would not be far behind.

As early as July 1956 signs of nationalization were apparent, as Undersecretary of State Herbert Hoover Jr. warned President Eisenhower that Egypt's nationalization of the Suez Canal might lead to a similar takeover of oil facilities in the region. The Suez crisis worried American policymakers, for sure, and Eisenhower certainly understood the warning. He did not, however, want to anger Arabs with direct Western military action. Should Nasser's move succeed, his enhanced status, the president feared, could lead to problems for the United States. In January 1958 Nasser's Arab nationalism spread to nearby Syria, and the two joined to become the United Arab Republic (UAR). Nasser and Egypt, American policymakers now recognized, were poised to dominate events in the Middle East.[6]

Eisenhower quickly moved to establish better relations with the Egyptian leader, recognizing the confederation a month later and soon offering American food aid under the Food for Peace program. Although the aid likely served the president's domestic economic agenda more than it addressed his Cold War concerns, it was clear he had turned away from his earlier aloof approach to Nasser.[7] It seemed that tensions had been reduced, and upon his inauguration President John F. Kennedy hoped to continue the positive engagement with the Egyptian leader. The new administration looked to increase food aid to Egypt, believing that Nasser could become a key figure in terms of American designs in the Middle East. Administration officials saw the aid as a long-term strategy to curtail Nasser's revolutionary designs for the region, but, just as important, they also saw it as a short-term strategy to reach compromise on United States–Israeli policy in the region.[8] Regardless of the development aid, however, "minor irritants," as one Kennedy aide called them, could threaten to frustrate progress, and war in Yemen proved to be one such case.[9]

A right-wing coup in Syria led to its withdrawal from the UAR in 1961, prompting Nasser to take a harder line when revolution erupted in Yemen the next year. In October he sent military aid to back the revolutionaries against Saudi-supported royalists. Crown Prince Faisal expressed his displeasure over Kennedy's rapprochement with Nasser. The new president hoped to appeal to less conservative regimes in the hope of acquiring them as potential allies in the Cold War, which from the start cast him in a poor light with the Saudi monarchy. King Saud admonished Kennedy for supporting Israel at the expense of its Arab neighbors and, owing to revolutionary pressures in the region, refused to renew the Americans' lease on the Dhahran Airbase. Saud also engaged in preliminary discussions with the Soviet Union regarding arms sales, which made matters even worse.[10] Saud's criticism of the United States did not fall on deaf ears, and Congress cut aid to Egypt in November 1963.[11] Many American policymakers regarded the substantial aid Nasser gave to Yemeni leftists as marking the end of American détente with Egypt. In addition, he remained friendly with the Soviets, backed the Palestine Liberation Organization, supported the Viet Cong, and criticized monarchies in Saudi Arabia and Iran allied to the United States. In American eyes, Nasser symbolized a Third World revolutionary of the worst kind.[12]

While not popular among American policymakers, Nasser's Arab nationalism appealed to many Saudi citizens. It spoke to their continued disgust with Arab–Israeli issues, French and British colonialism in North Africa and the Arabian Gulf, and American corporate control of the kingdom's oil wealth. Almost all of these criticisms found popular appeal in Saudi Arabia. As the historian Toby Craig Jones shows, criticism of the American oil company, while still a "red line" to Saudi officials, emerged popularly by the mid-1950s. While Arab nationalism may not have appealed to the monarchy, it clearly spoke to the Saudi people in the Eastern Province.[13] Nasser's attraction in the region remained powerful. Eisenhower had tried to contain it with anticommunist appeals embedded in the Eisenhower Doctrine, but his economic approach found limited support in Congress. So instead the president in 1957 looked to King Saud as a regional counterweight to Arab nationalism. Perhaps Saud's role as protector of Mecca and Medina could, as the administration hoped, broaden the king's regional following. Certainly Aramco hoped to benefit from its similar appeals to Saud's and Saudi Arabia's Islamic identity. Unfortunately, it was a foolish attempt given Saud's poor reputation at home and abroad. Saud, however, accepted the role cast for him by Washington, lowering his popularity among many in

Saudi Arabia even further. In the end, he was no match for Nasser. Saud's continued health problems, his lavish spending, and his poor governance damaged his ability to lead, even among his supporters in the House of Saud. After his family pushed him aside in favor of his brother, Prince Faisal, leadership squabbles would plague the kingdom for some time.[14]

Whereas Eisenhower had unsuccessfully turned to Saud as a regional Islamic leader, in the mid-1960s King Faisal looked to Islamic unity as a counter to Arab unity, which, as Jones notes, "helped animate dissent among Saudi Arabian Aramco employees."[15] Faisal toured the Muslim world as Nasser stepped up his backing of revolutionaries in Yemen in 1966. To Americans, Faisal's actions were a welcome attempt by a regional ally to combat Arab nationalism and Soviet encroachments in the region. Through new arms purchases from Britain and the United States, Faisal hoped to strengthen his position as a major regional power broker.[16]

Oil executives hoped to hold on to the concession, but the corporate image as a partner in the kingdom's nation building began to be replaced, not from within the company but from outside, as Saudi Arabia began to narrate its own future more actively. As the historian Robert Vitalis writes, "The ARAMCO Americans could hardly control the future of even the story that Saudis would begin to tell about them."[17] It was, however, more than a story about Americans in Saudi Arabia and who would be able to tell that past. It was a story about nation building, too. In the 1960s Saudi Arabia began to narrate its own path forward, and Aramco seemed willing to talk of its social and economic development programs in the past tense. It was not as if Aramco's notion of development had been achieved; it was simply that the company no longer believed continued engagement with the monarchy in this way benefited corporate interests. According to O'Dea's study, Aramco's talk of a transformative role might have a negative impact.[18] It was a foreign firm operating in Saudi Arabia for its own benefit, and by the end of the sixties it was clear that control of Saudi resources could no longer remain in the hands of an American company.

Growing concerns over nationalization and oil embargoes had put the West on notice. Indeed, oil became a powerful weapon, as Saudi Arabia suspended oil shipments to the United States and Britain after war erupted between Israel and its neighbors in 1967. One Aramco vice president worried aloud as Arabs and Israelis marched toward war that Aramco would be nationalized, "if not today, then tomorrow."[19] He was not far off. On

June 7 the Saudi oil minister, Ahmad Zaki Yamani, ordered Aramco to cease shipments of oil to both nations, and a following discussion raised the possibility of the future nationalization of the company. The West was able to forestall major short-term losses during the brief embargo, but it was now manifest that Aramco and other Western oil firms served the producing nations, not the other way around. Egypt's swift defeat in the war of 1967 humiliated Nasser, and soon after oil-rich states agreed to provide substantial monetary aid to Egypt and Jordan, half of which came from Saudi Arabia. As the historian Rachel Bronson put it, Nasser no longer represented a threat to Saudi Arabia: he "was now on the Saudi payroll."[20]

Events in Saudi Arabia during the summer of 1967 indicated without a doubt that Aramco's presence was growing increasingly unpopular. American and Aramco officials worried that Arab–Israeli disputes could provoke a violent response from Saudi Arabs against American installations in the kingdom. On June 7, 1967, a crowd of over four hundred Arab workers and others in Dhahran rioted for nearly twelve hours, attacking Aramco facilities, residences, and property as well as the consulate office and U.S. government facilities at the Dhahran Airbase. These events led to the evacuation of hundreds of Aramco's American personnel. The day before, after hearing radio announcements that American aid was being delivered to Israel, Arab protesters disrupted activities in Ras Tanura, where refined oil was being loaded onto tankers. Arab workers began to stage walkouts, heightening the company's concern. This was the middle of a week of violence that at one point had Aramco families evacuated to a school gymnasium for safety. Saudi Arabia's Public Safety Forces were on hand, but the rioters did not retreat until the better-trained and better-equipped Saudi National Guard arrived in force.[21] This disturbance, combined with continued upsets over work stoppages, intensified fears. While a U.S. government study concluded that there was no hard evidence to justify anxiety, over a decade of work-related conflict at Aramco regarding pay, benefits, and housing had in fact reached a climax.[22]

Work toward the nationalization—or participation, as Yamani called it—of Aramco had begun before the Arab–Israeli war of 1967, but the crisis allowed Yamani to place himself in a more powerful position regarding Aramco's future in Saudi Arabia. Vice President Frank Jungers, who headed up concession affairs, was convinced that American support of Israel was the biggest obstacle for Aramco by the late 1960s, owing largely to political pressure. The distinction the monarchy drew in 1948 between U.S. policy in Israel and the American corporation no longer existed. By 1968 Yamani had become a member of Aramco's executive committee, the company policy-making body.[23]

In the early 1970s, as Americans' energy usage continued to increase, the need for foreign oil deepened. Imports, restricted by quotas that Eisenhower imposed, could not keep pace, as domestic production was at full capacity by 1972. Lasting reliance on imports was the way of the future, but events in the Middle East would drive prices up and limit American corporate control further. In October 1973 Egypt and Syria attacked Israel, and the United States soon provided Israel with substantial material support. King Faisal had earlier promised Anwar Sadat of Egypt that he would use Saudi oil as a weapon against Israel's allies, if necessary. Just as the fighting commenced, OPEC and oil company representatives met to discuss pricing but failed to come to mutually acceptable terms. Gulf state members decided on their own to raise prices by 70 percent, and soon after they announced a series of production cuts and an embargo against the United States. The embargo would be far more difficult than rising prices for Americans to manage, owing to the cuts in production and increases in demand. In December OPEC doubled prices. With the onset of war in 1973 and the ensuing embargo, OPEC had seized control over pricing and production: the oil companies were no longer holding a winning hand. As Bronson notes, "The balance of power in the region, which had begun to shift from Egypt to Saudi Arabia after 1967, was solidified after 1973."[24]

Aramco's concession did not end, as some had feared it would, with swift nationalization. Befitting the company's long presence in the region, when nationalization occurred, it happened relatively slowly and with terms benefiting the American oil firms as much as the monarchy. After the 1967 conflict it was politically more difficult for Aramco to retain control of its concession. The company lobbied U.S. government officials who visited the corporate headquarters in Dhahran, hoping to tilt American policy in the region away from Israel and toward Arab states. American military aid to Israel, however, continued, and the company, to its dismay, became linked to this policy. The realities Aramco faced on the ground contributed heavily to the movement known as participation in Saudi Arabia and as nationalization throughout the world. Yamani, a young, Western-educated lawyer, pushed the company to open itself to greater Saudi participation in the oil operations. Jungers claimed he was unsure whether Yamani was naïve or clever, but given the wave of nationalizations in the region it was clear that time was running out for Western control of Middle East oil, and Yamani understood this shift. By 1973 Aramco had given the monarchy a 25 percent stake in the company.[25] The next year, the monarchy gained a 60 percent share, and negotiations began for a complete transition to Saudi ownership. In the spring of 1976 Aramco and Saudi Arabia worked out a final deal: Saudi Arabia would gain outright control of the company—rights and assets—but Aramco would continue to operate in the kingdom. In return for its service to Saudi Arabia, the company, through its extensive distribution and marketing networks, would be allowed to market 80 percent of Saudi oil, which it would buy at a reduced price. While the arrangement was agreed to in principle and dictated relations from that point forward, the monarchy did not sign it until 1990, finally ending Aramco's concession in Saudi Arabia.[26]

Aramco succeeded in Saudi Arabia where other Western firms failed. Of course the presence of oil makes an oil company valuable on some level, but corporate diplomacy mattered. A company like Bechtel, for instance, had different sorts of interactions with the House of Saud. Often with Aramco's support, Bechtel worked out contracts with the Saudi monarchy to bring in heavy construction equipment and engage in various building projects, many in coordination with the oil company. Bechtel found that it, like Aramco, would be called into service by royalty when minor repairs to appliances were needed or when upgrades to facilities at the palace were desired. Saudis seemed to recognize that Bechtel made a great deal of money in the kingdom, and some in the monarchy began to question the spending. Soon, Saudi Arabia fell behind in payments, and by mid-1950 it owed the construction firm $2 million. Steve Coll notes in his recent book on the Bin Laden family that the company's head, Stephen Bechtel, wondered if working in Saudi Arabia cost more in "headaches" than it was worth. The king's sons fought over how money was being spent, including how much was going to Bechtel, and the firm found it difficult, as Coll states, "to adapt to the royal family's way of business." The businessman Mohammed Bin Laden, however, had no difficulty eventually winning numerous contracts as a result of his flexibility and dutiful service to the monarchy. Aramco's more long-term successes compared to Bechtel's signals the importance of Aramco's diplomacy in its dealings with the monarchy.[27]

The end of Aramco's control of Saudi oil coincided with the end of Rostow's dreams of state-led modernization. Although Aramco's role in Saudi nation building had come to an end, the Saudi monarchy soon embarked on its own journey, building infrastructure, updating medical facilities, and expanding agricultural production. The future of Saudi Arabia would not be written by Aramco; rather, the path taken by the kingdom would be chosen from within. Aramco's exit, ironically, came at the same time that modernization theory began to undergo a radical change in the 1980s, one that imagined development taking place in ways very similar to those organized and promoted by Aramco. Development specialists in the era of President Ronald Reagan called for "structural adjustment," which meant the removal of the state from the process of modernization. The Washington Consensus advocated market solutions to development as opposed to state-directed ones. The U.S. government and the World Bank urged privatization, foreign investment, and corporate partnerships in places like Saudi Arabia, just as Aramco had absolved its supposed partnership in Saudi development and reduced its investment in Saudi society.[28] The legacy of Aramco in this context is tellingly and poignantly relevant, but it is also forgotten.

Notes

Introduction

1. Robert H. Scholl, Statement to the House, "Winning the Cold War: The U.S. Ideological Offensive," Subcommittee on International Organizations and Movements of the Committee on Foreign Affairs, Hearing, April 30, May 1, May 8, 1963, 201–8; Nick Cullather, "Development Doctrine and Modernization Theory," in *Encyclopedia of American Foreign Policy*, ed. Alexander DeConde, Richard Dean Burns, Fredrik Logevall, and Louise B. Ketz (New York: Scribner, 2002), 1:471–91. For more on American business abroad, see Victoria de Grazia, *Irresistible Empire: America's Advance through 20th-Century Europe* (Cambridge: Harvard University Press, 2005); Robert Vitalis, *America's Kingdom: Mythmaking on the Saudi Oil Frontier* (Stanford: Stanford University Press, 2007).

2. John R. Suman, "Middle Eastern Oil and Its Importance to the World," speech, Dallas, Texas, October 5, 1948, folder, Exxon Corporation: Subject Files: Corporate Public Affairs: Speeches, Addresses and Statements: Suman, John R., box 2.207/L13D, ExxonMobil Historical Collection, Dolph Briscoe Center for American History, University of Texas, Austin, Austin Texas (hereafter cited as ExxonMobil Papers).

3. Harry S. Truman, Second Inaugural Address, 20 January 1949, www.trumanlibrary.org. For a discussion of how social inventions such as living standards impact American interactions with the world, see de Grazia, *Irresistible Empire*.

4. Stanley Andrews, "Oil Development Aids Point 4 Activities," *Oil Forum*, November 1952, 388, 391–98, 379.

5. Cullather, "Development Doctrine and Modernization Theory."

6. Toby Craig Jones, *Desert Kingdom: How Oil and Water Forged Modern Saudi Arabia* (Cambridge: Harvard University Press, 2010).

7. Wayne C. Taylor and John Lindeman, *The Creole Petroleum Corporation in Venezuela* (Washington, DC: National Planning Association, 1955); Wayne Chatfield Taylor, *The Firestone Operations in Liberia* (Washington, DC: National Planning Association, 1956); Stacy May and Galo Plaza, *The United Fruit Company in Latin America* (Washington, DC: National Planning Association, 1958); Subbiah Kannappan and Eugene W. Burgess, *Aluminum Limited in India* (Washington, DC: National Planning Association, 1961); Vitalis, *America's Kingdom*; Daniel Yergin, *The Prize: The Epic Quest for Oil, Money and Power* (New York: Simon and Schuster, 1991).

8. Vitalis, *America's Kingdom*.

9. "A Special Issue: Partners in Growth," *Aramco World Magazine*, January/February 1977; John Lawton and Arthur Clark, "Foundations: A Decade of Development," *Aramco World Magazine*, November/December 1982, 1–3; Jones, *Desert Kingdom*, 1.

10. Yergin, *The Prize*: David S. Painter, *Oil and the American Century: The Political Economy of U.S. Foreign Oil Policy, 1941–1954* (Baltimore: Johns Hopkins University Press, 1986); Aaron David Miller, *Search for Security: Saudi Arabian Oil and American Foreign Policy, 1939–1949* (Chapel Hill: University of North Carolina Press, 1980); see also Michael B. Stoff, *Oil, War, and American Security: The Search for a National Policy on Foreign Oil, 1941–1947* (New Haven: Yale University Press, 1980); Irvine H. Anderson, *ARAMCO, the United States and Saudi Arabia: A Study of the Dynamics of Foreign Oil Policy, 1931–1950* (Princeton: Princeton University Press, 1981); Stephen J. Randall, *United States Foreign Oil Policy, 1911–1948: For Profits and Security* (Kingston: McGill-Queen's University Press, 1985).

11. Douglas Little, *American Orientalism: The United States and the Middle East since 1945*, 3rd ed. (Chapel Hill: University of North Carolina Press, 2008), 41–48.

12. Peter L. Hanh, *Crisis and Crossfire: The United States and the Middle East Since 1945* (Washington, DC: Potomac Books, 2005), 2; Yergin, *The Prize*, 194; Ussama Makdisi, *Faith Misplaced: The Broken Promise of U.S.–Arab Relations: 1821–2003* (New York: PublicAffairs, 2010), 2.

13. Rachel Bronson, *Thicker Than Oil: America's Uneasy Partnership with Saudi Arabia* (Oxford: Oxford University Press, 2006), 11–20.

14. Little, *American Orientalism*, 41–52.

15. Yergin, *The Prize*, 410; Painter, *Oil and the American Century*, 96.

16. Painter, *Oil and the American Century*; Miller, *Search for Security*; Stoff, *Oil, War, and American Security*; Anderson, *ARAMCO, the United States and Saudi Arabia*; Randall, *United States Foreign Oil Policy*.

17. Irvine Anderson is the exception, although his corporate sources consist almost exclusively of personal interviews.

18. Lloyd C. Gardner, *Three Kings: The Rise of an American Empire in the Middle East after World War II* (New York: New Press, 2009), 4, 9.

19. David S. Painter, "The Marshall Plan and Oil," *Cold War History* 9 (May 2009): 151–75.

20. Melvin P. Leffler, "National Security and U.S. Foreign Policy," in *Origins of the Cold War: An International History*, 2nd ed., ed. Melvyn P. Leffler and David S. Painter (New York: Routledge, 2005), 11–41.

21. Little, *American Orientalism*, 121–30.

22. Hahn, *Crisis and Crossfire*, 31–42; Bronson, *Thicker Than Oil*, 21–25.

23. Matthew F. Jacobs, *Imagining the Middle East: The Building of an American Foreign Policy, 1911–1967* (Chapel Hill: University of North Carolina Press, 2011), 51–88; Bronson, *Thicker Than Oil*, 27, 71–74.

24. David Ekbladh, *The Great American Mission: Modernization and the Construction of an American World Order* (Princeton: Princeton University Press, 2010); Matthew Connelly, "Seeing Beyond the State: The Population Control Movement and the Problem of Sovereignty," *Past and Present* 193 (November 2006): 197–233; Matthew Connelly, *Fatal Misconception: The Struggle to Control World Population* (Cambridge: Harvard University Press, 2008); Manela Erez, "Pox on Your Narrative: Writing Disease Control into Cold War History," *Diplomatic History* 34 (April 2010): 299–323; Nils Gilman, *Mandarins of the Future: Modernization Theory in Cold War America* (Baltimore: Johns Hopkins University Press, 2003); Michael E. Latham, *Modernization as Ideology: American Social Science and "Nation Building" in the Kennedy Era* (Chapel Hill: University of North Carolina Press, 2000); David Ekbladh, "Mr. TVA: Grass-Roots Development, David Lilienthal, and the Rise and Fall of the Tennessee Valley Authority as a Symbol of U.S. Overseas Development, 1931–1973," *Diplomatic History* 26 (July 2002): 335–74; Nick Cullather, "Damming Afghanistan: Modernization in a Buffer State," *Journal of American History* 89 (September 2002): 511–37; Nick Cullather, "Miracles of

Modernization: The Green Revolution and the Apotheosis of Technology," *Diplomatic History* 28 (April 2004): 221–54. See also the Special Forum on Modernization as a Global Project in *Diplomatic History* 33 (June 2009).

25. Early works include Latham, *Modernization as Ideology;* Gilman, *Mandarins of the Future;* Amy L. S. Staples, *The Birth of Development: How the World Bank, Food and Agriculture Organization, and World Health Organization Changed the World, 1941–1965* (Kent: Kent State University Press, 2006); David C. Engerman, Nils Gilman, Mark H. Haefele, and Michael E. Latham, eds., *Staging Growth: Modernization, Development, and the Global Cold War* (Amherst: University of Massachusetts Press, 2003).

26. Bradley R. Simpson, *Economists with Guns: Authoritarian Development and U.S.-Indonesian Relations, 1961–1968* (Stanford: Stanford University Press, 2008); Gregg Brazinsky, *Nation Building in South Korea: Koreans, Americans, and the Making of Democracy* (Chapel Hill: University of North Carolina Press, 2009).

27. Ekbladh, *The Great American Mission;* Nick Cullather, *The Hungry World: America's Cold War Battle against Poverty in Asia* (Cambridge: Harvard University Press, 2010); Jeremy Kuzmarov, *Modernizing Repression: Police Training and Nation Building in the American Century* (Amherst: University of Massachusetts Press, 2012); Cullather, "Miracles of Modernization." See also the Special Forum on Modernization as a Global Project in *Diplomatic History* 33 (June 2009).

28. John F. Kennedy, Inaugural Address, January 20, 1961, Miller Center of Public Affairs, University of Virginia, Digital Archives, http://millercenter.org.

29. Latham, *Modernization as Ideology.*

30. Michael E. Latham, *The Right Kind of Revolution: Modernization, Development, and U.S. Foreign Policy from the Cold War to the Present* (Ithaca: Cornell University Press, 2011), 41–53.

31. Gilman, *Mandarins of the Future,* 11.

32. American diplomatic historians have increasingly begun to explore these questions and investigate modernization more globally. See, for instance, the Special Forum on Modernization as a Global Project, in *Diplomatic History* 33 (June 2009): 371–512. See also Ekbladh, *The Great American Mission;* Cullather, *The Hungry World.*

33. Latham, *The Right Kind of Revolution,* 47.

34. James Terry Duce, untitled speech to the Council on Foreign Relations, January 25, 1956, box 2, Philip C. McConnell Papers, 1931–1963, Hoover Institution Archives, Stanford, CA (hereafter cited as McConnell Papers).

35. Vitalis, *America's Kingdom.*

36. Jones, *Desert Kingdom.*

37. Richard Drayton, *Nature's Government: Science, Imperial Britain, and the 'Improvement' of the World* (New Haven: Yale University Press, 2000).

1. Aramco's World

1. Robert Vitalis, *America's Kingdom: Mythmaking on the Saudi Oil Frontier* (Stanford: Stanford University Press, 2007); William E. Mulligan, Biographical Information on George Rentz, folder 53, box 1, William E. Mulligan Papers, Archives and Special Collections, Georgetown University, Washington, DC (hereafter cited as Mulligan Papers).

2. Toby Craig Jones, *Desert Kingdom: How Oil and Water Forged Modern Saudi Arabia* (Cambridge: Harvard University Press, 2010).

3. Roy Lebkicher, *Handbooks for American Employees,* vol. 1, part 1, *Aramco and World Oil,* rev. ed. (New York: Russell F. Moore, 1952), preface. The material in the original handbook

(1950) was also published, in a reorganized fashion, as *The Arabia of Ibn Saud* and distributed to a broader audience upon request.

4. Wallace Stegner, *Discovery! The Search for Arabian Oil,* as abridged in *Aramco World Magazine* (Beirut: Middle East Export Press, 1971), 1.

5. Paul N. Edwards, *The Closed World: Computers and the Politics of Discourse in Cold War America* (Cambridge: MIT Press, 1996).

6. Roland Marchand, *Creating the Corporate Soul: The Rise of Public Relations and Corporate Imagery in American Big Business* (Berkeley: University of California Press, 1998); Vitalis, *America's Kingdom;* Margaret R. Somers, "Narrativity, Narrative Identity, and Social Action: Rethinking English Working-Class Formation," *Social Science History* 16 (Winter 1992): 604. David E. Nye refers to "representational strategies" that emerge to situate corporate identity. See David E. Nye, *Image Worlds: Corporate Identities at General Electric, 1891–1930* (Cambridge: MIT Press, 1985), 152; Robert Vitalis, "Wallace Stegner's Arabian Discovery: The Imperial Entailments of Continental Vision," Working paper 8, International Center for Advanced Studies, New York University, 2003, 2, 30; Robert Vitalis, "Black Gold, White Crude: An Essay on American Exceptionalism, Hierarchy, and Hegemony in the Gulf," *Diplomatic History* 26 (Spring 2002): 202.

7. Vitalis, "Wallace Stegner's Arabian Discovery," 2, 30; Vitalis, *America's Kingdom.*

8. Daniel Yergin, *The Prize: The Epic Quest for Oil, Money and Power* (New York: Simon and Schuster, 1991), 289; for a discussion of Twitchell's work in Saudi Arabia, see K. S. Twitchell and Edward Jabra Jurji, *Saudi Arabia: With an Account of the Development of its Natural Resources* (Princeton: Princeton University Press, 1947); H. St. J. B. Philby, *Arabian Jubilee* (London: Robert Hale, 1952); and H. St. J. B. Philby, "Britain and Arabia," *Nineteenth Century and After* 117 (1935): 571–84.

9. Quoted in James E. O'Brien, "Odyssey of a Journeyman Lawyer," oral history conducted by Carle Hicke (1981–89), Regional Oral History Office, Bancroft Library, University of California, Berkeley, 1993, 191–94.

10. Moreover, there is evidence that more broadly in the Middle East the United States represented something different to those who had experienced Western imperialism. See Rashid Khalidi, *Resurrecting Empire: Western Footprints and American's Perilous Path in the Middle East* (London: I. B. Tauris, 2004).

11. "Astute Ibn Saud," *Newsweek,* August 21, 1939, 21.

12. Marjorie McFarland, "Sheik of Standard Oil," *Living Age,* February 1940, 541. Lloyd Hamilton reported to *Collier's* in 1945 that the king stated that American "imperial designs" were not the same as those of the British. The Saudis are reported to have stated, "And besides . . . you are so far away." See Marquis Childs, "All the King's Oil," *Collier's,* August 18, 1945, 47.

13. Khalidi, *Resurrecting Empire.* Khalidi argues that there was a general perception in the Middle East before the end of the Second World War that the United States, given the experiences in the region with European imperialism, indeed represented something different to many Arabs. See also Ussama Makdisi, *Faith Misplaced: The Broken Promise of U.S–Arab Relations: 1821–2003* (New York: PublicAffairs, 2010).

14. William A. Eddy, *F.D.R. Meets Ibn Saud* (New York: American Friends of the Middle East, 1954), 35.

15. John C. Henry, "Ibn Saud Rubs a Magic Lamp," *Nation's Business,* January 1948, 38.

16. Quoted in Inge Kaiser, "Oil, Blood and Sand," *New Republic,* December 17, 1945, 831.

17. T. E. Lawrence, *Seven Pillars of Wisdom: A Triumph* (Garden City, NY: Doubleday, Doran, 1935). See also Charles M. Doughty, *Travels in Arabia Deserta* (Cambridge: Cambridge University Press, 1888).

18. William Norman Ewer, "Oil in the Arabian Desert," *Living Age,* October 1945, 105.

19. Alexei Vassiliev, *The History of Saudi Arabia* (London: Al-Saqi Books, 1998); Joseph Kostiner, *The Making of Saudi Arabia, 1911–1936: From Chieftaincy to Monarchical State* (New York: Oxford University Press, 1993); and Madawi Al-Rasheed, *A History of Saudi Arabia* (New York: Cambridge University Press, 2002).

20. H. St. J. B. Philby, *Arabian Oil Ventures* (Washington, DC: Middle East Institute, 1964), 53.

21. Vassiliev, *The History of Saudi Arabia,* 311–15.

22. "As the Arabs Do," *Newsweek,* November 8, 1948, 61–64; Arabian American Oil Company, *Basic Arabic: Flash Card Supplement* (Arabian American Oil Company, c1950); Arabian American Oil Company, *Introduction to Spoken Arabic of Eastern Arabia* (Arabian American Oil Company, 1950).

23. "As the Arabs Do."

24. Frank Jungers, "From Construction Engineer to CEO and Chairman of Aramco, 1941–1978," oral history conducted by Carole Hicke (1992), in "American Perspectives of Aramco, the Saudi-Arabian Oil-Producing Company, 1930s to 1980s," Regional Oral History Office, Bancroft Library, University of California, Berkeley, 1995, 1–7; interview with Frank Jungers, Frontline, "House of Saud," www.pbs.org; Bob Waters, "1941–1949: Pre-Saudi Arabia," www.aramcoexpats.com; Robert M. Hallett, "Many Hues to Desert Oil," *Christian Science Monitor,* April 23, 1949, 1–3.

25. *Aramco World,* June 1955, 1–2.

26. Waters, "1941–1949: Pre-Saudi Arabia."

27. Grant C. Butler, *Kings and Camels: An American in Saudi Arabia* (New York: Devin-Adair, 1960), 181–99.

28. Waters's memoirs contain a number of stories of cultural misunderstanding between American and Arab employees. For instance, see "Arabian Return Chapter VIII: The Long Hot Summer," www.aramcoexpats.com.

29. The handbook was republished in 1952 and then updated versions emerged in 1960, 1968, and 1980.

30. Lebkicher, *Handbooks for American Employees,* ii.

31. Ibid., iv.

32. Solon T. Kimball, "American Culture in Saudi Arabia," paper presented at a meeting of the Section of Oceanography and Meteorology, Section of Anthropology, February 27, 1956, 471–72, folder 23, box 1, Mulligan Papers; Vitalis, "Black Gold, White Crude," 200; James W. Loewen, *Sundown Towns: A Hidden Dimension of American Racism* (New York: Touchstone, 2006).

33. Vitalis, "Black Gold, White Crude," 201–4; Michael Edward Dobe, "A Long Slow Tutelage in Western Ways of Work: Industrial Education and the Containment of Nationalism in Anglo-Iranian and Aramco, 1921–1963" (PhD diss., Rutgers University, 2008).

34. Michael B. Stoff, *Oil, War, and American Security: The Search for a National Policy on Foreign Oil, 1941–1947* (New Haven: Yale University Press, 1980); Aaron David Miller, *Search for Security: Saudi Arabian Oil and American Foreign Policy, 1939–1949* (Chapel Hill: University of North Carolina Press, 1980); Yergin, *The Prize*; Parker T. Hart, *Saudi Arabia and the United States: Birth of a Security Partnership* (Bloomington: Indiana University Press, 1998).

35. Parker T. Hart, "General Observations Regarding Dhahran and Bahrein," folder 801-886, box 1, Confidential File, 1941–1945, Dhahran Consulate, Record Group 84, Foreign Service Posts of the Department of State, National Archives at College Park, College Park, MD (hereafter cited as NACP); quote from Hart to Eddy, February 5, 1945, folder 801-886, box 1, Confidential File, 1941–1945, Dhahran Consulate, RG 84, NACP.

36. Hart to Near East Division, Department of State, July 24, 1945, folder 801-886, box 1, Confidential File, 1941–1945, Dhahran Consulate, RG 84, NACP.

37. Clarence McIntosh, Memorandum for Files, October 15, 1945, folder 801-886, box 1, Confidential File, 1941–1945, Dhahran Consulate, RG 84, NACP.

38. "Interview with Parker T. Hart," conducted by William Roy Crawford, January 27, 1989, The Foreign Affairs Oral History Collection of the Association for Diplomatic Studies and Training, http://memory.loc.gov/ammem/collections/diplomacy/, s.v. "Parker T. Hart."

39. Childs to McGhee, February 24, 1950, J. Rives Childs Papers, Special Collections, University of Virginia Library (hereafter cited as Childs Papers), 1–10.

40. "Interview with Hermann Frederick Eilts," conducted by William D. Brewer, January 27, 1989, The Foreign Affairs Oral History Collection of the Association for Diplomatic Studies and Training, http://memory.loc.gov/ammem/collections/diplomacy/, s.v. "Hermann Frederick Eilts."

41. Arabian American Oil Company, "Donations, Contributions, and Assistance to Saudi Arabia, 1931–1970," folder 10, box 5, Mulligan Papers, 47.

42. J. B. Kelly, *Eastern Arabian Frontiers* (New York: Frederick A. Praeger, 1964), 141–47; Nathan J. Citino, *From Arab Nationalism to OPEC: Eisenhower, King Sa'ud, and the Making of U.S.–Saudi Relations* (Bloomington: Indiana University Press, 2002), 21–26; Memorandum of Conversation, Aramco officials and Judge Manley O. Hudson, April 25, 1950, *Foreign Relations of the United States, 1950* (Washington, DC: U.S. Government Printing Office, 1950), 5:45 (hereafter cited as *FRUS*).

43. F. S. Vidal, *The Aramco Reports on Al-Hasa and Oman,* vol. 2: *The Oasis of Al-Hasa* (Cambridge: Cambridge Archive Editions, 1990; original edition, Dhahran, Saudi Arabia: Arabian American Oil Company, 1950).

44. George Rentz and William Mulligan, *The Aramco Reports on Al-Hasa and Oman,* vol. 1: *The Eastern Reaches of Al-Hasa Province* (Cambridge: Cambridge Archive Editions, 1990; original edition, Dhahran, Saudi Arabia: Arabian American Oil Company, 1950); George Rentz, *Oman and the Southern Shore of the Persian Gulf* (orig. pub. 1952) in *Oman and the South-Eastern Shore of Arabia,* ed. Raghid El-Solh (Berkshire, UK: Ithaca Press, 1997).

45. Research Department of the British Foreign Office, "Comment on Rentz's Book on S. E. Arabia," February 25, 1954, in Rentz, *Oman and the South-Eastern Shore of Arabia;* see also Kelly, *Eastern Arabian Frontiers.*

46. Citino, *From Arab Nationalism to OPEC;* Tore Tingvold Petersen, "Anglo-American Rivalry in the Middle East: The Struggle for the Buraimi Oasis, 1951–1957," *International History Review* 14 (February 1992): 71–91.

47. Alexander Melamid, "The Buraimi Oasis Dispute," *Middle Eastern Affairs* 7 (1956): 51–62; Petersen, "Anglo-American Rivalry in the Middle East"; Rentz, *Oman and the South-Eastern Shore of the Persian Gulf,* 115. Rentz states that there were nine villages; Melamid claims there were eight.

48. "Log of Activities—William E. Mulligan, on Exploration Field Party Liaison," April 16, 1949, folder 20, "Mulligan, William E. – Correspondence, 1941–49," box 11, Mulligan Papers.

49. William E. Mulligan, memorandum, April 22, 1949, folder 20, "Mulligan, William E. – Correspondence, 1941–49," box 11, Mulligan Papers.

50. Stobbart to Holm, April 22, 1949, folder 20, "Mulligan, William E. – Correspondence, 1941–49," box 11, Mulligan Papers.

51. Melamid, "The Buraimi Oasis Dispute," 58.

52. Citino, *From Arab Nationalism to OPEC,* 21; W. Taylor Fain, *American Ascendance and British Retreat in the Persian Gulf Region* (New York: Palgrave Macmillan, 2008), 63. The Iraq Petroleum Company (IPC) was a jointly owned subsidiary of multiple firms, among them

British and American companies. Arranged in the 1920s, Standard Oil of New Jersey and Standard Oil of New York were just two of a collection of American firms that shared a 23.75 percent share. Royal Dutch / Shell (British), the Anglo Persian / Iranian Oil Company (British, with government shares), and Compagnie Française des Pétroles (French) each held 23.75 percent. The remaining 5 percent went to Calouste Gulbenkian, the Armenian dealmaker who negotiated the consortium. See Yergin, *The Prize;* Memorandum of Conversation, April 20, 1950, *FRUS, 1950,* 5:38.

53. Kelly, *Eastern Arabian Frontiers,* 145; Citino, *From Arab Nationalism to OPEC,* 21–26.

54. Memorandum of Conversation, January 31, 1950, *FRUS, 1950,* 5:18; Memorandum of Conversation, April 20, 1950, *FRUS, 1950,* 5:38; Memorandum of Conversation, April 25, 1950, *FRUS, 1950,* 5:45.

55. Memorandum of Conversation, March 19, 1951, *FRUS, 1951,* 6:286.

56. Memorandum of Conversation, January 31, 1950, *FRUS, 1950,* 5:18; Memorandum of Conversation, April 25, 1950, *FRUS, 1950,* 5:45.

57. Kelly, *Eastern Arabian Frontiers,* 294.

58. Al-Rasheed, *A History of Saudi Arabia,* 11–19.

59. Truman to Abdul Aziz Ibn Saud, October 31, 1950, *FRUS, 1950,* 5:1190–91.

60. Memorandum of Conversation, May 19, 1953, *FRUS, 1951–1954,* 9:1, 96; Memorandum of Conversation, May 19, 1953, *FRUS, 1951–1954,* 9:1, 99.

61. Citino, *From Arab Nationalism to OPEC,* 19, 28.

62. Chargé in Saudi Arabia to Department of State, May 14, 1952, *FRUS, 1951–1954,* 9:2469.

63. Citino, *From Arab Nationalism to OPEC,* 21–31; Melamid, "The Buraimi Oasis Dispute," 59.

64. Citino, *From Arab Nationalism to OPEC,* 61–64; Petersen, "Anglo-American Rivalry in the Middle East," 72; Melamid, "The Buraimi Oasis Dispute," 58; Tore T. Petersen, *The Middle East between the Great Powers: Anglo-American Conflict and Cooperation, 1951–7* (London: Palgrave Macmillan, 2000); Fain, *American Ascendance and British Retreat.*

65. "Jurisdictional Dispute of Saudi Arabia," Paper Prepared in the Department of State for the London Foreign Ministers Meeting in May, April 20, 1950, *FRUS, 1950,* 5:40.

66. Acheson to U.S. Embassy in the UK, November 20, 1950, *FRUS, 1950,* 5:117.

67. *Arbitration Agreement between the Government of the United Kingdom (acting on behalf of the Ruler of Abu Dhabi and His Highness the Sultan Said bin Taimur) and the Government of Saudi Arabia,* Jeddah, July 30, 1954, in Kelly, *Eastern Arabian Frontiers,* appendix A, 281–92; telegram, Wadsworth to Department of State, July 31, 1954, *FRUS, 1951–1954,* 9, part 2: 2611–15, note 2.

68. Petersen, "Anglo-American Rivalry in the Middle East," 83.

69. Citino, *From Arab Nationalism to OPEC,* 64.

70. Ibid., 81–82.

71. Petersen, "Anglo-American Rivalry in the Middle East," 84; Citino, *From Arab Nationalism to OPEC,* 84.

72. Fain, *American Ascendance and British Retreat,* 61–68; quote in Petersen, *The Middle East between Great Powers,* 51–59.

73. Fain, *American Ascendance and British Retreat,* 111–18.

74. Kelly, *Eastern Arabian Frontiers,* 268.

75. Saudi Arabia and United Arab Emirates, "Agreement on the Delimitation of Boundaries," 21 August 1974, United Nations Treaty Collection, http://treaties.un.org.

76. Memorandum of Conversation, March 19, 1951, *FRUS, 1951,* 5:281–97.

77. Rentz, *Oman and the Southern Shore of the Persian Gulf,* xxv.

78. Ibid., 111–20.

79. Research Department of the British Foreign Office, "Comment on Rentz's Book on S.

E. Arabia," February 25, 1954, in Rentz, *Oman and the South-Eastern Shore of Arabia;* see also Kelly, *Eastern Arabian Frontiers.*

80. United States Record of the First Session of the United States–United Kingdom Talks on Middle East Oil, April 5, 1954, *FRUS, 1952–1954,* vol. 9, pt. 1, 799.

81. Memorandum of Conversation, Buraimi Dispute, May 27, 1954, *FRUS, 1951–1954,* vol. 9, pt.1, 822.

82. Memorandum of Conversation, April 3, 1953, *FRUS, 1952–1954,* vol. 9, pt. 2, 2533; Memorandum of Conversations, April 16, 1953, *FRUS, 1952–1954,* vol. 9, pt. 2, 2535.

83. Moline to Eakens, February 16, 1954, *FRUS, 1952–1954,* vol. 9, pt. 2, 2578.

84. Memorandum of Conversation, "Buraimi Dispute: Aramco's Interests in latest British Proposals," March 10, 1954, *FRUS, 1952–1954,* vol. 9, pt. 2, 2581–87.

85. Memorandum of Conversation, June 25, 1954, *FRUS, 1952–1954,* Western Europe and Canada, pt. 1, 1054.

86. Manuel Castells, *The Power of Identity* (Malden, MA: Blackwell, 2004); Charles Tilly, "Citizenship, Identity and Social History," in *Citizenship, Identity and Social History,* ed. Charles Tilly (Cambridge, Cambridge University Press, 1995), 1–18; David Campbell, *Writing Security: United States Foreign Policy and the Politics of Identity* (Minneapolis: University of Minnesota Press, 1992). Campbell argues that states create identity through the promotion of various dangers that fall outside the proscribed normative self-definition, the boundaries of which are "secured by the representation of danger integral to foreign policy." See Campbell, *Writing Security,* 3.

87. Marchand, *Creating the Corporate Soul,* 5; Richard Drayton, *Nature's Government: Science, Imperial Britain, and the 'Improvement' of the World* (New Haven: Yale University Press, 2000).

2. Constructing Balance

1. "Tracks in the Sand," *Aramco World,* April 1951, 1, 7; "Railroad Opened," *Aramco World,* November 1951, 12.

2. *Aramco World,* June 1952, 7.

3. See Julio Moreno's discussion of similar, American-styled advertisements in Mexico after the Second World War. Julio Moreno, *Yankee Don't Go Home! Mexican Nationalism, American Business Culture, and the Shaping of Modern Mexico, 1920–1950* (Chapel Hill: University of North Carolina Press, 2003).

4. William L. Owen, "Negotiations and Legal Affairs of Aramco, 1941–1980," oral history conducted by Carole Hicke (1992), in "American Perspectives of Aramco, the Saudi-Arabian Oil-Producing Company, 1930s to 1980s," Regional Oral History Office, Bancroft Library, University of California, Berkeley, 1995, 315.

5. Edward Shils, *Political Development in the New States* (The Hague: Mouton, 1962), 31–32; Edward Shils, *The Intellectual between Tradition and Modernity: The Indian Situation* (The Hague: Mouton, 1961), 11–12.

6. Matthew F. Jacobs, *Imagining the Middle East: The Building of an American Foreign Policy, 1911–1967* (Chapel Hill: University of North Carolina Press, 2011), 71–79.

7. Ibid., 88.

8. Ibid., 141–49.

9. Ibid., 58.

10. William A. Stoltzfus Jr., quoted in Robert D. Kaplan, *The Arabists: The Romance of an American Elite* (New York: Free Press, 1993), 2.

11. Daniel Lerner, *The Passing of Traditional Society: Modernizing the Middle East* (Glencoe, IL: Free Press, 1958), 46.

12. Ibid., 163.

13. Ibid., 163, 45.

14. Nils Gilman, *Mandarins of the Future: Modernization Theory in Cold War America* (Baltimore: Johns Hopkins University Press, 2003), 14.

15. Ibid., 11–16.

16. Nimrod Raphaeli, "Demands for Reforms in Saudi Arabia," *Middle Eastern Studies* 41 (July 2005): 511–32.

17. Madawi Al-Rasheed, *A History of Saudi Arabia* (New York: Cambridge University Press, 2002), 11, 51.

18. J. Loder Park, "Sidelights on Ibn Saud and the Mecca Situation: Interview with H. St. J. B. Philby," in *Documents on the History of Saudi Arabia*, vol. 1, *The Unification of Central Arabia Under Ibn Saud, 1901–1925*, ed. Ibrahim al-Rashid (Salisbury, NC: Documentary Publications, 1976), 205.

19. K. D. Twitchell, "Importance of Position of Abdul Aziz Ibn Saud, King of Saudi Arabia," May 14, 1941, in *Saudi Arabia Enters the Modern World: Secret U.S. Documents on the Emergence of the Kingdom of Saudi Arabia as a World Power, 1936–1949*, ed. Ibrahim al-Rashid (Salisbury, NC: Documentary Publications, 1980), 71–76.

20. Mir Zohair Husain, *Islam and the Muslim World* (Dubuque, IA: McGraw-Hill, 2006); F. E. Peters, *The Hajj: The Muslim Pilgrimage to Mecca and the Holy Places* (Princeton: Princeton University Press: 1994); William Spencer, *Middle East*, 11th ed. (Dubuque, IA: McGraw-Hill, 2007).

21. H. St. J. B. Philby, *A Pilgrim in Arabia* (London: Robert Hale, 1946); Edward A. Salisbury, "The Port to Paradise," *Asia* 24 (1924): 21–26.

22. Leon Krajewski, "Mekka Bound: An Account of Il Hadj," *The Living Age*, February 6, 1926, 301–7; "The Sudan: Pilgrims Ordeal," *Time*, April 13, 1953.

23. Clayson W. Aldridge, "Growing Modernization of the Hedjaz," in *Documents on the History of Saudi Arabia*, vol. 2, *The Consolidation of Power in Central Arabia Under Ibn Saud, 1921–1928*, ed. Ibrahim al-Rashid (Salisbury, NC: Documentary Publications, 1976), 150.

24. Quoted in Philby, *A Pilgrim in Arabia*, 11–19.

25. Translation of the Italian monthly review "Oriente Moderno," March 1935, in Leo J. Callanan, "The Pilgrimage to Mecca, 1931–35, and Saudi Arabian Finances," August 17, 1935, in *Documents on the History of Saudi Arabia*, vol. 3, *Establishment of the Kingdom of Saudi Arabia under Ibn Saud, 1921–1935*, ed. Ibrahim al-Rashid (Salisbury, NC: Documentary Publications, 1976), 206, 201–10; and Callanan to State, August 17, 1935, ibid., 211–12.

26. J. Rives Childs to Secretary of State, January 19, 1948, in al-Rashid, *Saudi Arabia Enters the Modern World*, 131–40.

27. H. St. J. B. Philby, "Southern Najd," *Geographical Journal* 55 (March 1920): 163; James A. Montgomery, "Arabia To-Day: An Essay in Contemporary History," *Journal of the American Oriental Society* 47 (April 1927): 91–132.

28. Joseph Kostiner, *The Making of Saudi Arabia, 1911–1936: From Chieftaincy to Monarchical State* (New York: Oxford University Press, 1993), 109.

29. Ibid., 109; Al-Rasheed, *A History of Saudi Arabia*, 11–20, 31, 41–46.

30. Kostiner, *The Making of Saudi Arabia*, 101–17.

31. J. Rives Childs to Secretary of State, January 19, 1948, in al-Rashid, *Saudi Arabia Enters the Modern World*, 140.

32. Al-Rasheed, *A History of Saudi Arabia*, 5.

33. Letter from Raymond Hare to Frederick Awalt. [Incident at Dhahran Air Field], November 25, 1951, RG 59, Records of the Department of State, Lot Files, the National Security Archive, George Washington University, www.gwu.edu.

34. Joyce Battle, "U.S. Propaganda in the Middle East: The Early Cold War Version," National Security Archive Electronic Briefing Book No. 78, December 13, 2002, National Security Archive, www2.gwu.edu.

35. Dispatch from Raymond Hare to the Department of State. [Proposed Saudi Pamphlet Program], January 8, 1952, RG 59, Records of the Department of State, Decimal Files, 1951–1954, available at National Security Archive, www2.gwu.edu.

36. Cable to the Department of State, [Saudi Arabia and U.S. Objectives], September 7, 1952, RG 59, Records of the Department of State, Decimal Files, 1951–1954, National Security Archive, www2.gwu.edu.

37. Battle, "U.S. Propaganda in the Middle East."

38. Letter from William A. Eddy to Dorothy Thompson, [Christian–Muslim Anticommunist Propaganda Theme], June 7, 1951, RG 59, Records of the Department of State, Lot Files, National Security Archive, www2.gwu.edu.

39. Executive Secretary Report to the United States, National Security Council, "United States Objectives and Policies with Respect to the Arab States and Israel" [Annex to NSC 129], April 7, 1952, National Security Archive, www2.gwu.edu.

40. Letter from Dwight D. Eisenhower to Edward L. R. Elson [Response to Letter on the Middle East], July 31, 1958, National Security Archive, www2.gwu.edu; see also Seth Jacobs, *America's Miracle Man in Vietnam: Ngo Dinh Diem, Religion, Race, and U.S. Intervention in Southeast Asia, 1951–1957* (Durham: Duke University Press, 2004).

41. Andrew J. Rotter, *Comrades at Odds: The United States and India, 1941–1964* (Ithaca: Cornell University Press, 2000). For a more extensive discussion of religion and American foreign relations, see Andrew Preston, *Sword of the Spirit, Shield of Faith: Religion in American War and Diplomacy* (New York: Alfred A. Knopf, 2012); Andrew Preston, "Bridging the Gap between the Sacred and the Secular in the History of American Foreign Relations," *Diplomatic History* 30 (November 2006): 781–812.

42. Orientation Program for New Employees, Orientation Checklist, August 7, 1976, folder 17, box 7, Mulligan Papers.

43. Armand P. Gelpi, "Aramco Medical Services: 1951–1969," oral history conducted by Carole Hicke (1997), in "Health and Disease in Saudi Arabia: The Aramco Experience, 1940s–1990s," Regional Oral History Office, Bancroft Library, University of California, Berkeley, 1998.

44. George Lenczowski, "Tradition and Reform in Saudi Arabia," *Current History* 52 (February 1967): 91–104, 115; "Slavery in Saudi Arabia Ended by Faisal Edict," *New York Times*, November 7, 1962.

45. Michael Sheldon Cheney, *Big Oilman from Arabia* (London: Heineman, 1958), 11.

46. Undated Report of the Local Government Relations Department on "Religious Obligations," folder 13, box 5, 13, Mulligan Papers.

47. Vitalis, *America's Kingdom: Mythmaking on the Saudi Oil Frontier* (Stanford: Stanford University Press, 2007), 92, 291–97.

48. Cheney, *Big Oilman from Arabia*, 54.

49. Anthony Cave Brown, *Oil, God, and Gold: The Story of Aramco and the Saudi Kings* (Boston: Houghton Mifflin, 1999), 59.

50. Solon Kimball, "American Culture in Saudi Arabia," *Transactions of the New York Academy of Sciences* 18 (1956): 475.

51. Owen, "Negotiations and Legal Affairs of Aramco, 1941–1980," 389.

52. "The Blue Flame," probable authors Robin S. Marsh and Russell L. Nicholson, late 1950s, www.aramco-brats.com (no longer available).

53. Kimball, "American Culture in Saudi Arabia," 475.

54. Undated Report of the Local Government Relations Department on "Religious Obligations," folder 13, box 5, Mulligan Papers.

55. Baldo Marinovic, "Financial Aspects of Aramco's Oil Operations, 1951–1985," oral history conducted by Carole Hicke (1992), in "American Perspectives of Aramco, the Saudi-

Arabian Oil-Producing Company, 1930s to 1980s," Regional Oral History Office, Bancroft Library, University of California, Berkeley, 1995, 280.

56. Memorandum from Frederick Awalt to Samuel K. C. Kopper. "Conversation with Prince Saud," March 10, 1952, RG 59, Records of the Department of State, Lot File, National Security Archive, www2.gwu.edu.

57. Kimball, "American Culture in Saudi Arabia," 471–73.

58. Raymond A. Hare to Frederick H. Awalt, November 25, 1951, RG 59, Records of the Department of States, Lot Files, National Security Archive, www2.gwu.edu.

59. Dana Adams Schmidt, "Saudis Expunge a Popular Image," *New York Times,* May 13, 1962; Wilton Wynn, "There's Gold in Footsteps of King Saud," *Chicago Daily Tribune,* January 27, 1957.

60. Dana Adams Schmidt, "Faisal Modernizes but with Caution," *New York Times Magazine,* November 1, 1964, 38.

61. Quoted in David Milne, "'Our Equivalent of Guerrilla Warfare': Walt Rostow and the Bombing of North Vietnam, 1961–1968," *Journal of Military History* 71 (January 2007): 201.

62. Lerner, *The Passing of Traditional Society,* 51–54; Benedict Anderson, *Imagined Communities: Reflections on the Origin and Spread of Nationalism* (London: Verso, 1983).

63. "Background Information," Aramco Television Programming, June 24, 1961, unbound report of the Public Relations Department, folder 18, box 4, Mulligan Papers.

64. Brown, *Oil, God, and Gold,* 281–84, 304.

65. *State Department Bulletin,* October 21, 1945, 623.

66. Douglas Little, *American Orientalism: The United States and the Middle East since 1945* (Chapel Hill: University of North Carolina Press, 2004), 81–87.

67. Henderson to Marshall, September 22, 1947, *Foreign Relations of the United States, 1947* (Washington, DC: U.S. Government Printing Office, 1947), 5:1151–58 (hereafter cited as *FRUS*).

68. Memorandum of Conversation by Secretary of State, May 12, 1948, *FRUS, 1948,* 5:971–77.

69. Dean Acheson, *Present at the Creation: My Years in the State Department* (New York: Norton, 1969), 169.

70. Tuck to Secretary of State, May 18, 1948, in *Secret History of the Oil Companies in the Middle East,* vol. 1, ed. William J. Kennedy (Salisbury, NC: Documentary Publications, 1979), 175.

71. Henderson to Secretary of State, May 26, 1948, in Kennedy, *Secret History,* 175.

72. Arabian American Oil Company, "Donations, Contributions, and Assistance to Saudi Arabia, 1931–1970, folder 10, box 5, Mulligan Papers, 47.

73. Robert Vitalis, "Black Gold, White Crude: An Essay on American Exceptionalism, Hierarchy, and Hegemony in the Gulf," *Diplomatic History* 26 (Spring 2002): 204.

74. Duce letter quoted in Immanuel Velikovsky, "Oil—The Dictator: The Slippery Master of American Policy Betrays the People to Their Enemies for Profit," *New York Post,* June 30, 1948, www.varchive.org.

75. Yergin, *The Prize: The Epic Quest for Oil, Money and Power* (New York: Simon and Schuster, 1991), 426.

76. Douglas Little, "Pipeline Politics: America, TAPLINE, and the Arabs," *Business History Review* 64 (Summer 1990): 265.

77. Elmer A. Carter, Investigating Commissioner, "Determination after Investigation and Conference: American Jewish Congress vs. Arabian American Oil Company," November 6, 1958, Central Decimal Files, 1951–1959, Record Group 59, General Records of the Department of State, National Archives at College Park, College Park, MD (hereafter cited as NACP with filing information).

78. Samuel J. Ravitch to US Ambassador to Saudi Arabia, July 10, 1956, Central Decimal Files, 1951–1959, RG 59, NACP; Alfred le S. Jenkins to Samuel J. Ravitch, July 24, 1956, Central Decimal Files, 1951–1959, RG 59, NACP.

79. "Aramco Denies Race Bias in Jobs," *Washington Post and Times Herald,* April 23, 1957.

80. Carter, Investigating Commissioner, "Determination after Investigation and Conference: American Jewish Congress vs. Arabian American Oil Company."

81. Dana Adams Schmidt, "U.S. Denies Aiding Bias Against Jews," *New York Times,* May 19, 1959; "Aramco's Ban Here on Jews Overruled," *New York Times,* July 16, 1959.

82. "Aramco's Ban Here on Jews Overruled," 1.

83. Sam Pope Brewer, "Aramco Queries Assailed as Bias," *New York Times,* April 6, 1960; Farnsworth Fowle, "S.C.A.D. Reopens Aramco Job Case," *New York Times,* January 9, 1962.

84. American Jewish Congress, Press Release, Richard Cohen, "AJCongress Asks SCAD for Prompt Action to Obtain Full Compliance by ARAMCO with New York Anti-Discrimination Law," folder 16, box 1113, American Civil Liberties Union Records, Seeley G. Mudd Manuscript Library, Princeton University, Princeton, NJ.

85. David Binder, "State Tells Aramco to Drop Its Policy of Excluding Jews," *New York Times,* September 28, 1962.

86. Thomas W. Lippman, *Inside the Mirage: America's Fragile Partnership with Saudi Arabia* (Boulder, CO: Westview Press, 2004), 217; Vitalis, *America's Kingdom,* 249; "Saudi Arabia Lets Jews in U.S. Units Serve on Her Soil," *New York Times,* June 10, 1963.

87. "Considerations for Testimony on Anti-boycott Legislation," February 29, 1977, folder 32, box 8, Mulligan Papers.

88. Jacobs, *Imagining the Middle East,* 81–89; Salim Yaqub, *Containing Arab Nationalism: The Eisenhower Doctrine and the Middle East* (Chapel Hill: University of North Carolina Press, 2004).

3. Curing Antiquity

1. Ivor Morgan, "Obstetrics/Gynecology: 1951–1967," oral history conducted by Carole Hicke (1997), in "Health and Disease in Saudi Arabia: The Aramco Experience, 1940s–1990s," Regional Oral History Office, Bancroft Library, University of California, Berkeley, 1998 (hereafter cited as "Health and Disease in Saudi Arabia"), 420.

2. Ibid., 420–21.

3. Ibid., 421.

4. Michel Foucault, *Birth of the Clinic: An Archaeology of Medical Perception,* trans. A. M. Sheridan Smith (New York: Pantheon Books, 1973); Robin Bunton and Alan Petersen, "Introduction: Foucault's Medicine," in *Foucault, Health and Medicine,* ed. Alan Petersen and Robin Bunton (London: Routledge, 1997), 1–11.

5. Ashis Nandy, *Return from Exile* (New Delhi: Oxford University Press, 1998), 146.

6. Arnold Toynbee, "Report for Aramco," Jidda to State, May 6, 1958, Central Decimal Files, 1951–1959, Record Group 59, General Records of the Department of State, National Archives at College Park, College Park, MD (hereafter cited as NACP); A. J. Toynbee, "Report for Aramco," box 19, Harry Roscoe Snyder Papers, Hoover Institution Archives, Stanford, CA (hereafter cited as Snyder Papers).

7. Foucault, *Birth of the Clinic.*

8. Michel Foucault, "Governmentality," *I & C* 6 (1979), 20.

9. Robert Perrine, "Internal Medicine at Abqaiq and Dhahran: 1961–1980," oral history conducted by Carole Hicke (1997), in "Health and Disease in Saudi Arabia," 524.

10. Memorandum to the File, "Status and Role of the Aged in Saudi Arab Society," June 1, 1960, folder 1, box 3, William E. Mulligan Papers, Archives and Special Collections, Georgetown University, Washington, DC (hereafter cited as Mulligan Papers).

11. Julius Taylor, "Surgeon and Medical Director," oral history conducted by Carole Hicke (1997), in "Health and Disease in Saudi Arabia," 222.

12. Morgan, "Obstetrics/Gynecology," 423; Taylor, "Surgeon and Medical Director," 222.

13. Taylor, "Surgeon and Medical Director," 222.

14. Ibid.

15. Perrine, "Internal Medicine at Abqaiq and Dhahran," 524.

16. Eleanor Abdella Doumato, "An 'Extra Legible Illustration' of the Christian Faith: Medicine, Medical Ethics and Missionaries in the Arabian Gulf," *Islam and Christian–Muslim Relations* 13, no. 4 (2002): 371–90.

17. Robert Oertley, "Ras Tanura, Abqaiq, and Dhahran Medical Facilities," oral history conducted by Carole Hicke (1997), in "Health and Disease in Saudi Arabia," 347.

18. Ibid., 349.

19. Ibid.

20. Perrine, "Internal Medicine at Abqaiq and Dhahran," 521–25. While the use of these remedies decreased, American medical science did not eradicate them. Local remedies continue into the twenty-first century. See B. H. Al-Awamy, "Evaluation of Commonly Used Tribal and Traditional Remedies in Saudi Arabia," *Saudi Medical Journal* 22 (2001): 1061–68.

21. James Steven Simmons, "Welcoming Address," *Industry and Tropical Health* 1 (1950): 11–15; Joyce Battle, ed., "U.S. Propaganda in the Middle East: The Early Cold War Version," National Security Archive Electronic Briefing Book No. 78, December 12, 2002, National Security Archive, www2.gwu.edu.

22. Daniel Headrick, *Tools of Empire: Technology and European Imperialism in the Nineteenth Century* (New York: Oxford University Press, 1981); David Arnold, "Introduction: Disease, Medicine and Empire, in *Imperial Medicine and Indigenous Societies,* ed. David Arnold (Manchester: Manchester University Press, 1988), 10; Roy MacLeod and Milton Lewis, eds., *Disease, Medicine, and Empire: Perspectives on Western Medicine and the Experience of European Expansion* (London: Routledge, 1988); Teresa A. Meade and Mark Walker, eds., *Science, Medicine, and Cultural Imperialism* (New York: St. Martins Press, 1991); Dorothy Porter, ed., *The History of Public Health and the Modern State* (Amsterdam: Rodopi, 1994); Randall Packard, "Visions of Postwar Health and Development and Their Impact on Public Health Interventions in the Developing World," in *International Development and the Social Sciences: Essays on the History of Politics of Knowledge,* ed. Frederick Cooper and Randall Packard (Berkeley: University of California Press, 1997), 91–115; William H. Schneider, ed., *Rockefeller Philanthropy and Modern Biomedicine: International Initiatives from World War I to the Cold War* (Bloomington: Indiana University Press, 2002); Frank Ninkovich, "The Rockefeller Foundation, China, and Cultural Change," *Journal of American History* 70 (1984): 791–820; Elizabeth Fee, "Public Health in the States: The United States," in *The History of Public Health and the Modern State,* ed. Dorothy Porter (Amsterdam: Rodopi, 1994), 221–75; Steven Palmer, "Central American Encounters with Rockefeller Public Health, 1911–1921," in *Close Encounters of Empire: Writing the Cultural History of U.S.–Latin American Relations,* ed. Gilbert M. Joseph, Catherine C. Legrand, and Ricardo D. Salvatore (Durham: Duke University Press, 1998), 311–32; Kristin Ruggiero, *Modernity in the Flesh: Medicine, Law, and Society in Turn-of-the-Century Argentina* (Stanford: Stanford University Press, 2004), 2.

23. Jonathan C. Brown, *Oil and Revolution in Mexico* (Berkeley: University of California Press, 1993), 311–16. The Iraq Petroleum Company, a jointly owned subsidiary of various Western oil interests, including Aramco's parent companies Standard Oil of New Jersey and Standard Oil of New York-Vacuum, brought enormous increases in wealth to Qatar, which resulted in development initiatives organized by the Qatari government. New medical facilities were once referred to as the "piece de resistance" of these improvements. See Wanda M. Jablonski, "From Oil to Free False Teeth, and Then Some," *Petroleum Week* 4 (April 12, 1957):

51–55; J. H. Bamberg, *The History of the British Petroleum Company: The Anglo-Iranian Years, 1921–1954*, vol. 2 (Cambridge: Cambridge University Press, 1994).

24. Randall M. Packard, "Postcolonial Medicine," in *Medicine in the 20th Century*, ed. Roger Cooter and John Pickstone (London: Harwood Academic, 2000), 91–112.

25. Quoted in Paul L. Armerding, *Doctors for the Kingdom: The Work of the American Mission Hospitals in the Kingdom of Saudi Arabia, 1911–1955* (Grand Rapids, MI: Wm. B. Eerdmans, 2003), 79.

26. Gerrit D. Van Peursem, "The Arabian Mission and Saudi-Arabia," *Muslim World* 38 (January 1948): 1–10.

27. Taylor, "Surgeon and Medical Director," 232.

28. Thomas C. Barger, *Out of the Blue: Letters from Arabia, 1937 to 1940: A Young American Geologist Explores the Deserts of Early Saudi Arabia* (Vista, CA: Selwa Press: 2000), 32.

29. Armand P. Gelpi, "Volume Introduction," in "Health and Disease in Saudi Arabia," i–xxiv.

30. Richard H. Daggy, "The Administration of Medical Care and Health Services by Aramco in Saudi Arabia," *The Medical Bulletin* 64 (March 1964): 3.

31. Richard H. Daggy, "Preventive Medicine in Saudi Arabia, 1941–1964," oral history conducted by Carole Hicke (1997), in "Health and Disease in Saudi Arabia," 19.

32. Thomas Osborne, "Medicine and Epistemology: Michel Foucault and the Liberality of Clinical Reason," *History of the Human Sciences* 5 (1992): 82.

33. Arabian American Oil Company, "Donations, Contributions, and Assistance to Saudi Arabia, 1931–1970," folder 10, box 5, Mulligan Papers, 3.

34. Taylor, "Surgeon and Medical Director," 181–83.

35. Oertley, "Ras Tanura, Abqaiq, and Dhahran Medical Facilities," 370.

36. Taylor, "Surgeon and Medical Director," 198; David Skory, Report, April 17, 1955, folder ca. 1955–1959: Arabian American Oil Company (2 of 4), box 6, Middle East Ventures of the Mobil Oil Company, 1951–1960, Special Collections, University of Virginia Library, Charlottesville, Virginia (hereafter cited as Mobil Papers). A clear indication of the positive impact medicine might have on diplomatic relations can be seen in similar discussions within the U.S. government. See Memorandum from Acheson to Eisenhower, "Urgent Request to You from King Ibn Saud for the Services of General Graham," August 9, 1951, folder: "Correspondence of Harry S. Truman regarding Palestine and Saudi Arabian Security," box 2, Papers of Parker T. Hart, Special Collections, University of Virginia Library (hereafter cited as Hart Papers). King 'Abd al-Aziz expressed his gratitude following Graham's medical mission, indicating a willingness to work on "mutual problems" together. See Letter from 'Abd al-Aziz to Harry Truman, March 3, 1952, folder: "Correspondence of Harry S. Truman regarding Palestine and Saudi Arabian Security," box 2, Hart Papers; William C. Marett, "Some Medical Problems Met in Saudi Arabia," *United States Armed Forces Medical Journal* 4 (1953): 33.

37. Tariq Ali, *The Clash of Fundamentalisms: Crusades, Jihad, and Modernity* (London: Verso, 2002).

38. Abdelrahman Munif, *Cities of Salt*, trans. Peter Theroux (New York: Vintage Books, 1987; originally published in Arabic, 1984).

39. "Control of Malaria," *Chronicle of the World Health Organization* 2 (July 1948): 146.

40. Alberto Missiroli, quoted in Packard, "Visions of Postwar Health," 96.

41. C.-E. A. Winslow, *The Cost of Sickness and the Price of Health*, World Health Organization Monograph Series, no. 7 (Geneva: World Health Organization, 1951).

42. R. Clinton Page and R. H. Daggy, "Aramco's Preventive Medicine Program," *Medical Bulletin* 16 (1956): 196.

43. Ibid.

44. Ibid.

45. Dorothy McComb, "Trachoma Project: 1951–1976," oral history conducted by Carole Hicke (1997), in "Health and Disease in Saudi Arabia," 320.

46. Arabian American Oil Company, Planning Committee, January 4, 1944, box 3, Philip C. McConnell Papers, 1931–1963, Hoover Institution Archives, Stanford, CA (hereafter cited as McConnell Papers).

47. Dhahran to State, Walter W. Birge Jr., September 12, 1945, Decimal Files, 1941–1949, RG 59, NACP, 6.

48. Ibid., 12.

49. Waldo E. Bailey, Memorandum, Jidda to State, August 18, 1947, Decimal Files, 1941–1949, RG 59, NACP.

50. J. Rives Childs, Memorandum, Jidda to State, October 25, 1948, Decimal Files, 1941–1949, RG 59, NACP.

51. Lorania K. Francis, "U.S. Hospital Oasis of Health for Arabs," *Los Angeles Times,* April 2, 1951.

52. Taylor, "Surgeon and Medical Director: 1951–1978," 186.

53. Ibid., 180.

54. Ibid., 190.

55. Ibid., 189.

56. Morgan, "Obstetrics/Gynecology: 1951–1967," 439.

57. Taylor, "Surgeon and Medical Director: 1951–1978," 189.

58. Morgan, "Obstetrics/Gynecology: 1951–1967," 440.

59. Arabian American Oil Company, "Donations, Contributions, and Assistance to Saudi Arabia, 1931–1970," folder 10, box 5, Mulligan Papers, 1–5.

60. Gelpi, "Aramco Medical Services: 1951–1969," oral history conducted by Carole Hicke (1997), in "Health and Disease in Saudi Arabia," 51–53.

61. Jidda to State, Walter K. Schwinn, Foreign Service Dispatch, February 2, 1960, Central Files of the Department of State, RG 59, 1961–1963, 886A.562/1-2060.

62. Jidda to State, John Evarts Horner, "Dosari Hospital Expected to Open May 1, 1961," December 16, 1961, Central Files of the Department of State, 1961–1963, RG 59, NACP.

63. Taylor, "Surgeon and Medical Director: 1951–1978," 215.

64. Gelpi, "Aramco Medical Services: 1951–1969," 54.

65. Taylor, "Surgeon and Medical Director: 1951–1978," 223.

66. Perrine, "Internal Medicine at Abqaiq and Dhahran," 522.

67. Toby Craig Jones, *Desert Kingdom: How Oil and Water Forged Modern Saudi Arabia* (Cambridge: Harvard University Press, 2010).

68. Jidda to State, Alfred le S. Jenkins, "Fortnightly Review of Events in Saudi Arabia, May 11–31, 1956," June 9, 1956, Central Decimal Files, 1951–1959, RG 59, NACP.

69. International Sanitary Regulations, *World Health Organization Technical Report Series* 41 (May 25, 1951), 1, 15.

70. Ibid.

71. Ministry of Health, Kingdom of Saudi Arabia, *Jeddah Quarantine Station* (Jeddah, Saudi Arabia: Asfahani Printers, April 2, 1956).

72. "International Sanitary Regulations," *WHO Technical Report Series* 41.

73. Jidda to State, Translation of Radio Mecca broadcast, June 3, 1956, Central Decimal Files, 1951–1959, RG 59, NACP.

74. F. E. Peters, *The Hajj: The Muslim Pilgrimage to Mecca and the Holy Places* (Princeton: Princeton University Press: 1994), 301–15.

75. A. H. Sadek, "Final Report: Quarantine Station – Jeddah," January 1956, unpublished

report by the World Health Organization, EM/EPID/5, Library of the World Health Organization Library, Geneva, Switzerland.

76. Gorson to Taggart, "USA Operations Mission to Saudi Arabia, 7 June 1954, folder Health and Sanitation, Records of the U.S. Foreign Assistance Agencies, 1941–1961, Mission to Saudi Arabia, Office of the Director, box 3, Subject Files, Central Files, 1951–1954, Health and Sanitation, Record Group 469, U.S. Foreign Assistance Agencies, 1941–1961, NACP.

77. Ministry of Health, Kingdom of Saudi Arabia, *Jeddah Quarantine Station.*

78. Taylor, "Surgeon and Medical Director: 1951–1978," 241.

4. Man-Made Disease

1. Richard H. Daggy, "Preventive Medicine in Saudi Arabia, 1941–1964," oral history conducted by Carole Hicke (1997), in "Health and Disease in Saudi Arabia: The Aramco Experience, 1940s–1990s," Regional Oral History Office, Bancroft Library, University of California, Berkeley, 1998 (hereafter cited as "Health and Disease in Saudi Arabia"), 2, 3, 9, 14–15; "When Malaria Met Its Match," *Al-Ayyam Al-Jamilah* (Fall 2001): 24–27; Daggy, letter, November 20, 1942, reprinted in the University of Minnesota Department of Agriculture, Division of Entomology and Economic Zoology Newsletter, vol. 5, no. 27 (February 1943): 4–7.

2. E. J. Pampana, "Malaria as a Problem for the WHO," draft of paper for Fourth International Congress on Tropical Medicine and Malaria, 10–15 May 1948, microfilm, 451-1-4, Archives of the World Health Organization, Geneva, Switzerland (hereafter cited as WHO Archive).

3. See Ian Tyrrell, "Reflections on the Transnational Turn in United States History: Theory and Practice," *Journal of Global History* 4 (2009): 453–74; David Thelen, "The Nation and Beyond: Transnational Perspectives on United States History—An Introduction," *Journal of American History* 86 (December 1999): 965–75; Matthew Connelly, "Seeing Beyond the State: The Population Control Movement and the Problem of Sovereignty," *Past and Present* 193 (November 2006): 197–233; James C. Scott, *Seeing Like a State: How Certain Schemes to Improve the Human Condition Have Failed* (New Haven: Yale University Press, 1999); Erez Manela, "Pox on Your Narrative: Writing Disease Control into Cold War History," *Diplomatic History* 34 (April 2010): 299–323.

4. George Rentz, memorandum, February 3, 1947, folder 13, box 2, William E. Mulligan Papers, Archives and Special Collections, Georgetown University, Washington, DC (hereafter cited as Mulligan Papers); J. V. Knight, Minutes of Relations Department Meeting, September 18, 1948, folder 13, box 2, Mulligan Papers.

5. F. S. Vidal, *The Aramco Reports on Al-Hasa and Oman*, vol. 2: *The Oasis of Al-Hasa* (Cambridge: Cambridge Archive Editions, 1990; original edition, Dhahran, Saudi Arabia: Arabian American Oil Company, 1950), vii.

6. Richard H. Daggy, "Malaria in Oases of Eastern Saudi Arabia," *American Journal of Tropical Medicine and Hygiene* 8 (1959): 223.

7. Quoted in Randall Packard, "Visions of Postwar Health and Development and Their Impact on Public Health Interventions in the Developing World," in *International Development and the Social Sciences: Essays on the History and Politics of Knowledge*, ed. Frederick Cooper and Randall M. Packard (Berkeley: University of California Press, 1998), 96; C-E. A. Winslow, *The Cost of Sickness and the Price of Health* (Geneva: World Health Organization, 1951); Inter-Regional Conference on Malaria for the Eastern Mediterranean and European Regions, Athens, 11–19 June 1956, and Advisory Meeting on Malaria Eradication in Egypt, Iran, Iraq, Lebanon, Saudi Arabia and Syria: [Report], 19 June 1956, 56–57, www.who.int; Frank M. Snowden, "'Fields of Death': Malaria in Italy, 1861–1962," *Modern Italy* 4 (1999): 25–57; "Ma-

laria Round the World," *American Journal of Public Health* 41 (January 1951): 132; "Control of Malaria," *Chronicle of the World Health Organization* 2 (July 1948): 146.

8. Randall M. Packard, "Roll Back Malaria, Roll in Development? Reassessing the Economic Burden of Malaria," *Population and Development Review* 35 (March 2009): 53–87; Randall Packard, "'Malaria Blocks Development' Revisited: The Role of Disease in the History of Agricultural Development in the Eastern and Northern Transvaal Lowveld, 1891–1960," *Journal of Southern African Studies* 27 (September 2001): 591–612.

9. Randall M. Packard, *The Making of a Tropical Disease: A Short History of Malaria* (Baltimore: Johns Hopkins University Press, 2007).

10. Sheldon Watts, "British Development Policies and Malaria, 1891–1929," *Past and Present* 165 (1999): 141–81; Ira Klein, "Development and Death: Reinterpreting Malaria, Economics and Ecology in British India," *Indian Economic and Social History Review* 23, no. 2 (2001): 141–79.

11. Peter J. Brown, "Socioeconomic and Demographic Effects of Malaria Eradication: A Comparison of Sri Lanka and Sardinia," *Social Science and Medicine* 22, no. 8 (1986): 847–59.

12. Sandra M. Sufian, *Healing the Land and the Nation: Malaria and the Zionist Project in Palestine, 1921–1947* (Chicago: University of Chicago Press, 2007); Packard, "Roll Back Malaria, Roll in Development?," 53–87; Marc Farley, *To Cast Out Disease: A History of the International Health Division of the Rockefeller Foundation (1911–1951)* (Oxford: Oxford University Press, 2004); Packard, "'Malaria Blocks Development' Revisited," 591–612; R. M. Packard, "'No Other Logical Choice': Global Malaria Eradication and the Politics of International Health in the Post-War Era," *Parassitologia* 40 (1998): 217–29; R. M. Packard and P. J. Brown, "Rethinking Health, Development, and Malaria: Historicizing a Cultural Model in International Health," *Medical Anthropology* 17 (1997): 181–94; Peter J. Brown, "Malaria, Miseria, and Underpopulation in Sardinia: The 'Malaria Blocks Development' Cultural Model," *Medical Anthropology* 17 (1997): 239–54; Randall M. Packard, "Malaria Dreams: Postwar Visions of Health and Development in the Third World," *Medical Anthropology* 17 (May 1997): 279–96.

13. Frank Snowden, *The Conquest of Malaria: Italy, 1901–1962* (New Haven: Yale University Press, 2006).

14. Alexanderina V. Schuler, *Malaria: Meeting the Global Challenge* (Boston: Gunn and Hain, 1985), 3; Margaret Humphreys, *Malaria: Poverty, Race, and Public Health in the United States* (Baltimore: Johns Hopkins University Press, 2001).

15. Gordon Harrison, *Mosquitoes, Malaria and Man: A History of the Hostilities since 1880* (New York: E. P. Dutton, 1978), 166–67; Humphreys, *Malaria*, 47–48.

16. James L. A. Webb Jr., *Humanity's Burden: A Global History of Malaria* (Cambridge: Cambridge University Press, 2009), 136.

17. Randall M. Packard and Paulo Gadehla, "A Land Filled with Mosquitoes: Fred L. Soper, the Rockefeller Foundation, and the Anopheles Gambiae Invasion of Brazil," *Parassitologia* 36 (1994): 197–213; Amy L. S. Staples, "Constructing International Identity: The World Bank, Food and Agriculture Organization, and World Health Organization, 1941–1965" (PhD diss., Ohio State University, 1998); Hughes Evans, "European Malaria Policy in the 1920s and 1930s: The Epidemiology of Minutiae," *Isis* 80 (March 1989): 40–59.

18. "Principles and Methods of Antimalarial Measures in Europe," Second General Report of the Malaria Commission, League of Nations, July 1927, 27–28, 88, WHO Archive.

19. This integrated approach reduced infections despite a continued, and continuing, focus on attacking the vector or parasite. See Packard, *The Making of a Tropical Disease*.

20. Humphreys, *Malaria*; see also Harry Cleaver, "Malaria and the Political Economy of Public Health," *International Journal of Health Service* 7 (1977): 557–79.

21. See Packard and Gadehla, "A Land Filled with Mosquitoes," 215–38; Nancy Elizabeth Gallagher, *Egypt's Other Wars: Epidemics and the Politics of Public Health* (Baltimore: Johns Hopkins University Press, 1990); Timothy Mitchell, *Rule of Experts: Egypt, Techno-Politics, Modernity* (Berkeley: University of California Press, 2002), 19–53. See also Brown, "Malaria, Miseria, and Underpopulation"; Packard, " 'No Other Logical Choice' "; Eric D. Carter, " 'God Bless General Peron': DDT and the Endgame of Malaria Eradication in Argentina in the 1940s," *Journal of the History of Medicine and Allied Sciences* 64 (2009): 78–122.

22. Quoted in Snowden, *The Conquest of Malaria,* 201; Malcolm Gladwell, "The Mosquito Killer," *New Yorker,* July 2, 2001, 42–51.

23. Robert Rice, "DDT," *New Yorker,* June 17, 1954, 31–56; John H. Perkins, "Reshaping Technology in Wartime: The Effect of Military Goals on Entomological Research and Insect-Control Practices," *Technology and Culture* 19 (April 1978): 169–86; Edmund P. Russell, "The Strange Career of DDT: Experts, Federal Capacity, and Environmentalism in World War II," *Technology and Culture* 40 (October 1999): 770–96.

24. These new technologies, Packard and Brown argue, "encouraged a narrow biomedical view of health and disease." Packard and Brown, "Rethinking Health, Development, and Malaria," 185.

25. David Arnold, *Colonizing the Body: State Medicine and Epidemic Disease in Nineteenth-Century India* (Berkeley: University of California Press, 1993); Paul C. Winther, *Anglo-European Science and the Rhetoric of Empire: Malaria, Opium, and British Rule in India, 1751–1895* (Lanham, MD: Lexington Books, 2003); Mark Harrison, *Public Health in British India: Anglo-Indian Preventive Medicine, 1851–1914* (Cambridge: Cambridge University Press, 2003).

26. Soma Hewa, *Colonialism, Tropical Disease and Imperial Medicine: Rockefeller Philanthropy in Sri Lanka* (Lanham, MD: University Press of America, 1995); Biswamoy Pati and Mark Harrison, "Introduction," in *Health, Medicine and Empire: Perspectives on Colonial India,* ed. Biswamoy Pati and Mark Harrison (London: Routledge, 2009), 1–36; Margaret Jones, *Health Policy in Britain's Model Colony: Ceylon (1901–1948)* (New Delhi: Orient Longman Private, 2004); Roy MacLeod, "Introduction," in *Disease, Medicine, and Empire: Perspectives on Western Medicine and the Experience of European Expansion,* ed. Roy MacLeod and Milton Lewis (London: Routledge, 1988).

27. Heather Bell, *Frontiers of Medicine in the Anglo-Egyptian Sudan, 1891–1940* (Oxford: Oxford University Press, 1999).

28. Richard H. Daggy and R. C. Page, "Aramco's Preventive Medicine Program," *Medical Bulletin* 16 (1956): 196.

29. Bell, *Frontiers of Medicine,* 108.

30. Arabian American Oil Company, "Donations, Contributions, and Assistance to Saudi Arabia: 1933–1970," January 1971, folder 10, box 5, Mulligan Papers.

31. Daggy, "Preventive Medicine in Saudi Arabia," 3.

32. Robert Vitalis, *America's Kingdom: Mythmaking on the Saudi Oil Frontier* (Stanford: Stanford University Press, 2007).

33. Armand P. Gelpi, "Aramco Medical Services, 1951–1969," oral history conducted by Carole Hicke (1997), in "Health and Disease in Saudi Arabia," 72.

34. Daggy, "Preventive Medicine in Saudi Arabia," 5.

35. Bell, *Frontiers of Medicine;* Norman Etherington, "Introduction," in *Missions and Empire,* ed. Norman Etherington (New York: Oxford University Press, 2005), 1–18.

36. "Closing in on Malaria," *Aramco World,* March 1961, 4.

37. Letter from Richard H. Daggy to E. J. Pampana, December 8, 1948, file, Saudi Arabia JKTI ss4/4 1944–1957, WHO Archive. WHO reported high rates as well; see H. R. Rafatjah, Report on Visit to Saudi Arabia, 9 November–6 December 1956, Annex I, file, Saudi Arabia

JKTI ss4/4 1944–1957, folder, SAA 1958 SJ1, WHO Archive, 3; quotes from Daggy, "Preventive Medicine in Saudi Arabia," 2–3, 7.

38. Saad E. D. Afifi, "Malaria Eradication in Pilot Projects with Special Reference to Saudi Arabia," Second Regional Conference on Malaria Eradication, Addis Ababa, November 16–21, 1959, in unpublished reports of the World Health Organization, EM/ME-Tech.2/11, WHO Archive.

39. Daggy, "Preventive Medicine in Saudi Arabia," 6–7.

40. Lyn Schumaker, "Malaria," in *Medicine in the Twentieth Century,* ed. Roger Cooter and John V. Pickstone (Amsterdam: Harwood Academic Publisher, 2000), 704–5; Gallagher, *Egypt's Other Wars,* 4.

41. Daggy, "Malaria in Oases of Eastern Saudi Arabia," 223, 243; Daggy, "Preventive Medicine in Saudi Arabia," 8.

42. See H. R. Carter, "'Man-Made' Malaria," *Southern Medical Journal* 16 (April 1923): 271–81; Justin Andrews, "What's Happening to Malaria in the U.S.A.?," *American Journal of Public Health* 38 (July 1948): 933; Justin Andrews, Griffith E. Quinby, and Alexander D. Langmuir, "Malaria Eradication in the United States," *American Journal of Public Health* 40 (November 1950): 1405.

43. *Reprint of Transactions of the Royal Society of Tropical Medicine and Hygiene,* vol. 38, no. 3, December 1944, P. A. Buxton, "Rough Notes: Anopheles Mosquitoes and Malaria in Arabia," file, Saudi Arabia JKT1 ss4/4 1944–1957, 209–10, WHO Archive.

44. Daggy, "Malaria in Oases of Eastern Saudi Arabia," 236.

45. Richard H. Daggy, "Oasis Malaria," General Discussion, Industry and Tropic Health, *Proceedings of the Industrial Health Conference* 5 (1957): 43.

46. "Closing in on Malaria," *Aramco World,* March 1961, 4.

47. Daggy, "Malaria in Oases of Eastern Saudi Arabia," 225, 243; Vidal, *The Oasis of al-Hasa,* 18; Daggy, "Oasis Malaria," 43–45. For more recent statistics on population densities see the UN Demographic Yearbook, 2006, http://unstats.un.org.

48. J. G. Hamilton, "The Start of an Agricultural Program in the Eastern Province," 12 April 1955 Report, Arabian American Oil Company, folder ca. 1955–1959: Arabian American Oil Company (2 of 4), box 6, Middle East Ventures of the Mobil Oil Company, 1951–1960, Special Collections, University of Virginia Library, Charlottesville, Virginia (hereafter cited as Mobil Papers); Karl S. Twitchell, U.S. Agricultural Mission, Field Notes, 13 November 1942, folder 5 1911–1967, box 7, Karl S. Twitchell Papers, Seeley G. Mudd Manuscript Library, Princeton, NJ (hereafter cited as Twitchell Papers).

49. Daggy, "Malaria in Oases of Eastern Saudi Arabia," 230, 243, 229; Daggy, "Preventive Medicine in Saudi Arabia," 8; Daggy, "Oasis Malaria," 43.

50. Daggy, "Malaria in Oases of Eastern Saudi Arabia," 285; J. G. Hamilton, "The Start of an Agricultural Program in the Eastern Province," Mobil Papers.

51. Vidal, *The Oasis of al-Hasa,* 135–36.

52. *Transactions of the Royal Society of Tropical Medicine and Hygiene,* 209.

53. Daggy, "Malaria in Oases of Eastern Saudi Arabia," 231–35.

54. Letter from Richard H. Daggy to E. J. Pampana, 8 December 1948, file, Saudi Arabia JKTI ss4/4 1944–1957, WHO Archive.

55. Daggy, "Malaria in Oases of Eastern Saudi Arabia," 266.

56. There were beneficial "by-products" for U.S. government campaigns. Improved health followed visits, and equipment was appropriately labeled, clarifying the involvement of the United States. See Eugene P. Campbell, Statement to the Senate on Malaria Eradication, Mutual Security Act of 1959, Committee on Foreign Relations, Hearing (U.S. Government Printing Office, 1959), 748.

57. Daggy, "Preventive Medicine in Saudi Arabia," 266.

58. Vidal, *The Oasis of al-Hasa,* vi–vii.

59. Gelpi, "Aramco Medical Services," 72. As part of the malaria survey, company personnel also gave smallpox vaccinations. See Arabian American Oil Company, "Donations, Contributions, and Assistance to Saudi Arabia: 1933–1970," folder 10, box 5, Mulligan Papers. Aramco sponsored other programs as well, like one to combat the prevalent eye disease trachoma, after first attempting to get the Rockefeller Foundation to fund it. See Duce to Fosdick, 5 June 1946, folder 2382, box 352, series 817, sub-series 1946, RG 2, Rockefeller Foundation Archives, Rockefeller Archive Center, Sleepy Hollow, New York (hereafter cited as Rockefeller Archive).

60. Daggy, "Preventive Medicine in Saudi Arabia," 5.

61. Daggy, "Oasis Malaria," 50–52; Daggy, "Malaria in Oases of Eastern Saudi Arabia," 266–76.

62. Daggy and Page, "Aramco's Preventive Medicine Program," 200–201.

63. Daggy, "Oasis Malaria," 5; Daggy, "Preventive Medicine in Saudi Arabia," 12; Richard H. Daggy, "Malariometric Evidence for DDT Resistance in Anopheles Stephensi in Oases of Eastern Saudi Arabia," *Proceedings of the Sixth Congress on Tropical Medicine and Malaria* 7 (1958): 317–24. Resistance to Dieldren also emerged. See R. L. Peffly, "Dieldrin-Resistant Anopheles Fluviatilis in Eastern Saudi Arabia," report for the World Health Organization, 15 August 1959, http://apps.who.int.

64. Daggy, "Malaria in Oases of Eastern Saudi Arabia," 276–77.

65. Ibid., 283; Daggy, "Preventive Medicine in Saudi Arabia," 12–13; Harrison, *Mosquitoes, Malaria and Man,* 88; Dorothy McComb, "Trachoma Project: 1951–1976," oral history conducted by Carole Hicke (1997), in "Health and Disease in Saudi Arabia," 320.

66. "Kill the Mosquito before it kills you" poster, box 1, Philip C. McConnell Papers, 1931–1963, Hoover Institution Archives, Stanford, CA (hereafter cited as McConnell Papers).

67. Richard H. Handschin, "Preventive Medicine and Medical Director: 1951–1968," oral history conducted by Carole Hicke (1997), in "Health and Disease in Saudi Arabia," 132–33.

68. Daggy, "Malaria in Oases of Eastern Saudi Arabia," 284.

69. Afifi, "Malaria Eradication Pilot Projects," 16–21. WHO reports indicate low rates of infection in the Eastern Province following Aramco's Malaria Control Program in 1956. See H. Mashaal, "Malaria Control and Demonstration Project, Saudi Arabia," 18 August 1956–19 February 1958," January 1959, unpublished reports of the World Health Organization, EM/MAL/37, Saudi Arabia 4, WHO Archive.

70. H. Debbagh, "Preliminary Planning of Eradication of Malaria in Saudi Arabia," 20 November 1957, unpublished report of the World Health Organization, WHO Archive.

71. Afifi, "Malaria Eradication Pilot Projects."

72. "Joint Government/WHO Malaria Review Mission to Saudi Arabia," July 1–23, 1985 (World Health Organization, January 1987), http://whqlibdoc.who.int.

73. G. J. de Almeida, "Assignment Report: Malaria Pre-Eradication Programme in Saudi Arabia," July 1963–December 1968," unpublished report of the World Health Organization, March 1969, WHO Archive.

74. H. R. Rafatjah, Report on Visit to Saudi Arabia, 9 November–6 December 1956, Annex I, file, Saudi Arabia JKTI ss4/4 1944–1957, folder, SAA 1958 SJ1, WHO Archive; quote from de Almeida, "Assignment Report: Malaria Pre-Eradication Programme in Saudi Arabia."

75. Rafatjah, "Report on Visit to Saudi Arabia."

76. J. H. Pull, "Report on Visit to the Malaria Pre-Eradication Programme," Saudi Arabia, 12–19 May 1967," file, JKTI ss4/4 1944–1957, folder, SAA 1966–1967 SJ2, WHO Archives.

77. R. Bahar, "Report on a Visit to Saudi Arabia," 5–23 February 1976, unpublished report of the World Health Organization, May 1976, WHO Archive; Pull, "Report on Malaria

Control Programme of the Kingdom of Saudi Arabia"; Al Tawfiq Ja, "Epidemiology of Travel Related Malaria in a non-Malarious area in Saudi Arabia," *Saudi Medical Journal* 27 (2006): 86–89; Layla A. Bashwari, Ahmed M. Mandil, Ahmed A. Bahnassy, Mariam A. Al-Shamsi, and Huda A. Bukhari, "Epidemiological Profile of Malaria in a University Hospital in the Eastern Region of Saudi Arabia," *Saudi Medical Journal* 22 (2001): 133–38.

78. Arabian American Oil Company Donations, Contributions, and Assistance to Saudi Arabia, 1931–1970, folder 10: "Donations, Contributions, and Assistance to Saudi Arabia, 1931–1970," box 5, Mulligan Papers, 8.

79. Duce to Fosdick, June 5, 1946, folder 2382, box 352, series 817, sub-series 1946, RG 2, Rockefeller Archive; Russell to Rockefeller, Memorandum to Mr. Rockefeller, December 7, 1934, folder 849, box 110, series 817, sub-series 1934, RG 2, General Correspondence, Rockefeller Archive; Strode to Duce, June 10, 1946, folder 2382, box 352, series 817, sub-series 1946, RG 2, Rockefeller Archive.

80. John C. Snyder, "The Harvard/Aramco Trachoma Project," oral history conducted by Carole Hicke (1997), in "Health and Disease in Saudi Arabia," 246.

81. Richard Handschin, "Preventive Medicine and Medical Director, 1951–1968" oral history conducted by Carole Hicke (1997), in "Health and Disease in Saudi Arabia," 134.

82. "At War With Trachoma," *Aramco World,* October 1960, 3.

83. Arabian American Oil Company Donations, Contributions, and Assistance to Saudi Arabia, 1931–1970, folder 10: "Donations, Contributions, and Assistance to Saudi Arabia, 1931–1970," box 5, Mulligan Papers, 7.

84. "At War With Trachoma," 1–6.

85. Dorothy McComb, "Trachoma Project, 1951–1976" oral history conducted by Carole Hicke (1997), in "Health and Disease in Saudi Arabia," 303; Roger L. Nichols, Edward S. Murray, Pamela P. Schott, and Dorothy E. McComb, "Trachoma Isolation Studies in Saudi Arabia from 1957 through 1969," in *Trachoma and Related Disorders Caused by Chlamydial Agents,* ed. Roger L. Nichols (Amsterdam: Excerpta Medica, 1971), 511–28.

86. Roger Nichols et al., "Trachoma Isolation Studies in Saudi Arabia," 526.

87. Elinor P. Nichols, "Roger Nichols and the Trachoma Project: 1951–1982," oral history conducted by Carole Hicke (1997), in "Health and Disease in Saudi Arabia," 285.

88. McComb, "Trachoma Project," 303.

89. Elinor Nichols, "Roger Nichols and the Trachoma Project," 269.

90. Roger Nichols et al., "Trachoma Isolation Studies in Saudi Arabia," 526.

91. McComb, "Trachoma Project," 304. Trachoma continued to exist in Saudi Arabia but with a dramatic decline in the incidence of infection. See Chandra G., "Trachoma in Eastern Province of Saudi Arabia," *Revue Internationale du Trachome et de Pathologie Oculaire Tropicale et Subtropicale et de Santé Publique* 67 (1992): 111–32.

92. McComb, "Trachoma Project," 320.

93. Gelpi, "Aramco Medical Services," 21–25.

94. Taylor, "Surgeon and Medical Director: 1951–1978," oral history conducted by Carole Hicke (1997), in "Health and Disease in Saudi Arabia," 227.

95. Ibid., 226.

96. "Health in Arabia" poster, box 2, McConnell Papers.

5. Aramco's Eden

1. "Daniel Da Cruz, "A Drop of Rain," *Aramco World Magazine,* July/August 1964, 21–29.

2. Ahmed Omer Fakry and Karl Saben Twitchell, *Report of the United States Agricultural Mission to Saudi Arabia* (Cairo, 1943), 77.

3. S. W. Edgecombe, "Brief Report on Visit to Saudi Arabia," March 29, 1955, folder ca.

1951–1959: Arabian American Oil Company (2 of 4), box 6, Middle East Ventures of the Mobil Oil Company, 1951–1960, Special Collections, University of Virginia Library, Charlottesville, Virginia (hereafter cited as Mobil Papers).

4. A. S. Helaissi, "The Bedouins and Tribal Life in Saudi Arabia," *International Social Science Journal* 11 (1959): 537.

5. Robert Vitalis, *America's Kingdom: Mythmaking on the Saudi Oil Frontier* (Stanford: Stanford University Press, 2007), 71–74.

6. Claire C. Robertson, "Black, White, and Red All Over: Beans, Women, and Agricultural Imperialism in Twentieth-Century Kenya," *Agricultural History* 71, no. 3 (Summer 1997): 251–99.

7. Nick Cullather, *The Hungry World: America's Cold War Battle Against Poverty in Asia* (Cambridge: Harvard University Press, 2010).

8. Glen Francis Brown, "The Geology and Ground Water of Al Kharj District, Nejd, Saudi Arabia" (PhD diss., Northwestern University, 1949), 1–5; K. S. Twitchell and Edward Jabra Jurji, *Saudi Arabia: With an Account of the Development of Its Natural Resources* (Princeton: Princeton University Press, 1947), 43.

9. D. G. Hogarth, "Some Recent Arabian Explorations," *Geographical Review* 11 (July 1921): 321–37.

10. H. St. J. B. Philby, "Southern Najd," *Geographical Journal* 55 (March 1920): 161–85.

11. Arabian American Oil Company, *Report of Operations to the Saudi Arab Government* (Dhahran, Saudi Arabia, 1949).

12. Arabian American Oil Company, *Report of Operations to the Saudi Arab Government* (Dhahran, Saudi Arabia, 1950).

13. Arabian American Oil Company, *Report of Operations to the Saudi Arab Government* (Dhahran, Saudi Arabia, 1957).

14. Wallace Stegner, "Discovery! The Story of Aramco Then: Chapter 14: The Frontier Closes," *Aramco World* (July/August, 1970), 11. The publishing of Stegner's book has an interesting history of its own. As Robert Vitalis details, Stegner's draft of 1956 took over a decade to be released. Aramco claimed that the delays related to Stegner's praise of Americans over Saudis, but, more accurately, it was Stegner's candid discussion of some of the problems in the Aramco–Saudi relationship that caused most of the delays. See Vitalis, *America's Kingdom*, 191–99.

15. "Arabs and Americans Join in Creating Modern 'Eden,'" *New York Herald Tribune,* May 16, 1948, folder 10, box 8, William E. Mulligan Papers, Archives and Special Collections, Georgetown University, Washington, DC (hereafter cited as Mulligan Papers); Lorania K. Francis, "Arab Farms Boom Under Americans," *Los Angeles Times,* March 28, 1951.

16. "Arabs and Americans Join in Creating Modern 'Eden.'"

17. Roy Lebkicher, *Handbooks for American Employees,* rev. ed., part 2, "The Work and Life of Aramco Employees" (New York: Russell F. Moore, 1952), 102.

18. Ibid.

19. Richard Drayton, *Nature's Government: Science, Imperial Britain, and the 'Improvement' of the World* (New Haven: Yale University Press, 2000), 231–57; Mike Davis, *Late Victorian Holocausts: El Nino Famines and the Making of the Third World* (London, Verso: 2001), 311–40; David C. Engerman, "American Knowledge and Global Power," *Diplomatic History* 31 (September 2007): 591–622; Robertson, "Black, White, and Red All Over," 251–99.

20. K. S. Twitchell, "Water Resources of Saudi Arabia," *Geographical Review* 34 (July 1944): 361–86; Fakry and Twitchell, *Report of the United States Agricultural Mission to Saudi Arabia,* 41.

21. F. S. Vidal, *The Aramco Reports on Al-Hasa and Oman,* vol. 2: *The Oasis of Al-Hasa* (Cambridge: Cambridge Archive Editions, 1990; original edition, Dhahran, Saudi Arabia: Arabian American Oil Company, 1950), 141–44; Twitchell, "Water Resources of Saudi Arabia," 382.

22. "Memorandum of Conversation," Division of Near Eastern Affairs, July 17, 1943, *Foreign Relations of the United States, 1943* (Washington, DC: U.S. Government Printing Office, 1943), 4:871–79 (hereafter cited as *FRUS*).

23. Joseph Kostiner, "On Instruments and Their Designers: The Ikhwan of Najd and the Emergence of the Saudi State," *Middle Eastern Studies* 21 (1985): 291–323.

24. D. Van Der Meulen, *The Wells of Ibn Sa'ud* (New York: Praeger, 1957), 205.

25. Douglas D. Crary, "Recent Agricultural Developments in Saudi Arabia," *Geographical Review* 41 (July 1951): 367.

26. At the time, the company operated under the name California Arabian Standard Oil Company (Casoc). For the sake of simplicity and consistency, I use the name Aramco throughout. Ibid.

27. Twitchell, "Water Resources of Saudi Arabia."

28. R. A. Bramkamp, T. C. Barger, and L. M. Snyder, "Report on Development of Saudi Arabia Government's Irrigation Project at Al Kharj, Saudi Arabia," California Arabian Standard Oil Company, June 29, 1941, folder 7, box 9, Karl S. Twitchell Papers, Seeley G. Mudd Manuscript Library, Princeton, NJ (hereafter cited as Twitchell Papers).

29. Fakry and Twitchell, *Report of the United States Agricultural Mission*, 47; Crary, "Recent Agricultural Developments in Saudi Arabia," 370; Twitchell, "Water Resources of Saudi Arabia," 380.

30. Political implications for agricultural development also played a substantial role in European colonial officials' minds dating back to the nineteenth century. The British government, for instance, made a strategic move to invest more heavily in its Caribbean colonies as a bulwark against American interests in the region while noting that France and Germany invested heavily and did much the same thing. See Drayton, *Nature's Government*, 259.

31. Vitalis, *America's Kingdom*, 81–82; Thomas W. Lippman, *Inside the Mirage: America's Fragile Partnership with Saudi Arabia* (Boulder, CO: Westview Press, 2004), 31–35; Melvyn P. Leffler, *A Preponderance of Power: National Security, the Truman Administration, and the Cold War* (Stanford: Stanford University Press, 1992), 71–81; Rachel Bronson, *Thicker Than Oil: America's Uneasy Partnership with Saudi Arabia* (Oxford: Oxford University Press, 2006), 41–49.

32. Fakry and Twitchell, *Report of the United States Agricultural Mission*, 5.

33. Hull to Kirk, telegram, February 6, 1942, *FRUS, 1942*, 4:561–62; A. A. Berle Jr. to Twitchell, March 19, 1942, *FRUS, 1942*, 4:565.

34. Sumner Wells to Franklin Roosevelt, February 12, 1942, *FRUS, 1942*, 4:562.

35. Franklin D. Roosevelt, "Draft Message from President to the King of Saudi Arabia (Ibn Saud)," February 13, 1942, *FRUS, 1942*, 4:563.

36. Wells to Kirk, Telegram, April 15, 1942, *FRUS, 1942*, 4:569.

37. Fakry and Twitchell, *Report of the United States Agricultural Mission*, 5; Daniel Yergin, *The Prize: The Epic Quest for Oil, Money and Power* (New York: Simon and Schuster, 1991), 281–89.

38. Twitchell and Jurji, *Saudi Arabia*, vii.

39. Ibid., 165.

40. Wells to Kirk, March 3, 1942, *FRUS, 1942*, 4:551–60.

41. Twitchell and Jurji, *Saudi Arabia*, 161–68.

42. Ibid., 169; Kirk to Hull, February 26, 1943, *FRUS, 1943*, 4:861–62.

43. Aramco chose to pay for the equipment, not charging future royalties. See Fred Davies, president of Casoc, to Twitchell, June 28, 1943, folder 1, box 5, Twitchell Papers; Twitchell and Jurji, *Saudi Arabia*, 172.

44. Crary, "Recent Agricultural Developments in Saudi Arabia," 367.

45. Fakry and Twitchell, *Report of the United States Agricultural Mission*, 5, 11; R. A. Bramkamp, T. C. Barger, and L. M. Snyder, "Report on Development of Saudi Arabia Government's Irrigation Project at Al Kharj, Saudi Arabia," California Arabian Standard Oil Company, June 29, 1941, folder 7, box 9, Twitchell Papers.

46. Fakry and Twitchell, *Report of the United States Agricultural Mission*, 41–46.

47. Ibid., 75.

48. Ibid., 71–78.

49. J. G. Hamilton to Twitchell, June 13, 1944, folder 3, box 4, Twitchell Papers.

50. Twitchell and Jurji, *Saudi Arabia*, 172; Fakry and Twitchell, *Report of the United States Agricultural Mission*, 13.

51. Twitchell and Jurji, *Saudi Arabia*, 176.

52. Fakry and Twitchell, *Report of the United States Agricultural Mission*, 41–67.

53. Ibid., 84; Drayton, *Nature's Government*, 232.

54. Nils E. Lind, "The United States Agricultural Mission Project at Al-Kharj," attached to memorandum, April 18, 1945, folder: 021-125.6, box 1, Confidential File, 1941–1945, Dhahran Consulate, Record Group 84, Foreign Service Posts of the Department of State, National Archives at College Park, College Park, MD (hereafter cited as NACP).

55. Twitchell and Jurji, *Saudi Arabia*, 172; footnote, *FRUS, 1944*, 5:708.

56. Lind, "The United States Agricultural Mission Project at Al-Kharj," attached to memorandum.

57. Eddy to Secretary of State, June 16, 1945, folder: 021-125.6, box 1, Confidential File, 1941–1945, Dhahran Consulate, RG 84, NACP.

58. Hart to State, Telegram, May 21, 1946, folder, 021-125.6, box 1, Confidential File, 1941–1945, Dhahran Consulate, RG 84, NACP; Crary, "Recent Agricultural Developments in Saudi Arabia," 369.

59. David A. Rogers, Monthly Progress Report, March 1946, folder AAMSA, box 2, Confidential File, 1941–1949, Dhahran Consulate, RG 84, NACP.

60. Eddy to State, Airgram, June 16, 1945, folder 021-125.6, box 1, Confidential File, 1941–1945, RG 84, Dhahran Consulate, NACP; Memorandum, summary of cable to Washington, DC, by Harris, Buchanan, Tannous, folder AAMSA, box 2, Confidential File, 1941–1949, Dhahran Consulate, RG 84, NACP.

61. Lind, "The United States Agricultural Mission Project at Al-Kharj."

62. Waldo B. Bailey to Secretary of State, January 16, 1947, folder AAMSA, box 2, Confidential File, 1941–1949, Dhahran Consulate, RG 84, NACP.

63. Hart to American Legation in Jidda, Saudi Arabia, folder AAMSA, box 2, Confidential File, 1941–1949, Dhahran Consulate, RG 84, NACP.

64. Richard H. Sanger, *The Arabian Peninsula* (Ithaca: Cornell University Press, 1954), 61–65.

65. Ibid., 63; Vitalis, *America's Kingdom*, 71–74.

66. Sanger, *The Arabian Peninsula*, 61–66.

67. Ibid., 61–68.

68. "Report on Al Kharj Agricultural Project," April 7, 1952, folder Agricultural—Reports—Comments, box 1, RG 469, U.S. Foreign Assistance Agencies, 1941–1961, NACP.

69. Lorania K. Francis, "Arab Farms Boom Under Americans," *Los Angeles Times*, March 28, 1951; "Report on Al Kharj Agricultural Project," 4.

70. Mildred Montgomery Logan, "The Arabs Call Me Madam Sam," *The Cattleman*, January 1952, 61–65.

71. Mildred Montgomery Logan, "I Like Being the Garden of Eden's First Lady," *The Cattleman*, October 1951, 31–31, 101–13.

72. Lippman, *Inside the Mirage,* 182.

73. Vitalis, *America's Kingdom,* 74; Steve Coll, *The Bin Ladens: An Arabian Family in the American Century* (New York: Penguin Press, 2008), 71–78.

74. R. P. Green, "Condensed Executive Audit Report: Al Kharj Farms, 1954," August 28, 1954, folder 10, box 8, Mulligan Papers.

75. T. M. Righter, "Field Audit Report No. 4: Al Kharj Farms, 1954," folder 10, box 8, Mulligan Papers.

76. H. St. J. B. Philby was an early and constant advocate of the king, but Western journalists as well as Aramco publications describe the king in this way. See Lebkicher, *Handbooks for American Employees.*

77. Mohammed Hossein Saleh Ebrahim, "Problems of Nomad Settlement in the Middle East with Special Reference to Saudi Arabia and the Haradh Project" (PhD diss., Cornell University, 1981), 149.

78. Joseph Kostiner, *The Making of Saudi Arabia, 1911–1936: From Chieftaincy to Monarchical State* (New York: Oxford University Press, 1993), 71–72.

79. Sanger, *The Arabian Peninsula,* 69.

80. Kostiner, "On Instruments and Their Designers," 303.

81. James C. Scott, *Seeing Like a State: How Certain Schemes to Improve the Human Condition Have Failed* (New Haven: Yale University Press, 1998).

82. Helaissi, "The Bedouins and Tribal Life in Saudi Arabia." He argues that by 1959 up to 60 percent of Saudi Arabia's population were nomadic Bedouin, not including, as he states, those Bedouin "which have adopted agriculture as a profession and settled in their own villages and towns."

83. Ibid., 531–33.

84. Ebrahim, "Problems of Nomad Settlement in the Middle East," 170–71.

85. Ibid., 151–53.

86. Donald P. Cole, "Bedouin of the Oil Fields," *Natural History* 82 (1973): 96.

87. Helaissi, "The Bedouins and Tribal Life in Saudi Arabia," 538; Lerner, *The Passing of Traditional Society: Modernizing the Middle East* (Glencoe, IL: Free Press, 1958).

88. Donald P. Cole, "Bedouin of the oil fields," *Natural History* 82 (1973): 91–100; Ebrahim, "Problems of Nomad Settlement in the Middle East," 152.

89. F. S. Vidal, *Bedouin Migrations in the Ghawar Oil Field, Saudi Arabia* (Miami, FL: Field Research Projects, 1975), 21–23.

90. Sanger, *The Arabian Peninsula,* 71–76; Twitchell and Jurji, *Saudi Arabia,* 176; Anthony B. Toth, "The Transformation of a Pastoral Economy: Bedouin and States in Northern Arabia, 1851–1950" (PhD diss., St. Anthony's College, October 2000), 42.

91. Cole, "Bedouin of the Oil Fields."

92. J. P. Mandaville, "Bedouin Settlement in Saudi Arabia: Its Effect on Company Operations," a report prepared by Aramco's Local Government Relations Department, December 1965, folder 16, box 7, Mulligan Papers, 1, 16.

93. Mohammed Hussein Al-Fiar, "The Faisal Settlement Project at Haradh, Saudi Arabia: A Study in Nomad Attitudes Toward Sedentarization" (PhD diss., Michigan State University, 1977), 97.

94. Helaissi, "The Bedouins and Tribal Life in Saudi Arabia," 181.

95. Mandaville, "Bedouin Settlement in Saudi Arabia," 1.

96. Ibid., 1–8.

97. Ibid., 1–9.

98. Vidal, "Bedouin Migrations in the Ghawar Oil Fields, Saudi Arabia," 25.

99. Ibid., 25.

100. Mandaville, "Bedouin Settlement in Saudi Arabia," 1–7.

101. Helaissi, "The Bedouins and Tribal Life in Saudi Arabia," 533.

102. Joseph M. Dodge, Comment by Joseph M. Dodge for the Meeting of the Senior Economic Officers, Paris, France, September 1955, folder Mr. Dodge (5), box 1, Dwight D. Eisenhower Presidential Library, Abilene, KS.

103. David Skory, "Saudi Arabian Agricultural Program," August 17, 1955, folder ca. 1951–1959: Arabian American Oil Company (2 of 4), box 6, Mobil Papers.

104. Crary, "Recent Agricultural Developments in Saudi Arabia," 371–81.

105. Ibid., 381.

106. Ibid., 371–83.

107. Vidal, *The Aramco Reports on Al-Hasa and Oman, 1951–1955,* 131–50.

108. J. G. Hamilton, "The Start of an Agricultural Program in the Eastern Province," report to the Arabian American Oil Company, April 12, 1955, folder ca. 1951–1959: Arabian American Oil Company (2 of 4), box 6, Mobil Papers.

109. Vidal, *The Aramco Reports on Al-Hasa and Oman, 1951–1955,* 141–70.

110. Edgecombe, "Brief Report on Visit to Saudi Arabia."

111. See Hamilton, "The Start of an Agricultural Program in the Eastern Province." Hamilton states that labor costs increased tenfold from 1941 to 1953.

112. Edgecombe, "Brief Report on Visit to Saudi Arabia."

113. Vidal, "Date Culture in the Oasis of Al-Hasa," *Middle East Journal* 8 (1954): 421–27.

114. Vidal, *The Oasis of Al-Hasa,* 150–51.

115. Hamilton "The Start of an Agricultural Program in the Eastern Province," 2.

116. Good wages tended to be associated with the oil industry. See Hamilton report, 3; Vidal, *The Oasis of Al-Hasa,* 151–53.

117. Ibid., vi.

118. Skory, "Saudi Arabian Agricultural Program."

119. Hamilton "The Start of an Agricultural Program in the Eastern Province."

120. Agreement for the Technical Cooperation Program in Agriculture between the Government of the United States of American and the Government of the Kingdom of Saudi Arabia, November 10, 1952, folder Agriculture Agreement, Program Guide, General Policies, Relations with OFAR, box 1, RG 469, NACP, 3.

121. Wadsworth to State, June 1, 1954, *FRUS, 1951–1954,* 9, part 2:2451–53.

122. Hamilton, "The Start of an Agricultural Program in the Eastern Province," 1; Vidal, *The Aramco Reports on Al-Hasa and Oman, 1951–1955,* vi.

123. Elie El Hajj, "The Greening of Saudi Arabia—A Cost/Benefit Analysis," *Arab Banker* (Autumn/Winter 2006): 41–50; Vahid Nowshirvani, "The Yellow Brick Road: Self-Sufficiency or Self-Enrichment in Saudi Agriculture," *MERIP Middle East Report,* no. 145, The Struggle for Food (March–April 1987): 1–13.

124. William L. Owen, "Negotiation and Legal Affairs of Aramco, 1941–1980," oral history conducted by Carole Hicke (1992), in "American Perspectives of Aramco, the Saudi-Arabian Oil-Producing Company, 1930s to 1980s," Regional Oral History Office, Bancroft Library, University of California, Berkeley, 1995; Edgecombe, "Brief Report on Visit to Saudi Arabia."

125. Hajj, "The Greening of Saudi Arabia;" Nowshirvani, "The Yellow Brick Road."

Conclusion

1. Thomas F. O'Dea, "Social Change in Saudi Arabia: Problems and Prospects," Confidential Report, prepared from research conducted by the special study group, February–August

1963, box 21, Harry Roscoe Snyder Papers, Hoover Institution Archives, Stanford, CA (hereafter cited as Snyder Papers).

2. W. W. Rostow, *The Stages of Economic Growth: A Non-Communist Manifesto* (Cambridge: Cambridge University Press, 1960); Daniel Lerner, *The Passing of Traditional Society: Modernizing the Middle East* (Glencoe, IL: Free Press, 1958).

3. O'Dea, "Social Change in Saudi Arabia: Problems and Prospects."

4. O'Dea's candor did not please the executives at Aramco, who attempted to suppress his negative findings. See Robert Vitalis, *America's Kingdom: Mythmaking on the Saudi Oil Frontier* (Stanford: Stanford University Press, 2007), 251–64.

5. Vitalis, *America's Kingdom*, 251–57.

6. Douglas Little, *American Orientalism: The United States and the Middle East since 1945*, 3rd ed. (Chapel Hill: University of North Carolina Press, 2008), 171–82.

7. Kristin L. Ahlberg, *Transplanting the Great Society: Lyndon Johnson and Food for Peace* (Columbia: University of Missouri Press, 2008), 21–23; Little, *American Orientalism*, 161–72.

8. Little, *American Orientalism*, 181–84; Matthew F. Jacobs, *Imagining the Middle East: The Building of an American Foreign Policy, 1911–1967* (Chapel Hill: University of North Carolina Press, 2011), 171–78; Lloyd C. Gardner, *Three Kings: The Rise of an American Empire in the Middle East after World War II* (New York: New Press, 2009), 205.

9. Quoted in Jacobs, *Imagining the Middle East*, 177.

10. Rachel Bronson, *Thicker Than Oil: America's Uneasy Partnership with Saudi Arabia* (Oxford: Oxford University Press, 2006), 71–79.

11. Little, *American Orientalism*, 181–86; Peter L. Hahn, *Crisis and Crossfire: The United States and the Middle East since 1945* (Washington, DC: Potomac Books, 2005), 41–45.

12. Gardner, *Three Kings*, 206; Hahn, *Crisis and Crossfire*, 45.

13. Toby Craig Jones, *Desert Kingdom: How Oil and Water Forged Modern Saudi Arabia* (Cambridge: Harvard University Press, 2010), 151–59.

14. Bronson, *Thicker Than Oil*, 71–77.

15. Jones, *Desert Kingdom*, 151–56.

16. Bronson, *Thicker Than Oil*, 91–94.

17. Vitalis, *America's Kingdom*, 264.

18. O'Dea, "Social Change in Saudi Arabia: Problems and Prospects."

19. Memorandum for the Record, Conversation with Aramco Representative, May 24, 1967, *Foreign Relations of the United States, 1961–1968* (Washington, DC: U.S. Government Printing Office, 2000), 21:419.

20. Bronson, *Thicker Than Oil*, 91–103.

21. E. R. Bishop, "Report of Study of Saudi Arabian Public Security Forces Riot Control Capabilities and Requirements," January 1969, folder Saudi Arabia, box 65, Record Group 286, Records of the Agency for International Development, National Archives at College Park, MD; R. W. "Brock" Powers, "Petroleum Geologist to Vice Chairman of Aramco, 1941–1980," oral history conducted by Carole Hicke (1992), in "American Perspectives of Aramco, the Saudi-Arabian Oil-Producing Company, 1930s to 1980s," Regional Oral History Office, Bancroft Library, University of California, Berkeley, 1995 (hereafter cited as "American Perspectives of Aramco"), 421–27; Anthony Cave Brown, *Oil, God, and Gold: The Story of Aramco and the Saudi Kings* (Boston: Houghton Mifflin, 1999), 261–75.

22. Bishop, "Report of Study of Saudi Arabian Public Security Forces Riot Control Capabilities and Requirements"; Vitalis, *America's Kingdom*.

23. Frank Jungers, "From Construction Engineer to CEO and Chairman of Aramco, 1941–1978," oral history conducted by Carole Hicke (1992), in "American Perspectives of Aramco," 88; Brown, *Oil, God, and Gold*, 265, 289.

24. Bronson, *Thicker Than Oil,* 101–23.

25. Brown, *Oil, God, and Gold,* 267; Phoebe Ann Marr, "Ahmed Zaki Yamini," biographical sketch, 1962, folder 67, box 1, Mulligan Papers; Jungers, "From Construction Engineer to CEO and Chairman of Aramco, 1941–1978," 90.

26. Daniel Yergin, *The Prize: The Epic Quest for Oil, Money and Power* (New York: Simon and Schuster, 1991), 651–52.

27. Steve Coll, *The Bin Ladens: An Arabian Family in the American Century* (New York: Penguin, 2008); Laton McCartney, *Friends in High Places, The Bechtel Story: The Most Secret Corporation and How It Engineered the World* (New York: Simon and Schuster, 1988).

28. Nick Cullather, "Development Doctrine and Modernization Theory," in *Encyclopedia of American Foreign Policy,* ed. Alexander DeConde, Richard Dean Burns, Fredrik Logevall, and Louise B. Ketz (New York: Scribner, 2002), 1:471–91; Charles Gore, "The Rise and Fall of the Washington Consensus as a Paradigm for Developing Countries," *World Development* 28 (May 2000): 781–804.

Index

CHAD H. PARKER is associate professor of history at the University of Louisiana at Lafayette. A native of Indiana, he now calls Acadiana home, along with his partner, Emily Deal, and their two cats.